What Place for the A Priori?

What Place for the A Priori?

EDITED BY

Michael J. Shaffer and Michael L. Veber

OPEN COURT
Chicago and La Salle, Illinois

To order books from Open Court, call toll-free 1-800-815-2280, or visit www.opencourtbooks.com.

Open Court Publishing Company is a division of Carus Publishing Company.

Copyright ©2011 by Carus Publishing Company

First printing 2011

All rights reserved. No part of this publication may be reproduced, stored in a retrieval system, or transmitted, in any form or by any means, electronic, mechanical, photocopying, recording, or otherwise, without the prior written permission of the publisher, Open Court Publishing Company, a division of Carus Publishing Company, 70 East Lake Street, Suite 300, Chicago IL, 60601.

Printed and bound in the United States of America.

Library of Congress Cataloging-in-Publication Data

What place for the a priori? / edited by Michael J. Shaffer and Michael L. Veber.
   p. cm.
   Includes bibliographical references and index.
   ISBN 978-0-8126-9660-8 (trade paper : alk. paper)
   1. A priori. 2. Knowledge, Theory of. I. Shaffer, Michael J., 1970-
II. Veber, Michael L. III. Title.
BD181.3.W43 2011
121'.3—dc22
                                              2010046329

Contents

Contributors   vii

Introduction   1
   Michael L. Veber and Michael J. Shaffer

1. No Place for the A Priori   9
   Michael Devitt

2. Evidence-based Psychotherapy: Values and the A Priori   33
   Edward Erwin

3. The Philosophical Insignificance of A Priori Knowledge   61
   David Papineau

4. Albert Casullo's *A Priori Justification*   85
   Anthony Brueckner

5. Experience as a Natural Kind: Reflections on Albert Casullo's *A Priori Justification*   93
   Robin Jeshion

6. Reply to my Critics: Anthony Brueckner and Robin Jeshion   111
   Albert Casullo

7. Epistemological Empiricism 137
   Harold I. Brown

8. A Dilemma for Naturalized Epistemology? 157
   Shane Oakley

9. A Reconsideration of the Status of Newton's Laws 177
   David J. Stump

10. The Constitutive A Priori and Epistemic Justification 193
    Michael J. Shaffer

11. A Priori Conjectural Knowledge in Physics: The Comprehensibility of the Universe 211
    Nicholas Maxwell

12. Terror of Knowing: Can an Empiricist Avoid Unwanted A Priori Knowledge? 241
    Ümit D. Yalçın

Index 259

Contributors

Harold I. Brown, *Northern Illinois University*
Anthony Brueckner, *University of California, Santa Barbara*
Albert Casullo, *University of Nebraska, Lincoln*
Michael Devitt, *The Graduate Center, City University of New York*
Edward Erwin, *University of Miami*
Robin Jeshion, *University of California, Riverside*
Nicholas Maxwell, *University College London*
Shane Oakley, *University of Miami*
David Papineau, *King's College London*
Michael J. Shaffer, *St. Cloud State University*
David J. Stump, *University of San Francisco*
Michael L. Veber, *East Carolina University*
Ümit D. Yalçın, *East Carolina University*

Introduction

MICHAEL L. VEBER and MICHAEL J. SHAFFER

There are essentially three important questions that arise concerning a priori knowledge. First, what is a priori knowledge? Second, is there any such knowledge? And, third, what is the connection between a priori knowledge and other kinds of knowledge, specifically what is the connection between a priori and a posteriori knowledge? This collection of original essays grapples with all of these questions from a number of different perspectives. This introduction provides a brief survey and history of the philosophical problem of a priori knowledge, its relationship with philosophical naturalism and brief summaries of each of the essays.

Here is one way that the problem of the a priori arises. There are a host of statements for which it at least initially appears that once we understand them, we can know that they are true without having to rely on any empirical evidence at all. Seemingly, no experience is necessary for knowledge in these sorts of cases. Familiar examples arise in a variety of different epistemic domains. These include mathematical truths such as "2 + 2 = 4," conceptual truths such as "All bachelors are unmarried men," and even seemingly substantive metaphysical theses such as "No object can be both red and green all over at the same time" and "Every event has a cause." All of these claims have been regarded as items of a priori knowledge at some time. The crucial upshot here is that if initial appearances are accurate about any one of these statements or others like them then sensory experience cannot be the only source of knowledge.

Rationalism is the view that the initial appearances here are accurate. Although rationalists often disagree among themselves about the details concerning the theory of a priori knowledge, they all fundamentally agree that in addition to sensory experience, there is another source of knowledge. This source has gone by different names including: "reason," "reflection," "intuition," and "intellectual insight." Until the twentieth century, it was generally agreed that something like one of these faculties was the only way to account for some of our most important kinds of knowledge, especially our knowledge of logic and mathematics.

Some early twentieth-century philosophers found that belief in a non-empirical source of cognition did not sit well with their philosophical scruples. But they were also reluctant to classify logical and mathematical knowledge as empirical. So rather than postulate a special source of knowledge, they made a compromise in denying that such propositions have factual content. Propositions of the sorts in question are not, as many of them were wont to say, "about the world." These kinds of propositions were supposed to be known a priori only in the sense that they are not known on the basis of experience. But, the story goes, this need not worry anyone because they are merely analytic statements that are true by definition.[1]

By the late twentieth century, this view had fallen out of favor for a number of reasons. As is well known, arguments going back to Quine 1951 led many to doubt the intelligibility of a distinction between statements that are true in virtue of meaning and statements that are true in virtue of the facts. Does "All bachelors are unmarried men" not assert something about the world? Specifically, does it not assert of every bachelor that he is both unmarried and a male? If the standard interpretation of statements like this is correct, then "All bachelors are unmarried men" asserts something not only about bachelors but also about every object in the universe. Everything in the universe is either not a bachelor or it is unmarried and a man. And why is it not true in virtue of the fact that every bachelor is both unmarried and male or that everything in the universe is either not a bachelor or unmarried and a man? Furthermore, even if there is an intelligible distinction to be made between analytic and synthetic truths, it is unclear how a semantic distinction should solve the epistemological problem. Calling a truth "analytic" does not explain how we know it.

Rather than causing a shift back towards traditional rationalism, doubts over the tenability of the early twentieth-century account of the a priori led to a more radical form of empiricism where there simply is no such thing as a priori knowledge at all. The figurehead of radical empiricism was, of course, Quine and his seminal works "Epistemology Naturalized" (1969) and "Two Dogmas of Empiricism" (1951). Quine introduced a novel empiricist approach to the problem of a priori knowledge. His explanation for the appearance of a priority in examples like those mentioned above was that the "location" of these statements in our web of belief causes some to mistake a difference in degree for a difference in kind. According to Quine, beliefs about logic and mathematics are more central to our belief system, less close to the less secure observations that form its periphery, and this

---

[1] A classic statement of this position can be found in Ayer 1952.

makes them less susceptible to criticism than other more ordinary obviously empirical beliefs. According to Quine misguided philosophers mistake this resilience for complete immunity and then mistakenly postulate some special nonempirical source of evidence.

According to radical empiricism, everything we know including mathematics, logic, and even philosophy (insofar as philosophy can be known) is known empirically. This sort of outlook is what underwrites that family of philosophical theories and metaphilosophical proposals known as naturalism. Whatever its guise, naturalized philosophy rides the waves of radical empiricism's popularity by emphasizing empirical methods and frowning on traditional rationalistic ones. Whether philosophical naturalism is correct or not, it reminds us of how fundamental the question of a priori knowledge and justification is. Those who believe that there is a priori knowledge very often view the very nature of philosophy, its purpose and method, in a much different way from those who do not.

In the last fifty years, radical empiricism and philosophical naturalism have gained wide popularity among epistemologists almost, some would say, to the point of becoming a philosophical orthodoxy. But the last decade or so has also seen a renaissance of interest in a priori knowledge. Some contemporary epistemologists are dissatisfied with purely empirical attempts to account for logic, mathematics, and some of the other examples of apparently a priori knowledge. In addition to emphasizing the appearance of a priority in these examples, proponents of a priori knowledge also offer what one might call impossibility arguments to the effect that these sorts of things could not be justified by appeal to sensory experience alone.

The opening essay, Michael Devitt's "No Place for the A Priori," is an attempt to undermine some of these impossibility arguments and also to undercut the initial motivation for endorsing any sort of belief in a priori knowledge in the first place. Devitt argues that even though we have, at present, no plausible account of how logical and mathematical knowledge are acquired through sensory experience, a reasonable person will back the empirical horse anyway. This is because, on the one hand, we have a relatively clear idea of how empirical knowledge works. Facts in the world cause experiences that then justify belief in those facts. On the other hand, he argues that the workings of a priori knowledge and justification remain completely obscure and mysterious even in the writings of advocates of a priori knowledge. In particular, he offers objections to theories of the a priori that have been given by Christopher Peacocke, George Bealer, and Laurence BonJour. His essay also includes a discussion of the problem of circularity that faces any empiricist attempt to justify empirical methods and he argues that rationalism ultimately faces the same sort of problem.

In the second essay, "Evidence-based Psychotherapy," Edward Erwin offers a defense of a priori justification within the context of psychotherapy. Some have pointed out that various kinds of value judgments play a crucial role in conducting psychotherapy and in evaluating its outcomes. Many go on to argue that these value judgments are (empirically) unverifiable and that this poses serious foundational problems for the discipline. In an effort to solve this problem, Erwin develops a theory that connects what is good for a patient to what he desires. His theory assumes that subjects can be a priori warranted in making certain kinds of value judgments on the basis of rational intuition. The bulk of the essay is devoted to defending that assumption. The essay serves as a complement to Devitt's in that many of the same lines of criticism are discussed. Nevertheless, Erwin arrives at the contrary conclusion.

The third essay is David Papineau's "The Philosophical Insignificance of A Priori Knowledge." As its title would indicate, Papineau's essay is a defense of philosophical naturalism applied to philosophy itself. Unlike Devitt, Papineau is willing to grant that some truths may be knowable a priori but, much like empiricists of the early twentieth century, he argues that such truths are merely analytic and therefore, in a sense, trivial. He parts company with early twentieth-century empiricists by arguing that the bulk of those propositions that are of philosophical interest are not a priori or conceptual in character; instead, they are empirical insofar as they are of interest at all.

Devitt, Erwin, and Papineau all believe that we have enough reason to decide today on the issue of whether there is any such thing as a priori knowledge or justification. In his recent book *A Priori Justification*, Albert Casullo (2003) argues that the issue is best regarded as an open question. His case is made by surveying the various kinds of arguments that have been made by defenders of a priori knowledge (including the impossibility arguments mentioned above), and the arguments from radical empiricists designed to show that all knowledge must be empirical. He concludes that the arguments on both sides fail. He then argues that settling the question should be a largely empirical endeavor. Contrary to what some have argued, Casullo claims that an empirical attempt to find a priori justification would not ultimately undermine belief in its existence.

The fourth and fifth essays in this volume are critical responses to Casullo's book and the sixth is a reply to those from the author himself. Anthony Brueckner opens his critique by challenging Casullo's claim that there is a shared concept of a priori justification that different philosophers attempt to analyze. Brueckner also takes issue with Casullo's way of defining the expression "a priori justification." According to Casullo, a priori justification is just nonexperiential justification. The project then becomes one of defining what an experience is. One of Brueckner's complaints is that Casullo's way of handling this problem is inconsistent with his own criticisms of the alternatives. Casullo rejects all of the usual ways of analyzing "experience" and proposes that it is best thought of as a natural kind term, a full understanding of which must await further empirical investigation. According to Brueckner, however, Casullo has effectively cut off any means we might have had for investigating the deeper nature of experience by undermining all of the previously proposed definitions. Brueckner also challenges Casullo's claim that a priori methods can be shown empirically to be truth conducive.

Casullo responds to Brueckner's worries over the role of conceptual analysis in the matter by agreeing that the notion of "a priori justification" is a term of art while denying that this precludes the possibility of conceptual analysis. He also makes a distinction between recognizing certain surface characteristics of experience and making those characteristics necessary and sufficient conditions for experience. This is used to explain how his own claim that experience can be further investigated is consistent with his rejection of the previously proposed analyses. Surface characteristics help fix reference of "experience" but they need not be part of its definition. Casullo also further elaborates how he thinks an empirical investigation of a priori sources of justification might work, if we find that such sources exist.

Jeshion's criticism of Casullo focuses primarily on his claim that "experience" is a natural kind term. Jeshion interprets this to mean that "experience" must ultimately pick out some sort of neurological state or process. She then offers a twin-earth style argument against this sort of view. We would ascribe experiences to our twin earth counterparts even if they turned out to be biologically different from us. Sameness of underlying biology is not necessary for sameness of experience. She concludes that experience is a functional concept and not a natural kind term. Jeshion also sketches (but does not ultimately endorse) an argument based on the much-discussed cases of blindsight. It may turn out that a blindsighted person is in the same neural state we are when receiving information about his environment but it is not obvious that he has a sensory experience. Thus experience is not a matter of neurobiology.

In response to Jeshion, Casullo argues that the appropriate level of analysis for any natural kind term must ultimately be determined by scientific considerations. Thus he rejects Jeshion's assumption that unless "experience" picks out a neurological state or process, it is not a natural kind term. It may be that "experience" is best analyzed at the level of psychology rather than neurobiology. To handle the worries about blindsight, Casullo offers a more mundane example designed to show that we have often have visual experiences without any associated phenomenology. Following up on a suggestion Jeshion makes at the end of her paper,

Casullo also discusses whether his proposal for how experience should be analyzed is meant to be reversionary.

Historically, the most prominent impossibility argument for the existence of a priori knowledge rested on the claim that mathematical, logical, and conceptual truths are known with certainty in the sense that no further evidence could ever make it rational to reject them. This sort of reason was often offered by proponents of the early twentieth-century analytic accounts of a priori knowledge. Since it is widely held that empirically supported propositions can always be overturned by further evidence, it is concluded that these sorts of things must be other than empirical.

In the seventh essay, Harold Brown argues that there are no a priori truths in this sense that play any substantive role in empirical science. As far as physical theory is concerned, everything is subject to challenge by empirical evidence. Brown argues by way of example that there may be a sense in which definitional truths cannot be overturned by empirical evidence but these definitional truths can, in light of empirical discovery, become irrelevant. Something similar is said for certain "framework principles," such as mathematical or geometric truths, that are thought to play a constitutive role in scientific theory. It may be that certain mathematical or geometric truths hold given a certain framework but empirical reasons can and must be given for accepting or rejecting those frameworks. Brown acknowledges that scientific practice may require principles akin to Kant's synthetic a priori but that the phenomenon of conceptual innovation in science undermines any claim to these principles being unrevisable. New discoveries necessitate the development new concepts that often override earlier conceptual commitments even if those earlier commitments were taken to be a priori. Brown finds affinities for this sort of view in the work of Sellars, Putnam, and Kuhn.

Another impossibility argument that frequently gets raised in defense of a priori knowledge is that the opposing view is somehow incoherent or self-defeating. Any argument for the claim that all evidence is empirical must either be empirical or a priori in nature. If it is empirical in nature, then the argument is circular. If it is a priori in nature then the conclusion is false and the argument is unsound. In "A Dilemma for Naturalized Epistemology?" Shane Oakley offers a formally articulated defense naturalistic empiricism against this sort of charge. To put it informally, he agrees that if naturalism is justified it must be justified by evidence from within empirical science. But the fact that an epistemological theory can only be supported by the sort of evidence that it countenances does not show that this support is viciously circular because any general epistemological theory will have this result.

Another way that philosophers have tried to argue that a purely empirical epistemology cannot succeed has its grounding in empirical science itself. The ninth, tenth, and eleventh essays all concern what has come to be called the constitutivist view of a priori knowledge. This view is rooted in the Kantian idea that in order for empirical knowledge to be possible, some principles must be accepted a priori. While Kant was primarily concerned with establishing this sort of view at the level of individual subjects, contemporary constitutivists tend argue for this view on the basis of scientific practice.

Using Newton's Laws as an example, David Stump defends the claim that certain principles are functionally a priori. They must be assumed prior to any empirical testing because they are so fundamental they are required for the very possibility of empirical test in the first place. Unlike others who have defended this sort of view (including Kant himself), Stump denies that these principles are apodictic or necessary. Nonetheless, we must grant them an epistemological status that differs in kind from normal empirical claims.

On the other side of this issue is Michael Shaffer's "The Constitutive A Priori and Epistemic Justification." He focuses on this sort of view as it is defended by Michael Friedman but much of what he says is relevant to Stump's defense of this view as well. A large part of Shaffer's critique concerns the justification of the constitutive a priori principles. According to him, these principles must either be mere conventions of language or empirical propositions. But neither of these suffices for being a priori in any interesting sense. Thus he concludes that Kantian constitutivism gives us no reason to believe in the existence of any substantive sort of a priori knowledge.

Nicholas Maxwell also defends a view of the a priori akin to Kantian constitutivism. His essay opens by pointing out the familiar problem of underdetermination in science along with the usual proposal for how to deal with it. Since so many rival theories can be compatible with our empirical data we must appeal to nonempirical considerations of simplicity, unity, and explanatory character. This, according to Maxwell, shows that science is a priori committed to the universe being a certain way. Science is possible only on the assumption that the universe is such that there are no disunified theories that are not either false or entailed by true unified theories. Thus, contrary to orthodox epistemology and philosophy of science, the practice of science involves commitment to the existence of substantive a priori knowledge. The bulk of Maxwell's paper is devoted to refining and defending this claim within his own philosophy of science, a view that he refers to as "aim-oriented empiricism."

Questions about how exactly a priori knowledge should be defined appear again in the final essay, Ümit Yalçin's "Terror of Knowing: Can an Empiricist Avoid Unwanted A Priori Knowledge?" Yalçin discusses a well-known problem for semantic externalism. According to semantic externalism, the content of a concept like "water" is at least partly constituted by the substance that it refers to, in this case, water. This seems to entail that one can only have the concept of water if there is water in his environment. And if we accept that we have a priori access to our own thoughts, this seems to entail that, since I can know a priori that I am thinking about water, I can know a priori that there is water in my environment. But the claim that there is water in my environment can only be known empirically, so either semantic externalism or one of our other assumptions must be mistaken. Yalçin argues that this argument fails and that this failure stems from a misunderstanding of the traditional a priori/a posteriori distinction. In arguing for this conclusion, Yalçin reminds us of the often overlooked fact that within empiricism there exists a long tradition of attempts to derive knowledge of the external world from knowledge of one's own mental states. This sort of empiricist would not find it surprising that one can know that water exists by reflection on his mental states and he would not call such knowledge a priori either.

REFERENCES

Ayer, A. J. 1952. *Language, Truth and Logic*. New York: Dover.
Casullo, A. 2003. *A Priori Justification*. New York: Oxford University Press.
Quine, W.V.O. 1951 Two Dogmas of Empiricism. *Philosophical Review* 60: 20–43.
———. 1969. Epistemology Naturalized. In *Ontological Relativity and Other Essays*, 69–90. New York: Columbia University Press.

[1]

No Place for the A Priori

MICHAEL DEVITT

1. Introduction

Why believe in the a priori? The answer is clear: there are many examples, drawn from mathematics, logic, and philosophy, of knowledge that does not seem to be empirical. It does not seem possible that this knowledge could be justified or revised "by experience." It *must* be justified in some other way, justified a priori.

So we have a motivation for the a priori. But there is a severe problem: the a priori seems deeply obscure. *What is it* for a belief to be justified a priori? What is the nature of this nonempirical method of justification? Without satisfactory answers the a priori is left mysterious.

In other works I have defended the naturalistic view that there is no a priori by attempting to undermine the motivation for the a priori and by demonstrating its obscurity (1996, 1998, 2002, 2005a,b).[1] In this essay, I shall summarize this attempt and then develop it further.

---

[1] On the naturalistic view, epistemology is part of science. It is important not to misunderstand this, as van Fraassen seems to (2000, 261–71). It goes without saying that *epistemology* implies the methods of science. But van Fraassen seems to take the naturalist view to be that *basic science, or special sciences like biology, medicine, and psychology*, imply the methods of science, a view that he rejects. That is not my view of naturalism (1997a, 75–79). I take *epistemology to be itself a special science*. As such it is no more simply implied by another science than is any other special science: it has the same sort of relative autonomy, and yet dependence on basic science, as other special sciences. So we should not go along with Quine's view that epistemology is a "chapter of psychology" (1969, 82). Naturalized epistemology, like any special science, applies the usual methods of science, whatever they may be, mostly taking established science for granted, to investigate its special realm. In the case of epistemology that realm is those very methods of science. The aim is to discover empirically how we humans learn, and should learn, about the world. We have no reason to suppose that the methods that have yielded knowledge elsewhere cannot yield knowledge in epistemology.

But I start with two preliminaries. First, what is the empirical method of justification? An answer starts from the metaphysical assumption that the worldly fact that p would make the belief that p true. The empirical justification of the belief is then to be found in its relationship to experiences that the worldly fact would cause. Justified beliefs are produced and/or sustained by experiences in a way that is appropriately sensitive to the way the world is. This is very brief and we shall return to the question later. Still it is hard to say much more.

Second, our concern with the a priori is with the *justification* of beliefs not primarily with their *source*. Experience is clearly not the source of many mental states: they are innate. Perhaps some of these are beliefs. I rather doubt this but suppose, nonetheless, that some were. That would raise two interesting questions. Could these innate beliefs be *innately justified*—justified, but not by the experiences of the believer—in a naturalistically respectable way? If so, would that justification fit the empirical model of justification we have briefly sketched?

There seem to be two naturalistically respectable possibilities for innate justification. The first starts with a belief of some of our distant ancestors, a belief formed as a result of experiences that justified it in the normal empirical way. Now suppose that the belief is extremely beneficial to the survival of those that hold it. Then there might be a process of natural selection leading in time to that belief being innate. That alone would not make the belief innately *justified* because its beneficial effects may have nothing to do with whether it is true; for example, one could imagine false religious beliefs being beneficial to survival. But suppose that the belief is as a matter of fact true and that it was *because it was true* that it was beneficial and hence selected for. Such an innate belief would have been produced by a reliable mechanism and I think we should count it as innately justified; this selection process would be a reliable way for us to inherit the justificatory work of those distant ancestors. And I think that this justification would fit the empirical model well enough.

It is worth noting that such innately justified beliefs would be a bit analogous to justified beliefs formed on the basis of testimony; for example, to learning that it is raining from someone reliable who has just experienced the rain. Of course, hearing testimony is an experience whereas receiving beliefs through your genes is not. Still in each case the believer's justification would be in a sense indirect, not coming from experiences directly produced by the worldly fact that makes the belief true.

The second possibility does not seem to fit the empirical model.[2] Again we start with a true belief of some of our distant ancestors. This time, how-

---

[2] I am much indebted to Kim Sterelny and Stephen Stich for eloquently bringing this possibility to my attention.

ever, they held that belief "by accident" *without any proper empirical justification at all.* The story then continues as before: suppose that because the belief is true it is extremely beneficial; it is then selected for and so becomes innate. Now if this belief is to count as justified, the justification must come entirely from the process of natural selection itself. No experiences of the worldly fact that makes the belief true played a role in producing or sustaining the belief in those distant ancestors: they simply happened on this belief which was beneficial because true and which was then selected for. Once again the belief would seem to have been produced by a reliable mechanism and should, I think, be counted as innately justified. Whereas the earlier first possibility is of an empirical justification *being inherited by natural selection* and so fits the empirical model well enough, this second possibility is of a justification *by natural selection itself* and so does not seem to fit the model at all.

I doubt that there are any innate beliefs and doubt even more that there are any that are innately justified in either of these possible ways. But if some were innately justified in the second possible way, a naturalistic philosopher would have to broaden his view of acceptable justification beyond empirical justification (as usually conceived). But this broadening would not give us anything like a priori justification (as usually conceived).[3] I shall ignore this possibility in what follows.

2. Undermining the Motivation

2.1. *The Naturalistic Alternative Summarized*

The task in undermining the motivation for the a priori is to show how the troublesome examples of allegedly a priori knowledge might be accounted for naturalistically. I have attempted this, drawing on Quine (1961, 1966,

---

[3] Nor, of course, does a much less interesting broadening to cover beliefs about one's own mental states that are justified by introspection. This discussion of innateness shows that Louise Antony is wrong in sensing a disagreement with me (2005a,b) over whether "a naturalized approach to knowledge requires repudiation of the a priori" (2004, 1). I repudiate an a priori that is committed to a nonnaturalistic justification whereas she defends an a priori that is "innateness plus reliability" (2). I am not against either innateness or a reliablist approach to knowledge. Antony goes on to claim that the a priori she defends "should be pretty satisfying" for those interested in the traditional notion (2). This is surely not so. What has interested nearly all philosophers under the name 'a priori' has been a nonnaturalistic way of justifying beliefs, as the citations in this present essay make plain. Furthermore, I would argue that what Antony counts as a priori is not close to being even coextensive with what the tradition counts; in particular, Antony would not count logical beliefs (in contrast to inferences), most philosophical beliefs, and a whole lot of ordinary analytic beliefs as a priori. I would also argue similarly against Georges Rey's reliablist defense of the a priori (1998), thus adding another criticism to my earlier ones (1998). In general, it seems to me a mistake for Antony,

1969, 1975) and before him Duhem (1954). In brief, the key is breaking free of a naive atomistic picture of justification. We must view justification in a more holistic way: beliefs, even whole theories, do not face the tribunal of experience alone, but in the company of auxiliary theories, background assumptions, and the like. Such holism is well supported by the revolution in the philosophy of science inspired by Thomas Kuhn (1970). In light of this holism, it is argued, we have no reason to believe that whereas scientific propositions, which are uncontroversially empirical, are confirmed in the holistic empirical way, the propositions of mathematics, logic, and philosophy are not; no reason to believe that there is a principled basis for drawing a line between what can be known this way and what cannot; no reason to believe that there is, in Quine's vivid metaphor, a seam in the web of belief.

I shall develop this view by considering in turn, in more detail, the problems posed for it by mathematics, philosophy, and logic.

2.2 Naturalism and Mathematics

Obviously, these brief remarks scarcely begin to solve the epistemological problem of mathematics. There are two reasons why this is not a great concern to the project of undermining the motivation for the a priori. First, as Georges Rey (1998) is fond of pointing out, we are not close to solving the epistemological problem of *anything*.[4] Since we do not have a serious theory that covers even the easiest examples of empirical knowledge—examples where experience plays its most direct role—the fact that we do not have one that covers the really difficult examples from mathematics hardly reflects on the claim that these are empirical too. We all agree that there *is* an empirical way of knowing. Beyond that, the present project needs only the claim that the empirical way is holistic. *We have no reason to believe that a serious theory would show that, whereas empirical scientific laws are confirmed in the holistic empirical way, the laws of mathematics are not.*

Second, there is a special reason for not expecting the epistemological problem of mathematics to be anywhere near solved: the *metaphysical* problem of mathematics—what mathematics is *about*—remains so intractable. How could we solve the epistemological problem when we remain in such

---

Rey, and other naturalistically-inclined philosophers—for example, Alvin Goldman (1999)—to attempt to "save the a priori." Epistemological naturalism is indeed a radical doctrine.

[4] This is not to deny that we have made progress in epistemology. Indeed, a good deal of the impressive scientific progress in recent centuries has come from learning how better to learn about the world (2005a, 110). Still these advances have not solved the basic epistemological problems.

darkness about the metaphysical one? The point is that we no longer have any reason to think that, *if we solved the metaphysical problem*, the epistemological problem would not be open to an empirical solution.[5]

I emphasize that this is not the claim that we now have anything close to an empirical justification of a mathematical proposition. It is the much weaker claim that we now have no good reason to think that such a justification could not be given. The weaker claim is all that is needed to undermine the motivation for the a priori. Furthermore, I am not denying the striking epistemological differences between mathematics and science. (i) There is an obvious difference between observing and inferring, and an obvious difference between inferring deductively and inferring nondeductively or "ampliatively." Where mathematical justification largely involves deductive inferences from "self-evident" assumptions in proofs, scientific justification largely involves ampliative inferences from observations in experiments. But the claim is that all these differences could be accommodated in the naturalistic picture; for example, that the justification of the self-evident assumptions could be empirical. (ii) Despite the holistic story, a scientific claim—even, say, the general theory of relativity—seems to answer fairly directly to certain evidence in a way that a mathematical claim does not. Nonetheless, the naturalist urges, this difference is just a matter of degree.[6]

2.3 Naturalism and Philosophy

George Bealer rightly points out that "in philosophy, the use of intuitions as evidence is... ubiquitous . . . these intuitions . . . determine the structure of contemporary debates in epistemology, metaphysics, and philosophy of logic, language, and mind." He goes on to say that "in our context when we speak of intuition, we mean 'rational intuition' or 'a priori intuition'" (1999, 30). This view of intuitions is, of course, fairly standard in philosophy. Indeed, it is common to suppose that only if intuitions are a priori can they play their evidential role in the characteristic "armchair" method of philosophy. From the naturalistic perspective, this common thought is mistaken. We have no need to see philosophical intuitions as a priori. We can see them as being members of a general class of empirical intuitions.

---

[5] I make a similar response (2005a, 107–8) to the common view that necessities can only be known a priori. There is no reason to believe that if we solved the metaphysical problem of necessity we would not be able to explain our knowledge of necessities empirically.

[6] This paragraph was prompted by some very helpful comments from John Bigelow and Kim Sterelny.

Consider these empirical intuitions. They are judgments that are empirical theory-laden "central-processor" responses to phenomena, differing from many other such judgments only in being immediate and unreflective, not based on any conscious reasoning. These intuitions are surely partly innate in origin but are usually and largely the result of past reflection on a lifetime of worldly experience.[7]

We are often right to trust a person's intuitions as evidence about some kind we are investigating. But we should trust them only to the degree that we have confidence in the person's empirically based expertise about that kind. Sometimes the folk may be as expert as anyone: intuitions laden with "folk theory" are the best we have to go on. Perhaps this is the case for a range of psychological kinds. For most kinds, it clearly is not: we should trust intuitions laden with established scientific theories. Consider, for example, a paleontologist in the field searching for fossils. She sees what seems to be a bit of white stone sticking through grey rock, and thinks "a pig's jawbone." This intuitive judgment is quick and unreflective. She may be quite sure but unable to explain just how she knows.[8] We trust her judgment in a way that we would not trust folk judgments because we know that it is the result of years of study and experience of old bones; she has become a *reliable indicator* of the properties of fossils. Similarly we trust the intuitions of the physicist over those of the folk about many aspects of the physical world where the folk have proved notoriously unreliable. And recent experiments have shown that we should have a similar attitude to many psychological intuitions. Thus, the cognitive psychologist, Edward Wisniewski, points out that "researchers who study behavior and thought within an experimental framework develop *better* intuitions about these phenomena than those of intuition researchers or lay people who do not study these phenomena within such a framework. The intuitions are better in the sense that they are more likely to be correct when subjected to experimental testing" (1998, 45).

Even where we are right to trust an intuition in the short run, nothing rests on it in the long run. We can look for more direct evidence in scientific tests. In such a scientific test we examine the reality the intuition is *about*; for example, we examine the paleontologist's white stone. These scientific examinations of reality, not intuitions about reality, are the primary source of evidence. The examinations may lead us to revise some of our ini-

---

[7] I have urged this view of intuitions before (1994; 1996, 48–86); see also Kornblith (1998). A more thorough treatment of intuitions is to be found in Devitt (2006a, ch. 7; 2006b).

[8] I owe this nice example to Sterelny. Gladwell (2005) has other nice examples: of art experts correctly judging an allegedly sixth-century Greek marble statue to be a fake; of the tennis coach, Vic Braden, correctly judging a serve to be a fault before the ball hits the ground.

tial intuitions. They will surely show us that the intuitions are far from a complete account of the relevant bit of reality.

Intuitions often arise in "thought experiments." Instead of real experiments that confront the expert with phenomena and ask her whether they are members of the kind F, we confront her with *descriptions* of phenomena and ask her whether she *would say* that they were members of F.[9] These thought experiments provide valuable clues to what the expert would intuitively identify as an F or a non-F if given the opportunity. They can do more: the descriptions that elicit the expert's response indicate richer intuitions that can be a useful guide to the nature of Fs. Some experiments may be difficult, perhaps impossible, to perform other than in thought. Valuable and useful as thought experiments may be in practice, they are dispensable in principle: we can make do with real experiments. And thought experiments call on the same empirically-based beliefs about the world as real experiments, and their results have the same empirical status.

In light of this, turn now to philosophical intuitions and the "armchair" method of philosophy. The traditional explanation of this method, illustrated by Bealer, is that philosophers are conducting thought experiments that probe their *concepts* to yield a priori *rational* intuitions; they are doing "conceptual analysis." The naturalistic explanation accepts that philosophers are conducting thought experiments but construes these differently. The philosophers are not probing concepts but rather *intuitions about kinds*. This is just as well because knowledge of concepts, being a species of semantic knowledge, is very hard to come by. In contrast, philosophers have acquired considerable knowledge of many kinds over a lifetime of acquaintance with them. The philosophers' intuitions that draw on this knowledge are not a priori but empirical. The philosophers are conducting thought experiments of the sort just described, counting themselves as experts about the kind in question. Thus, consider "the analysis of knowledge," a famous example of the method and one that Bealer discusses (1992, 100). The philosopher, as expert as anyone in identifying cases of knowledge, confronts descriptions of epistemic situations and considers whether the situations are cases of knowledge. On the basis of these empirical intuitions about cases the philosopher constructs an empirical theory about the nature of knowledge. The naturalist does not deny armchair intuitions a role in philosophy but does deny that their role has to be seen as a priori: the intuitions reflect an empirically-based expertise in the identification of kinds.

---

[9] There are other things we might ask—for example, "What would happen?"—but these are beside our concerns. Gendler 2003 is a nice summary of views about thought experiments.

So I am urging that philosophical intuitions should be seen as empirical central-processor responses to phenomena. This view has the great advantage of being theoretically modest: it treats these intuitions like intuitions in general. It accommodates the evidential role that intuitions play in philosophy without resort to the a priori.

2.4 Naturalism and Logic

The naturalistic alternative seems to face a difficulty with logic. For, on this alternative, experience justifies beliefs in the interior of the web via logical links with beliefs at the periphery, via logical links with beliefs "close to experience." But these justifications depend on the logical links themselves being justified: clearly a belief is not justified by other beliefs unless those others give it *genuine support*. And, many will claim, the justification of these links could not come from experience; it has to be a priori. Laurence BonJour has put the problem vividly: "if there is no a priori insight...no prediction will follow any more than any other . . . any . . . sort of connection between the parts of the system will become essentially arbitrary" (2001b, 679). "The rejection of all a priori justification is tantamount to intellectual suicide" (2001a, 626). In brief, the problem is that logic must be seen as a priori because we need logic to get evidence for or against anything.

To assess this problem we need to start with an important distinction. On the one hand, there are the rules that govern a person's practice in forming beliefs, that constitute her "evidential system" (Field 1996, 1998). These must include rules for forming beliefs from perceptual experiences and the logical rules that concern us here, rules for inferring one belief from another. On the other hand, there are assumptions or theories *about* such rules. Thus it is one thing for a rule of inference R—for example, *modus ponens*—to be among the rules that govern a person's thinking; it is another thing to theorize that R does so govern.[10] And it is also another thing to theorize about R's justification. So we have two types of *epistemological theorizing* about R that contrast with the *epistemic activity* of inferring according to R. The first type of theorizing is a piece of descriptive epistemology, the second, a piece of normative epistemology. The normative concern about the justification of R is with whether it gives

---

[10] In actual fact, we surely do not infer simply in accord with *modus ponens*, as Gilbert Harman has made plain (1999, 18–23): if we believe that p and that if p then q we *might* indeed infer that q but we might be so convinced of not q that we infer in accord with *modus tollens* and abandon our belief that p. The relations between psychological processes of inference, even of good inference, and logical implications is complex. Still, *modus ponens* is surely involved in some of our inferences and those inferences are good only because *modus ponens* is valid.

epistemic warrant to its conclusion when it operates on true premises; the concern is whether it is a *good* rule.

A belief we form about the epistemic status of a rule, like any other belief, raises an epistemic question: Is the belief justified? To avoid confusion, I shall in future talk of the *goodness* of rules rather than of their justification, and continue to talk of the *justification* of beliefs.

Against this background, we can now frame the issue. It is clearly the case that for beliefs arrived at by a process governed by R to be justified then the following must be true:

TR: R is a good rule.

And the issue is: What is the justification of TR? How do we know that R is a good rule?

We have seen that BonJour thinks that the justification must be by an a priori insight or rational intuition. And so too does Bealer (1992, 100–102; 1999, 30–34) who describes the intuition as an "intellectual seeming." This view may seem appealing if R is a rule of deductive logic like *modus ponens*, for we do at least *have* a lot of insight into deductive rules. But many, perhaps most, of the rules that govern our epistemic practices are ampliative rules. And these are rules that we do not have much insight into, whether a priori or not. We can, of course, wave our hands and talk of enumerative induction, abduction, simplicity, and the like, but we are unable to characterize these in the sort of detail that would come close to capturing the rules that must constitute our actual evidential systems; for example, we are unable to specify when an explanation is good, let alone the best, or when we should take the belief that all observed Fs have been G to justify the belief that all Fs are G. Aside from that, some of these vague rules are controversial; for example, scientific realists love abduction, Bas van Fraassen does not. In sum, when we move beyond deduction, we have few if any specific and uncontroversial rules to be insightful about. The nonskeptics among us will share the very general insight that, *whatever the rules that govern our epistemic practices may be*, those rules are for the most part good. So, if S is the sum of these largely unknown rules, if S is our evidential system, we believe

TS: The rules in S are for the most part good.

Now if the claim facing the naturalist is that TS is justified a priori the claim hardly seems tempting, given that we don't know what S is. It seems more plausible to view our general insight that TS is true as supported by the empirical success of S, whatever S may be. Similarly, someone afloat on a boat may not know the methods by which it was built but, noting its seaworthiness, infers that the methods, whatever they were, are good. In sum, when we focus on the largely unknown ampliative parts of S, our confidence in S seems as empirical as anything. To that extent, TS does not even appear to be justified by a priori insight.

Be that as it may, it will be thought that, at least, our insights into specific deductive rules like *modus ponens* are a priori. But why must we see the support for the deductive rules as different in principle from that for the ampliative rules? We need to have confidence in S as a whole if we are to avoid skepticism. We can see that confidence as coming from the overall empirical success of S. Then the justification of our belief in the deductive parts of S is no different in principle from that in the ampliative parts. Similarly, all parts of S are empirically *revisable*. Thus, suppose that experience leads us to abandon TS in favor of TS', a theory that recommends an evidential system S' built around a nonclassical logic. Then clearly we should use S' instead of S. In this way our logical practices are themselves open to rational revision in the light of experience.[11] These practices are far from "arbitrary": they are recommended by an experience-based epistemology.

This raises what may seem to be the most serious problem for naturalism. On the one hand, I talk of TS being justified by the empirical success of S. Yet that alleged justification must come via S itself. So, the attempt to support TS seems circular. On the other hand, I talk of the possibility of experience leading us to abandon TS in favor of TS'. Yet experience must be brought to bear on TS by using S and so could not show that TS is false and hence that we ought not to use S. The attempt to refute TS seems self-defeating.

A naturalist might attempt to respond to this by appealing to Quine?s famous metaphor of Neurath's boat. Quine likens our web of belief to a boat that we continually rebuild whilst staying afloat on it. We can rebuild any part of the boat—by replacement or addition—but in so doing we must take a stand on the rest of the boat for the moment. So we cannot rebuild it all at once. Similarly, we can justify or revise any part of our knowledge but in so doing we must accept the rest for the time being. So we cannot justify or revise it all at once. So the claim that one of S's rules, say R, is good or not could be supported by an argument that uses *other* rules of S but not R itself; thus, perhaps one could use inductive and deductive rules to justify the view that abduction should or should not be

---

[11] Hartry Field has urged on me that even if the empirical justification of logic has some plausibility, the empirical revision of it has not: we have no reason to believe that any evidential system we would find acceptable would allow this sort of empirical revision of logic. Perhaps not. But then we have no reason to believe that an acceptable system would *not* allow the revision. Perhaps I would be wiser to follow Field's advice and remain neutral on the matter of empirical revision, resting the naturalist case on the empirical justification of logic.

revised. There would be nothing circular or self-defeating about that. So if we could do that for claims about *each* rule of S in turn, we could justify or revise TS without circularity or self-defeat. And the justification or revision would be naturalistically kosher.

This is an attractive idea but I doubt that such a justification or revision of an epistemic rule would be generally available. In thinking about this it is important to remember that S must include rules governing its own potential replacement, rules governing the choice between TS and its rival TS' that recommends a different system S'. It is hard to see how these rules, vaguely indicated by the Neurath metaphor, could themselves be justified or revised in the Neurath way.[12]

In what follows I shall consider only the circularity problem, setting aside the self-defeat problem.[13] We must start by distinguishing "premise-circularity" from "rule-circularity." An argument is premise-circular if it aims to establish a conclusion that *is assumed as a premise in that very argument*. Premise-circularity is obviously reprehensible. But my argument for TS is not guilty of it because it does not use TS as a premise. An argument is rule-circular if it aims to establish a conclusion that *asserts that the rules used in that very argument are justified*. My argument tries to establish TS which asserts the justification of S, the system used in that argument to establish TS. So the argument is certainly rule-circular. Guided by the Neurath image, the argument accepts the nonepistemological part of our web for the moment and seeks to justify the epistemological part, TS. And that justification is governed by just the same rules that govern the justification of anything, the rules of S.

Rule circularity is not *obviously* reprehensible and some think it is not reprehensible at all (Papineau 1993; Psillos 1999). But there are two reasons for concern about it brought out nicely by Paul Boghossian (2000; 2001). The first reason is that even though rule circularity is not blatantly question begging like premise circularity it still has a question-begging air. For, in general, an argument for some conclusion can be criticized "either by questioning one of its premises or by questioning the implicated rule of inference R (Boghossian 2000, 246)." If R is questioned, one would have to defend it by justifying the belief that it is a good rule: one would have to justify TR. So in the rule-circular case where the conclusion of the argument is TR itself, the use of R may seem to beg the question. At least, as Boghossian points out (2000, 251–53) drawing on Michael Dummett (1991, 202), it seems to beg the question of the skeptic who genuinely doubts TR. Yet it is not clear that it begs the question of someone who does not doubt TR but is simply looking for a justification for his belief in it.

---

[12] I discuss this problem elsewhere in responding to Field (Devitt 1998, 61–63).
[13] But see Devitt 2005a, 110–11.

The naturalist may feel that he need lose no sleep over failing to satisfy the skeptic. But then there is the second reason for concern about rule circularity, what Boghossian calls "bad company": "unless constraints are placed on the acceptability of rule-circular arguments, . . . we will be able to justify all manner of absurd rules of inference," for example Prior's notorious rule of 'tonk'-introduction (2000, 247). As Crispin Wright says, "a rule-circular 'justification' would seem to be available for any rule whatever" (2001, 50). This is unacceptable: we clearly do need some constraint on rule-circular arguments.

So more work needs to be done on the legitimacy of rule-circularity.[14] But this should not be a cause for rejoicing among apriorists. First, it has not been shown that rule circularity is always illegitimate or that it is illegitimate in the naturalist's argument for *TS*. Second, and more important, any justification that the apriorist might offer of *TS* would *also* involve a sort of rule-circularity. Consider the rationalists, BonJour and Bealer, for example. According to them we form some beliefs on the basis of a priori intuitions or intellectual seemings, a process that is analogous to the uncontroversial forming of beliefs on the basis of perception. One respect in which the processes are analogous is that they are both noninferential. We might crudely state the rule for the perceptual process:

P: In normal conditions, if you have a perceptual experience that *p*—if it perceptually seems to you that *p*—then believe that *p*.

The rationalist idea is that there is also a rule that we might crudely state:

I: In normal conditions, if you have an a priori intuition that *p*—if it intellectually seems to you that *p*—then believe that *p*.

So, according to the rationalist, *I* is part of our evidential system *S* and hence is one of the rules that *TS* claims to be good. Now the rationalist is as obliged to justify *TS* as the naturalist. How could he do that? He would have to appeal ultimately to a priori intuitions. And that is indeed what BonJour and Bealer *do* appeal to, as already noted. So the rationalist justification of *TS* uses *I*, one the very rules that, according to the rationalist, *TS* claims to be good. So the justification is rule-circular.

The moral of this is that *any* justification of an epistemological belief in our evidential system, including our logic, whether apriorist or naturalist,

---

[14] Boghossian (2000, 248–51) proposes that a rule-circular argument is in order provided that the rule in question is meaning-constituting. This presupposes, as Boghossian acknowledges, a conceptual-role account of the meaning of the logical constants. Wright 2001 is a detailed and interesting critical discussion of Boghossian's proposal.

will be rule-circular (assuming that the Neurath way fails). So it is no skin off the nose of my project in this part of the paper that the naturalist justification must be rule-circular. For, that project is to undermine the motivation for thinking that that there must be a priori knowledge by showing that all beliefs could be justified empirically. Manifestly, the fact that any naturalist's justification of the epistemological belief must be rule-circular provides no motivation for the a priori given that any apriorist's justification must also be rule-circular. Of course, there would be a motivation if it could be established that the apriorist's rule-circularity is legitimate but the naturalist's is not. But the chances of finding a non-question-begging argument to this effect seem close to nil. So the project is intact.

Everyone agrees that there is an empirical way of knowing. The Duhem-Quine thesis, supported by the history of science, is that this way of knowing is holistic. I have argued that we have no good reason to think that our troublesome knowledge of mathematics, philosophy, and logic could not be accommodated within this holistic empirical picture. We are far short of a detailed epistemology for this knowledge, of course, but we are far short of a detailed epistemology for any knowledge. Now, if I am right about all this, we have clearly removed the theoretical need to seek another, a priori, way of knowing. This is the first part of the case against the a priori, but it cannot stand alone. The rest of the case is that the whole idea of the a priori is deeply obscure.

Many will remain unconvinced of the possibility of an empirical justification of the troublesome knowledge and will continue to think that the justification of this knowledge must be a priori. This thought would be rational if there were any grounds for optimism about the a priori. But, I shall now argue, there are no such grounds, only grounds for pessimism. If this is right, it is not rational to believe in the a priori.

3. Demonstrating the Obscurity

3.1 What Is A Priori Knowledge?

The aim in this part is to show that the whole idea of the a priori is too obscure for it to feature in a good explanation of our knowledge of anything. If this is right, we have a nice abduction: the *best* explanation of all knowledge is an empirical one.

We are presented with a range of examples of alleged a priori knowledge. But what are we to make of the allegation? What is the nature of a priori knowledge? We have the characterization: it is knowledge "*not* derived from experience" and so *not* justified in the empirical way; "a warrant . . . is a priori if neither sense experiences nor sense-perceptual beliefs are referred to or relied upon to contribute to the justificational force particular to that warrant" (Burge 1998, 3). But what we need if we are to take the a priori way seriously is a *positive* characterization, not just a negative one. We need to describe a process for justifying a belief that is different from the empirical way and that we have some reason for thinking is actual. We need some idea of what a priori knowledge *is* not just what it *is not*.[15]

Why? After all, I have been emphasizing how little we know ultimately about *empirical* justification. So why pick on the a priori?[16] The answer is that there are two crucial differences in the epistemic status of the two alleged methods of justification. First, the existence of the empirical method is not in question: everyone believes in it. In contrast, the existence of the a priori way is very much in question. Second, even though we do not have a serious theory of the empirical way, we do have an intuitively clear and appealing general idea of this way, of "learning from experience." It starts, as noted (sec. 1), from the metaphysical assumption that the worldly fact that p would make the belief that p true. A belief is justified if it is formed and/or sustained by the experiences of a mind/brain in a way that is appropriately sensitive to the putative fact that p. Many instruments—thermometers, voltmeters, etc.—are similarly sensitive to the world. Of course, the mind/brain differs from these instruments: beliefs are much more complex than the "information states" of instruments and their sensitivity to the world is mediated, in a holistic way, by many others.

---

[15] I shall not be concerned with the issue of the fallibility of claims to a priori knowledge, interesting though the issue is. Georges Rey describes the view that such claims might be wrong as "banal fallibilism" (1998, 26) and mocks the idea that traditional rationalists rejected such fallibilism. I am inclined to think that he is wrong about this, given their extreme Cartesianism about the mind. In any case, contemporary rationalists like BonJour and Bealer do not reject fallibilism. This is, of course, wise given the sad history of mistaken claims to a priori knowledge (Kornblith 2000, 67–70). But then, however we understand the view that claims to a priori knowledge can be mistaken, it looks as if those claims could do little epistemic work. One way to understand the view is that although the *process* of a priori justification is infallible, yielding outputs that are not open to empirical revision, a person might be mistaken in thinking she has gone through that process and so might make mistaken *claims* to a priori knowledge. But then for those claims to do any epistemic work we would need evidence, presumably empirical evidence, that they had been arrived at by the approved a priori process. Getting that evidence is surely going to be hard, particularly if I am right in arguing below that we do not know enough about this alleged process to know what to look for. Another way to understand the view is that the a priori process itself is fallible, yielding results that are open to empirical revision. But then it looks as if claims to a priori knowledge could do even less work. For, even if we knew that the claims had been arrived at by the a priori process, we would still need to assess them, in the usual holistic way, against the empirical evidence to see if they should be revised. This note was prompted by a helpful correspondence with Hilary Kornblith about his 2000.

[16] Bealer (1999, 52, n. 23) makes a point along these lines.

Still, the mind/brain is similar enough to the instruments to make empirical justification quite unmysterious, despite the sad lack of details. In contrast, we do not have the beginnings of an idea of what the a priori way might be; we lack not just a serious theory but *any idea at all*.

3.2 The Traditional Analyticity Explanation

The difficulty in giving a positive characterization of a priori knowledge is well-demonstrated by the failure of traditional attempts based on analyticity. A typical example of alleged a priori knowledge is our belief that

(B) All bachelors are unmarried.

Now, according to the tradition,

(1) The content of the concept <bachelor> is the same as that of <adult unmarried male>,

thus making (B) analytic. This seemed promising for an account of a priori knowledge because it was thought that, simply in virtue of *having* a concept, a person was in possession of "tacit knowledge" *about* the concept; in virtue of having <bachelor>, a person tacitly knew (1). So a person's conceptual competence gave her privileged "Cartesian" access to facts about concepts. The required nonempirical process of justification was thought to be one that exploited this access, a reflective process of inspecting the contents of concepts to yield knowledge of the relations between them which in turn yielded such knowledge as (B). This alleged process is that of "conceptual analysis."

Even if we grant that we have this Cartesian access to conceptual facts like (1), the account fails. For how would a person get from (1) to (B)? By arguing along the following lines. From (1) she infers

(2) The content of <All bachelors are unmarried> is the same as that of <All adult unmarried males are unmarried>

From this and

(3) <All adult unmarried males are unmarried> is true,

we can then infer

(4) <All bachelors are unmarried> is true,

and hence conclude (B). *But where did the justification of (3) come from?* It does no good to say, rightly, that the <All adult unmarried males are unmarried> is a *logical* truth, for what justifies logical truths? Logical truths were, of course, one of the main things that we were supposed to know a priori. Yet, no satisfactory nonempirical account has ever been given of how we could justify logical truths. And what about the inferences in this argument? (B) will be justified only if the view that these inferences are good is justified (2.4). Where does that justification come from? Without an answer to these questions about the justification of logic we have still not explained a nonempirical way of knowing.

In any case, we should not grant the Cartesian view that conceptual competence gives privileged access to contents, despite its great popularity. I urge a much more modest view of competence according to which it is an *ability or skill* that need not involve any tacit theory, any semantic propositional knowledge; it is knowledge-how not knowledge-that (1996). Why then should we believe the immodest Cartesian view, particularly since it is almost entirely unargued?

The content of a person's thought is constituted by relational properties of some sort: "internal" ones involving inferential relations among thoughts and "external" ones involving certain direct causal relations to the world. Take one of those relations. Why suppose that, simply in virtue of her thought *having* that relation, reflection must lead her to *believe that* it does? Even if reflection does, why suppose that, simply in virtue of that relation *partly constituting the content* of her thought, reflection must lead her to *believe that* it does? Most important of all, even if reflection did lead to these beliefs, why suppose that, simply in virtue of her competence, this process of belief formation *justifies* the beliefs, or gives them any special epistemic authority, and thus turns them into *knowledge*? These suppositions seem gratuitous. We need a plausible explanation of this allegedly nonempirical process of belief formation and justification.

Of course, if one *were* justified in believing (1), and took logic for granted, then one would have a route to justifying <All bachelors are unmarried> other that the usual empirical route arising from experiencing the non-semantic world. But the point is that there is no reason to believe in a Cartesian route to justifying (1). The route to justifying (1) would be that of empirical semantics.[17]

---

[17] Stipulating contents might provide an unusual example of an empirical semantic route to justifying the likes of (1). A person does not, as a matter of fact, stipulate (1), does not stipulate that the content of her <bachelor> concept is the same as that of <adult unmarried male>, but suppose that she did. If her memory of such matters is reliable then any time later that she remembers the stipulation she will be justified in believing (1). But remembering is an empirical process.

This having been said, the naturalist may, from the perspective of a reliablist epistemology, have to allow a truth in the traditional explanation, albeit not one that is any help to the a priori.[18] Suppose that (1), or something similar, really were the case. Then anyone who has the concept <bachelor> might be disposed to believe the necessary proposition <All bachelors are unmarried>. She might be disposed to believe this even though she did not have the Cartesian access to her concepts that would yield semantic knowledge of (1) (or, indeed, an empirical semantic theory that would yield this knowledge). She might be disposed to believe it simply in virtue of the fact that <unmarried> *did* partly constitute <bachelor>. A consequence of this is that acquiring <bachelor> would be a reliable way of coming to this true belief. So, a reliablist must then allow that her belief is justified (although, of course, she does not know its justification). That would be a truth in the traditional explanation. But this is no help to the a priori. It would show that the empirical process of acquiring a concept involved a process that justifies a necessary belief. But that justification does not differ in any epistemologically significant way from the empirical justification of a contingent belief, for example of <All bachelors are envied>: there is still no Cartesian route to justification. Just the same sort of empirically reliable mechanism must be in place in both cases for the beliefs to be justified. The difference between the cases is strictly semantic: if the mechanism appropriate for the justification of <All bachelors are unmarried> is not in place, then the person will not have the concept <bachelor> and hence will not even entertain that proposition; there is no analogue of this with <All bachelors are envied>.[19]

Let us turn now to the views of some contemporary apriorists as further evidence of the difficulty of explaining the a priori. I think that we can predict that any attempted explanation will involve Cartesianism and/or taking logic for granted. And if the a priori is left unexplained, it is left mysterious, even mystical.

3.3 Christopher Peacocke

Peacocke follows the tradition in thinking that the sort of understanding that comes with possessing a concept yields a priori knowledge: "it is intuitive that understanding makes available some a priori ways of coming to know propositions" (2005, 751). "The theory of possession conditions is the crucial resource on which truth-conditional theories need to draw in explaining why certain ways of coming to know are a priori ways" (753).

---

[18] I am indebted to Bob Kirk for making me to see this.
[19] For a defense of this view, see Devitt 1996 (30–36); 1997b (356–58).

He proposes what he calls a "metasemantic theory of the a priori" which is illustrated in the following claim about conjunction: "the possession condition for the concept of conjunction . . . will entail that thinkers must find the transition from A&B to A compelling" (753). Peacocke thinks that this compulsion reflects tacit knowledge of the nature of the concept that can yield a priori knowledge of the inference from A&B to A. "The moderate rationalist holds that any case of a priori status can be explained as such by appeal to the nature of the concepts involved in the content known a priori" (755).

I do not question the compulsion that comes with understanding conjunction. But what is left unexplained is how this compulsion, or anything else about the possession conditions of the concept of conjunction, yields the *justification* that would turn a belief in the inference from A&B to A into knowledge. Peacocke's account presupposes a Cartesian access to the possession conditions of a concept, an access which I have just argued that we have no reason to believe that we have. But even if we went along with this Cartesianism, it is unclear where the justification would come from. Thus suppose that a person has Cartesian access to the fact that a certain inferential role constitutes the content of a concept. And suppose that this inferential role makes the concept a concept of conjunction. How would that justify the person's view that an inference from A&B to A is *good*? How do we get from knowledge of the content of a concept to knowledge of logic? It is hard to see how an answer to this will not take our knowledge of logic for granted.

In sum, I think that Peacocke's account suffers from the same defects as the traditional one.

3.4 George Bealer

For Bealer, as we have noted, a priori knowledge arises from "rational intuitions," "intellectual seemings." He emphasizes that these intuitions have a particular phenomenology: "After a moment's reflection you 'just see'" the truth of De Morgan's Law (1992, 103; see also 107; 1999, 30). But what justifies these allegedly a priori intuitions? Bealer, like Peacocke, looks to our grasp of concepts for the answer: the tie "between intuitions and the truth . . . is simply a consequence of what, by definition, it is to possess— to understand—the concepts involved in our intuitions (1999, 29–30). Bealer distinguishes possessing a concept merely "nominally" from possessing it "determinately." Possessing it nominally is compatible with the sort of "misunderstanding" exemplified in Tyler Burge's case (1979) of someone who wrongly thinks that arthritis can be in the thigh; and with the sort of "incomplete" understanding exemplified in Burge's case of someone who does not know whether or not a contract must be written.

But such misunderstanding or incomplete understanding is incompatible with possessing a concept determinately (1999). In other words, determinate possession requires having a true theory of what the concept is about. Bealer then sets out to give an account of determinate possession. His sensitivity to various problems leads, over many pages, to an account that is fiendishly complicated (38–47). However, I think that we can abstract from these complications.

But, first, a word on the phenomenology. Bealer places a good deal of weight on the phenomenology of having what is thought to be an a priori intuition. This is common among apriorists; see, for example, Alvin Plantinga (1993, 106). What needs to be emphasized is that nothing in the experience of having an intuition supports the view that *it is a priori* or, indeed, supports *any* view of what justifies the intuition. In particular, it does not show that the insight is not justified in a holistic empirical way. This theoretical issue is way beyond anything in the phenomenology.

Turn now to Bealer's account of the determinate possession of a concept. We can abstract from the complications of this account because everything hinges on one key aspect of it: the view that if having intuition I is partly constitutive of possessing concept C (in the sense defined/explained), and a person possesses C and has I, then I is true. And, of course, Bealer thinks that there are such concepts and intuitions (otherwise there would be no a priori knowledge). Suppose that this were so. Why would I be justified? More importantly, what would make that justification a priori? The truth in the traditional analyticity explanation that we allowed earlier (3.2) shows how the justification could be empirical. Coming to possess C is an empirical process. If having I is partly constitutive of possessing C then we could find the justification of I in that empirical process. The very same empirical process leads to both the justification and the possession. Clearly if the justification of I is to be a priori it has to be found in some other process.

Bealer owes us an account of this a priori process. It is helpful to compare what one supposes he must say with the traditional explanation of the a priori. On that explanation, first, Cartesian access was alleged to yield knowledge of the relation between, say, <bachelor> and <unmarried>; see (1). To get from this to the knowledge that all bachelors are unmarried, (B), we needed, second, to apply knowledge of logic. I objected to both of these features. I take it that if Bealer has an explanation of a priori justification it must be a two-step one also, but one resting solely on Cartesian access and hence able to do without the appeal to logic. First, simply in virtue of possessing C a person must tacitly know that having I is partly constitutive of this possession and, second, hence must tacitly know that I is true. Now even if one thinks that people have *some* Cartesian access, it would be bold indeed to think that they have *this much*. Thus, suppose that we grant the first step, how do we make the massive leap to the truth of *I* that comes with the second? Remember that Putnam (1975) and two-factor theorists have proposed theories according to which having certain beliefs (e.g. that all lemons are yellow) is partly constitutive of possessing a concept *even though the beliefs may be false*. Yet, according to the explanation we are attributing to Bealer, simply in virtue of possessing *C* and hence knowing that the possession is partly constituted by having *I*, a person must *thereby* know that *I* is true, thus falsifying the semantic theories of Putnam and others. This is very hard to buy. Indeed, it would really amount to little more than the claim that *I* simply *is* justified a priori without any explanation of how it is. Perhaps Bealer has in mind some other explanation.

3.5 Laurence BonJour

Finally, let us consider BonJour. He rests a priori justification on "rational insight": "a priori justification occurs when the mind directly or intuitively sees or grasps or apprehends . . . a necessary fact about the nature or structure of reality" (1998, 1516). So, our problem of explaining the a priori becomes that of explaining rational insight. Where is the *justification* to be found in this quasi-perceptual process of apprehending a necessary fact?

BonJour offers the beginnings of an explanation but he does not claim much for it (180–86).[20] Indeed, with admirable frankness, he acknowledges that "we do not presently have anything close" to an adequate explanation of rational insight (2001b, 674). That seems to leave the a priori deeply mysterious. Not according to BonJour: "the supposed mystery pertaining to rationalism . . . has been . . . greatly exaggerated" (1998, 31); allegations that rationalism is "objectionably mysterious, perhaps even somehow occult" "are very hard to take seriously" (107–8); "the capacity for rational insight, though fundamental and irreducible, is in no way puzzling or especially in need of further explanation" (16).[21]

What is the source of this extraordinary confidence in an unexplained and apparently mysterious capacity? It comes partly from the earlier-rejected view (2.5) that to deny the a priori is to commit "intellectual sui-

---

[20] In my view (2005a, 113), and that of others (Boghossian 2001 and Rey 2001), BonJour's explanation is very unpromising. (BonJour 2005a,b,c and Devitt 2005a,b constitute a debate over the a priori.)

[21] Bealer is also anxious to resist the charge that the a priori knowledge arises from "a supernatural power or a magical inner voice or anything of that sort" (1992, 101; see also 1999, 29–30).

cide." But it comes also from "the intuitive or phenomenological appearances" of rational insight (107): BonJour thinks that these appearances, when examining examples of alleged a priori knowledge, provide a *prima facie* case for rationalism that is "extremely obvious and compelling" (99). I have just rejected the force of this sort of appeal to phenomenology (3.4).

So, in my view, BonJour leaves the a priori unexplained and mysterious. I shall end with a few more remarks about the hopelessness of explaining it and the extent of the mystery.

3.6 The Mystery of the A Priori

Although we do not have a serious theory of empirical justification, we do have an intuitively clear and appealing idea, an idea that treats the mind/brain as an instrument sensitive, via experience, to the way the world is (3.1). We would certainly like to know a lot more about this but it is not in the least mysterious. The contrast with allegedly a priori justification is stark. What sort of link *could* there be between the mind/brain and the external world, other than via experience, that would make states of the mind/brain likely to be true about the world? What nonexperiential link to reality could support insights into its necessary character? There is a high correlation between the logical facts of the world and our beliefs about those facts which can only be explained by supposing that there are connections between those beliefs and facts. If those connections are not via experience, they do indeed seem occult.

At this point, it remains a mystery what it would be for something to be known a priori. Any attempt to remove this mystery must find a path between the Scylla of describing something that is not a priori knowledge because its justification is empirical and the Charybdis of describing something that is not knowledge at all because it has no justification.[22] The evidence suggests that there is no such path. Hankering after a priori knowledge is hankering after the unattainable.

Our knowledge of many things has not yet been given a satisfactory empirical explanation just as the evolution of many organisms has not yet been given a satisfactory Darwinian explanation. But it is no more appropriate to respond to the former by claiming that the knowledge is a priori than to respond to the latter by claiming that the evolution is by "intelligent design." These responses have no scientific substance: they simply label the present absence of a satisfactory explanation.

---

[22] I argue (1998), in effect, that Rey's attempt (1998) to give a reliablist account of the a priori falls victim to Charybdis.

The nice abduction is established: our knowledge of mathematics, philosophy and logic cannot be explained a priori; an empirical explanation of it is the best.[23]

REFERENCES

Antony, L. 2004. A Naturalized Approach to the *A Priori*. In *Epistemology: Philosophical Issues 14, 2004*, ed. E. Sosa and E Villanueva, 1–17. Cambridge, MA: Blackwell Publishers.
Bealer, G. 1992. The Incoherence of Empiricism. *The Aristotelian Society*, supp. vol. 66: 99–138.
———. 1999. A Theory of the A Priori. *Philosophical Perspectives, 13, Epistemology, 1999*. Cambridge, MA: Blackwell Publishers, 29–55.
Boghossian, P. 2000. Knowledge of Logic. In Boghossian and Peacocke 2000, 229–54.
———. 2001. How Are Objective Epistemic Reasons Possible? *Philosophical Studies* 106: 1–40.
Boghossian, P., and C. Peacocke, eds. 2000. *New Essays on the A Priori*. Oxford: Clarendon Press.
BonJour, L. 1998. *In Defense of Pure Reason: A Rationalist Account of A Priori Justification*. Cambridge: Cambridge University Press.
———. 2001a. Precis of *In Defense of Pure Reason*. *Philosophy and Phenomenological Research* 63: 625–31.
———. 2001b. Replies. *Philosophy and Phenomenological Research* 63: 673–98.
———. 2005a. In Defense of A Priori Reasons. In Sosa and Steup 2005, 98–105.
———. 2005b. Reply to Devitt. In Sosa and Steup 2005, 115–18.
———. 2005c. Last Rejoinder. In Sosa and Steup 2005, 120–22.
Burge, T. 1979. Individualism and the Mental. In *Midwest Studies in Philosophy*, vol. 4: *Studies in Metaphysics*, ed. P. A. French, T. E. Uehling Jr., and H. K. Wettstein, 73–21. Minneapolis: University of Minnesota Press.
———. 1998. Computer Proof, Apriori Knowledge, and Other Minds. In *Philosophical Perspectives, 12, Language, Mind, and Ontology, 1998*, ed. J. Tomberlin, 1–38. Cambridge, MA: Blackwell Publishers.
DePaul, M. R., and W. Ramsey, eds. 1998. *Rethinking Intuition: The Psychology of Intuition and Its Role in Philosophical Inquiry*. London: Rowman and Littlefield Publishers.
Devitt, M. 1994. The Methodology of Naturalistic Semantics. *Journal of Philosophy* 91: 545–72.
———. 1996. *Coming to Our Senses: A Naturalistic Program for Semantic Localism*. New York: Cambridge University Press.

---

[23] Earlier versions of this paper were delivered at Macquarie University and at the Eastern Division Conference of the American Philosophical Association in New York, December 2005. I am grateful for comments at those meetings, particularly those of James Pryor.

———. 1997a. *Realism and Truth.* 2nd ed. with new Afterword. Princeton: Princeton University Press.
———. 1997b. Responses to the Maribor Papers. In *The Maribor Papers in Naturalized Semantics*, ed. D. Jutronic, 353–411. Maribor: Pedagoska fakulteta Maribor.
———. 1998. Naturalism and the *A Priori. Philosophical Studies* 92: 45–65.
———. 2002. Underdetermination and Realism. In *Realism and Relativism: Philosophical Issues, 12, 2002*, ed. E. Sosa and E. Villanueva, 26–50. Cambridge, MA: Blackwell Publishers.
———. 2005a. There is No A Priori. In Sosa and Steup 2005, 105–15.
———. 2005b. Reply to BonJour. In Sosa and Steup 2005, 118–20.
———. 2006a. *Ignorance of Language.* Oxford: Oxford University Press.
———. 2006b. Intuitions in Linguistics. *British Journal for the Philosophy of Science* 57: 481–513.
Duhem, P. [1906] 1954. *The Aim and Structure of Physical Theory.* Trans. P. Wiener. Princeton: Princeton University Press.
Dummett, M. 1991. *Logical Basis of Metaphysics.* London: Duckworth.
Field, H. 1996. The A Prioricity of Logic. *Proceedings of the Aristotelian Society* 96: 1–21.
Field, H. 1998. Epistemological Nonfactualism and the A Prioricity of Logic. *Philosophical Studies* 92: 1–24.
Gendler, T. S. 2003. Thought Experiments. In *Encyclopedia of Cognitive Science*, vol. 4, ed. L. Nadel, 388–94. London: Nature Publishing Group.
Gladwell, M. 2005. *Blink: The Power of Thinking Without Thinking.* New York: Little, Brown.
Goldman, A. 1999. A Priori Warrant and Naturalistic Epistemology. In *Philosophical Perspectives, 13, Epistemology, 1999*, ed. J. Tomberlin, 1–28. Cambridge, MA: Blackwell Publishers.
Harman, G. 1999. *Reasoning, Meaning, and Mind.* Oxford: Clarendon Press.
Kornblith, H. 1998. The Role of Intuition in Philosophical Inquiry: An Account with no Unnatural Ingredients. In DePaul and Ramsey 1998, 129–41.
———. 2000. The Impurity of Reason. *Pacific Philosophical Quarterly* 81: 67–89.
Papineau, D. 1993. *Philosophical Naturalism.* Oxford: Blackwell Publishers.
Peacocke, C. 2005. The A Priori. In *The Oxford Handbook of Contemporary Philosophy*, ed. F. Jackson and M. Smith, 739–63. Oxford: Oxford University Press.
Plantinga, A. 1993. *Warrant and Proper Function.* New York: Oxford University Press
Psillos, S. 1999. *Scientific Realism: How Science Tracks Truth.* New York: Routledge.
Putnam, H. 1975. *Mind, Language and Reality: Philosophical Papers*, vol. 2. Cambridge: Cambridge University Press
Quine, W. V. O. [1953] 1961. Two Dogmas of Empiricism. In *From a Logical Point of View*, 2nd ed., 20–46 Cambridge, MA: Harvard University Press.
———. 1966. The Scope and Language of Science. In *The Ways of Paradox and Other Essays.* New York: Random House, 215–32.

———. 1969. Epistemology Naturalized. In *Ontological Relativity and Other Essays*. New York: Random House, 69–90.

———. 1975. The Nature of Natural Knowledge. In *Mind and Language*, ed. S. Guttenplan, 67–81. Oxford: Clarendon Press.

Rey, G. 1998. A Naturalistic A Priori. *Philosophical Studies* 92: 25–43.

———. 2001. Digging Deeper for the *A Priori*. *Philosophy and Phenomenological Research* 63: 649–56.

Sosa, E., and M. Steup, eds. 2005. *Contemporary Debates in Epistemology*. Cambridge, MA: Blackwell Publishers.

Van Fraassen, B. C. 2000. The False Hopes of Traditional Epistemology. *Philosophy and Phenomenological Research* 40: 253–80.

Wisniewski, E. J. 1998. The Psychology of Intuitions. In DePaul and Ramsey 1998, 45–58.

Wright, C. 2001. On Basic Logical Knowledge: Reflections on Paul Boghossian's "How Are Objective Epistemic Reasons Possible?" *Philosophical Studies* 106: 41–85.

[2]

Evidence-based Psychotherapy: Values and the A Priori

EDWARD ERWIN

The idea of developing an evidence-based science of psychotherapy (Erwin 2006) is only now beginning to take root in the discipline and many are skeptical about its prospects. In this essay, I will try to answer a widely held and deep objection. The objection is that unverifiable value judgments must be systematically presupposed in psychotherapy research and practice. My counterargument appeals to a certain theory of value, the theory of defective desires, which in turn presupposes a controversial thesis about a priori warrant. I discuss the theory of value in part 1 and issues about a priori justification in part 2.

1. The Theory of Defective Desires

The theory of defective desires is a "desire theory" in that it connects nonmoral value judgments—for example, that a certain treatment was beneficial to a client—to an agent's desires. One of the best-known theories of this type was developed by Richard Brandt in his classic *A Theory of the Good and the Right* (1979).

Brandt's theory employs a single category of what I will call "defective desires": the category of irrational desires. The satisfaction of irrational desires is not good for the individual, on Brandt's theory, and the satisfaction of rational desires is good. One of Brandt's novel ideas is that one identifies irrational desires by seeing if they would survive what he calls "cognitive correction." Those that would not are irrational; those that would are rational.

I argue (Erwin 2006, ch. 1) that Brandt's single category of irrational desires is not enough; that in most cases, there is no way to tell if a rational desire would survive cognitive correction or if an irrational desire would be extinguished by it; and that Brandt's answer to the skeptic fails.

The theory I now wish to develop uses multiple categories of defective desires; it does not rely on Brandt's cognitive therapy, the effects of which have never been established; and it provides a different answer than Brandt's to the skeptic.

In a typical case of desire satisfaction, i.e., where someone obtains the object of the desire, there is a gain to the person, a benefit accrues. In certain other cases, however, the subject experiences no gain. I am not referring here to instances where someone gains a benefit but subsequent events make it not worth having. For example, a teenager is given a car that he badly wants but two weeks later becomes a quadriplegic as the result of a driving accident. The teenager did benefit from receiving the object of his desire. He wanted the car, and receiving it was beneficial to him; it is just that later events produced pain that outweighed the initial reward. In many of the cases of interest here, however, it is not that subsequent events nullify the initial benefit; rather, there is no initial benefit, at least no net benefit. In another class of cases of interest, the mere having of the desire, given other facts, is bad for the person. I shall refer to desires that malfunction in either of these two ways—their satisfaction yields no initial net gain to the individual or their possession reduces the overall benefits possessed by the person—as "defective desires." This is not intended, however, to be a definition of "defective desire." I shall not even try to give an informative definition but will treat "defective desire" as a theoretical term used to pick out a certain class of desires: namely, those that generally reduce the persons' overall good or generally lead to no benefit even if they are satisfied. In rare cases, the satisfaction of a defective desire does yield some unanticipated benefit, but typically that does not happen.

The theory consists of three parts, each of which needs to be worked out in much greater detail than I do here. I think that each part can be developed further, but if I am wrong then the theory itself is defective (of course, it might be no good for other reasons as well).

Part 1 of the theory consists of a system of diagnostic categories somewhat similar to the DSM categories, the diagnostic and statistical categories used by the American Psychiatric Association, but their function is not to diagnose mental health problems but to classify desires that are defective in some way or other. If the account in part 1 can be made specific and plausible, it may be of use to both the researcher and practitioner in deciding whether a therapeutic outcome is beneficial to the patient or some other party who is the intended beneficiary of the treatment.

Part 2 of the theory consists of statements purporting to explain why the desires classified as defective in part 1 typically produce no gain to the subject or why their mere possession is bad for the individual. In stating parts 1 and 2 of the theory, I assume that we can sometimes tell when the satisfaction of a desire produces a benefit. We often know, I am assuming, that when people desire things that truly make them happy, or give them more autonomy (whether or not there is a concomitant gain in happiness), or enable them to avoid or eliminate severe pain, the results are generally beneficial to them, at least in the short run, when they obtain the objects of their desires. In making this assumption about our background information, I am deliberately, but temporarily, begging the question against a skeptic who argues that no value judgment of any kind can ever be justified. Part 3 of the theory takes up the issue raised by this sort of skeptic. It is here that the issue of a priori justification enters.

There are three concepts that should be introduced here. One is the concept of what is good for an individual; the second is the idea of the intrinsically desired; the third is the concept of the instrumentally desired.

Many writers on the good distinguish between intrinsic goods (things that are good in and of themselves) and instrumental goods (things that are good only because their possession leads to some further good). On this account, if happiness is the only intrinsic good, as hedonism claims, then a psychotherapy outcome is good if and only if it makes the client happier. Many writers on psychotherapy, however, dispute hedonism, and argue that psychotherapy outcomes are sometimes beneficial when they lead to no increase in happiness but enhance the client's autonomy or provide some other benefit. Some also argue a thesis about the ranking of intrinsic goods. For the purposes of psychotherapy, they say, the most important intrinsic good is autonomy, not happiness or pleasure (Holmes and Lindley 1989, 142; Thompson 1990, 13; Kovel 1978).

Problems raised in the psychotherapy literature about how one establishes that happiness or autonomy is intrinsically good and or about establishing the correct ranking of intrinsic goods are very difficult, perhaps intractable. The theory I want to explore avoids these problems because it makes no use of the concept of the intrinsically good. There is no need for my purposes to prove that something is "intrinsically good," where this is taken to mean, in part, *intrinsically good for everyone*, or to prove that one intrinsic good is better than another. In assessing psychotherapeutic outcomes, we are generally interested in identifying a good result for a *particular* client. This determination, ultimately, raises a question about what is good for that single individual, which may or may not be identical with what is intrinsically good for other people (see Erwin 1997, 32–33 on this point). What is good for a client, moreover, is not identical with what she believes to be good for her. People can make mistakes in their beliefs about what benefits them.

It will also help to introduce the concept of what someone "desires intrinsically" (Brandt 1996). I want something intrinsically just if I want it for its own sake. We can refer to such a desire as "an intrinsic desire," and all other desires as "instrumental desires." In contrast to intrinsic goods, what someone desires intrinsically can be determined empirically.

1.1 Categories of Defective Desires

Here is a start at developing a scheme of categories relevant to the evaluation of psychotherapy outcomes.

a. *Irrational Desires or Aversions*: These are the sort talked about by Brandt's theory, those that stem partly from faulty reasoning or incorrect information. It can be misleading to call some of these desires "irrational" if saying this suggests wild irrationality, but this is not what Brandt meant. "Irrational" is to be understood so that it applies when the agent desires something because of a logical error or otherwise unsupported or false belief, even if the mistake is a modest one.

The most obvious cases involve instrumental desires. A client wants to achieve an improved score on a certain type of personality test or a test for depression, but only because his therapist has convinced him that the test is valid, when in fact it is not. Another client wants to punish her father because her therapist has persuaded her that she has repressed the memory of her father's sexual abuse, when, in fact, there has been no repression and no sexual abuse. These are cases of defective instrumental desires, but even intrinsic desires may originate from unwarranted beliefs. A child may want for its own sake something not good for him or her because the child lacks the competence to process evidence for certain beliefs. An adult may intrinsically desire a certain life style involving, say, total chastity, because of some religious or philosophical belief; yet if the underlying belief is not true, then satisfaction of the desire may yield no benefit.

b. *Absolute Musts*: The concept of an "absolute must" was introduced by Albert Ellis (see the discussion in Dryden 1991), who points out that psychological problems often develop when someone transmutes a simple preference into something he or she simply "must" have. My preference for X becomes "Because I like X, I absolutely must have it. Otherwise, my life will be ruined." My desire that a certain woman love me may, at first, be nondefective in that its satisfaction would bring me great joy, but suppose that the desire becomes deformed, and turns into "Because I love her, I absolutely must have her love." This new desire may be bad for me if it takes control of my life and yet cannot possibly be satisfied.

c. *Conditioned Phobic Desires*: I may desire to avoid flying on airplanes or riding on elevators, but the satisfaction of these desires may provide no net benefit to me, or no benefit at all. Some aversions of this sort may be due to false or unwarranted beliefs; in such cases, they fall into the first category.

Phobic desires due to traumatic conditioning fall into a different category; they would be defective even if they were to remain intact after cognitive appraisal or cognitive correction of the sort envisioned by Brandt. Someone gives me a rational argument for the proposition that venturing out of my house to go to work is quite unlikely to pose any grave threat. I am convinced by the argument, but because of the traumatic experience I suffered several months ago, I still desire never to leave my house. The rational argument does not eliminate the defective desire.

Because I sincerely want to stay indoors, someone who helps me satisfy my agoraphobic desire may be benefiting me to some degree, but, all things considered, staying in the house is not a benefit.

How many phobias are due to cognitive deficits and how many to some sort of conditioning, either classical or operant, is a disputed question in clinical psychology. Joseph Wolpe (1993) estimates that about two thirds of maladaptive fears are classically conditioned and only one third cognitively based. On the basis of this estimate, he concludes that in the treatment of phobic fears, cognitive therapy of any sort is likely to work in only about one third of all cases. Whether Wolpe is right or not about this exact ratio (for some doubts see Erwin 1997, 121–23), it is likely that some phobic desires will, because of their etiology, survive cognitive treatment.

d. *Obsessional or Compulsive Desires*: A client may be obsessed with something, say excellence in her scientific work, and the satisfaction of the obsessional desire may provide substantial benefits, but other sorts of obsessional or compulsive desires, say those that meet the criteria of DSM IV, may be defective. A client wants to go through a time-consuming ritual before working, or wants to wash his hands a hundred times a day, but gains little or no benefit from the satisfaction of the desire.

e. *Autistic and Other Psychotic Desires*: Some of the things that an autistic child desires, such as food and warmth, are obviously beneficial; others that spring directly from the autistic condition are not. The child may desire to bang his head against the wall until it is bloodied or want to rip out his fingernails, but the satisfaction of neither desire is beneficial to the child. Similar remarks apply to some of the desires of schizophrenics and those suffering from a bipolar disorder.

In cases of autistic or psychotic desires, unlike irrational desires, neither logic nor false beliefs, nor conditioning, may have anything to do with defectiveness. An autistic child may gain no benefit at all from head banging, but the desire to bang his or her head is probably not due to a false belief or faulty conditioning from nurses, as was once thought. The desire is likely due to a genetic or neurological defect. If that defect could be removed, the desire for head banging or other forms of self-mutilation would presumably vanish.

Defective desire theory, as described so far, can be developed as a purely empirical theory. We can generally decide whether someone instrumentally or intrinsically desires something by asking the person or by observing his or her behavior. Given all of our background evidence, there can be little doubt that many people instrumentally desire to have food and shelter, and that most people intrinsically desire to be happy, even if that is not the only thing they desire intrinsically. Even without an operational definition of the concept of a defective desire, we can, furthermore, form reasonable empirical hypotheses about the kinds of desires that are often defective by looking at the ways desires malfunction, and we can then develop additional categories of defective desires of relevance to psychotherapy. It still needs to be explained, however, why satisfaction of the desires in the categories just listed is in most cases not good for the person. What follows are some explanatory hypotheses.

1.2 Losing the Connection between Desire Satisfaction and the Good

Although some philosophers might question this assertion, on my view, there is no single factor that explains all failures of desires to connect to the good. Here are what appear to be several independent factors that can explain why the connection between desire satisfaction and the good of the client has been lost:

a. *Defeat of a Relevant Desire-condition*: The good-denying mechanism operative in cases of irrational desires is, typically, defeat of a causally necessary condition for retention of the desire. A woman with an irrational desire for X wants X only because she believes that condition C holds and would not want X if it were not to hold; in fact, C does not hold. The client, for example, becomes convinced by her therapist that an increase in ego strength will help with her excessive drinking, but if she were to discover that she was wrong in believing this, then she would not want to achieve the goal set by the therapist, unless she had some additional reason to want an increase in ego strength.

The explanation of why desire satisfaction is not good producing in this sort of case is obvious: If meeting the goal is desirable for the person only if she wants to meet that goal provided that a certain condition is met, and the condition is not met if her belief is false, then meeting the goal is not desirable for her. Not all cases of irrational belief, however, are so simple. A client may greatly desire insight into the cause of her problems only because she believes that understanding their origin will make the problems vanish, but later, after finding out that this does not happen, she may come to desire the insight for its own sake. Before it seemed to her that insight was good because of a causal connection between its attainment and problem resolution; it now seems to her that gaining insight is good for her whether or not it resolves her problems. In such a case, the insight may be genuinely beneficial to the client even though the original basis for the desire turned out to be wrong.

In another kind of case, someone may desire something because of a false belief and stop desiring it once the truth is discovered; yet, unknown to the person, the thing may be beneficial anyway. Desiring something is not a necessary condition for something being good for a person. Because of these complexities, there is no logical guarantee that merely because a desire is irrational, the thing desired is of no benefit to the person. Neither the therapist nor the researcher, however, needs logical guarantees to make an assessment. If the person wants a certain therapeutic outcome only because he believes that something is true, say, that the outcome measure is valid, and the belief is false, there will generally be evidence, even if it is not conclusive, that the result is not beneficial to the client—provided that certain other conditions are met, especially that there is no other visible reason for thinking the thing of value to the person.

In cases where we are right about what someone will believe after learning the facts, why is the truth of the prediction "S will cease to desire X once she realizes that condition C is not met" a reason for believing that obtaining X will not be beneficial (assuming there is no other reason for thinking the thing valuable)? The answer is: If the client realizes her error and no longer has a desire for X, then it will seem to her that the formerly desired end is not a benefit for her. Why is this "seeming to be not beneficial" a reason to believe that X is truly not beneficial? I will try to answer that question in part 2.

b. *Futile Desires*: What explains the defectiveness of "absolute musts" is that they are futile desires that have become so transformed that they take control of a person's life but have no chance of satisfaction. My continuing to love a woman who will never love me may itself be good for me, but the transformation of this desire into "I must have her love me or my life will be ruined" may be bad for me because its mere possession in this form leads to serious psychological problems or just general misery.

c. *Incoherent Desires*: A set of desires, unlike a group of propositions, cannot be logically inconsistent, but they can be incoherent in the sense that they cannot be jointly satisfied. Taken by itself, each of a set of desires may be nondefective, but when combined with other desires, the satisfaction of one or more of the desires may produce no good for the subject. For example, a client may want power for its own sake, but its pursuit may cause the sacrifice of something equally valued, or valued even more, such as reputation, integrity, or contentment.

This factor explains why many conditioned phobic desires or aversions are defective. If I am agoraphobic because of some traumatic experience, I may obtain some benefit from never leaving my house. Consequently, anyone who does something to enable me to fulfill my phobic desire may be doing me some good, but I have other desires, such as the desire to work and travel, and they cannot be jointly satisfied while my desire to stay home is satisfied. The result is that I would be better off if the desire to perpetually stay home were extinguished rather than satisfied.

   d. *The Priority of Second-Order Desires*: Just as the phobic client may get some minimal gain from satisfying a phobic desire, many obsessional and compulsive desires that are defective may produce some good for the individual when satisfied, but not all things considered. The reason is that the person may have a second order desire to get rid of the first order desire and have a greater preference for the satisfaction of the second-order desire. A compulsive gambler may benefit from being given the opportunity to gamble, something he ardently desires to do, but if compulsive gambling has ruined him financially, he may have a second-order desire that is even more important: the desire to extinguish the desire to gamble.

   Some of these cases are also cases of incoherent desires; so a single desire can fall into both categories c and d. This overlap does not matter, but there is nevertheless a difference worth marking. The desire of the agoraphobic to travel and go to work is a first order desire that is inconsistent with the desire to stay home, but this first order desire is one that people typically have. In contrast, the desire to extinguish the desire to gamble is a second-order desire; people tend to have it only when the desire to gamble has led to problems.

   Either the incoherence of a set of desires or the priority of second order desires may also explain the defectiveness of the desire of an autistic child to mutilate himself. Even if the satisfaction of the desire yields some benefit, it is likely to be far outweighed by the resulting pain. Without knowing what goes on in the mind of an autistic child, it may be difficult to know whether the child has a second-order desire to be rid of the desire to mutilate, but even if there is no such desire, it is reasonable to believe, based on a great deal of empirical evidence, that the child is likely to desire the absence of searing pain; this desire cannot be satisfied jointly with the desire to mutilate one's self.

   The priority of second-order desires also explains defectiveness in certain cases where the desire malfunction is not due to a false belief, traumatic conditioning, or defective biology. For example, a woman suffering from bulimia nervosa may derive some minimal benefit from satisfaction of her desire to purge herself of food, but the end result is not a benefit all things considered, except in special cases, as when a movie actress requires a thin physique to prosper in her career. What makes the desire to purge defective in many cases is that the person has a second-order desire to stop purging, for obvious reasons: Purging every day can be quite unpleasant. The gain from purging may be minimal compared to the loss from not satisfying the second-order desire not to purge. If that were not so, as might be true where the weight reduction from purging were to bring tremendous benefits, the desire to purge might not be defective and would probably not be the stimulus for seeing a psychotherapist.

2. A Priori Justification

In assuming that we can sometimes tell whether people benefit from having their desires fulfilled, I am obviously, as already mentioned, begging important questions against the skeptic. I now turn to some of them, although others will be set to one side in order to proceed more quickly to the epistemological issues. One issue I will not discuss here concerns counterexamples to all desire-theories of the good (for a good discussion of some of these issues see Heathwood 2005). My conclusion, hence, will be conditional: Such and such is true if these other issues can be satisfactorily resolved. I shall also assume without giving any argument here that (1) categorical value judgments, which are the focus of the theory of defective desires, are either true or false, and, (2) contrary to what John Mackie has powerfully argued (1977), they are not all false (for the arguments for these twin assumptions see Erwin 2006, although both of my assumptions have also been argued for in the philosophical literature by others). If these twin claims are true, the remaining key issue is epistemological: Can some categorical value judgments be objectively warranted (i.e., warranted not merely relative to what some group or individual believes)? Some, pretty clearly, can be translated into empirical judgments, which in turn can be justified through empirical observation. The proposition expressed by "Roger Bannister was, for a time, the best miler, in the world" is equivalent to "Roger Bannister was, for a time, the fastest miler in the world." The latter has been confirmed by empirical observation, assuming that there were none faster than the milers he routinely beat. There are other examples where something close to a translation can be given (see Scriven 1994), but neither my example about Roger Bannister nor Scriven's examples is of much help in explaining how to justify psychotherapeutic outcome evaluations, which are not equivalent to empirical judgments. Absent reducibility to empirical judgments, the normative claims of interest here appear to be impossible to prove empirically, at least in practice. For this reason, I will assume that the only options for warranting these judgments are: a priori justification or skepticism. If this assumption were mistaken, then this would only help my case for developing an evidence-based science of psychotherapy (Erwin 2006), although it might make appeal to defective desire theory unnecessary.

Assuming that a priori justification is crucial for my project, I need to answer those who are skeptical about all a priori evidence, as well as those who are not but who draw the a priori evidential line at the border of logic and mathematics. I will begin with the more general sort of skepticism.

2.1 General Doubts about the A Priori

Some naturalists (e.g, Devitt 1998) base their skepticism about the a priori partly on Quinean arguments. As is widely known, in the last section of "Two Dogmas of Empiricism" (1951) Quine uses his ideas about the web of belief and holism to show that any sentence or proposition is vulnerable to the possibility of empirical disconfirmation. On this basis, Quine further concludes that "analyticity" (so-called) is a matter of degree; others take Quine to have shown either that there are no necessary truths or no truths knowable a priori. In reply, I argued in Erwin 1970 (311) and in Erwin 1978 (284–85) that propositions that are knowable a priori, or are analytically or necessarily true can, at least in principle, be empirically disconfirmed. Hence, arguments that appeal to Quine's revisablity argument to show that nothing can be justified a priori, or that there are no analytically true or necessarily true propositions must rest on a mistake.

To take one example of such a mistake, consider L. W. Sumner and John Woods (1969) argument. Writing in reference to Quine's last two sections of "Two Dogmas of Empiricism," they say: "There he (Quine) says explicitly that no statement is immune from revision. If so, then there is no statement whose falsity is impossible; but this is to say that no true statement is necessary, that there are no necessary truths" (9).

As I point out in Erwin 1978, the mistake here is to move from "no statement is immune from revision" to "there is no statement whose falsity is impossible." The statement that a particular proposition is logically necessary and that, therefore, its falsity is logically impossible does not logically entail that it is immune to revision. The distributive principles of logic might be necessarily true and yet empirical results from quantum mechanics may at one time have disconfirmed them (whether they were ever in fact empirically disconfirmed is controversial; see Erwin 1978). Empirical disconfirmation of a logically necessary truth is not a contradiction.

An analogous mistake is often made about analyticity. Saying that there are analytically true statements does not entail that some statements are immune from the possibility of empirical disconfirmation (for arguments that analytically truths are not immune from empirical revision see Erwin 1970; 1978).

A third mistake, analogous to the first two, concerns the a priori. Some philosophers have argued that because there are no statements that are confirmed "come what may," there are no statements that are warranted a priori (Putnam 1983; Devitt 1997). Although Quine never proved that no statement is confirmed come what may—indeed his ideas of holism and the web of belief were never specified beyond the metaphorical level—his thesis about revision, with a minor qualification, can be defended on other grounds. With a few possible exceptions irrelevant to the point at issue here, all statements can at least in principle be empirically disconfirmed (Erwin 1970), including basic principles of logic, but the argument against a priori warranting nevertheless fails because it contains another premise, one that is false.

The mistake in the argument about the a priori is the assumption that saying that a proposition has been warranted a priori logically implies that it cannot be empirically disconfirmed. There is no such implication. Putnam and others simply added to the idea of an a priori truth the idea of certitude, or as Putnam sometimes puts it, the idea of a proposition that is "confirmed no matter what" (Putnam 1983, 87). Delete this idea from the concept of the a priori and the Quine-Putnam-Devitt argument against the a priori collapses.

One could, of course, just stipulate that by definition a proposition is known priori only if it is known with certitude or is confirmed no matter what the evidence might be, but, then, the a priori and a posteriori distinction ceases to be exhaustive. We would need three concepts: the a priori (in Putnam's sense, which requires unrevisability or certitude), the a posteriori, and the "a priori" defined as applicable to propositions that can be warranted nonempirically but are still subject to empirical disconfirmation. Thus, if intuitions can support a judgment, then the judgment can be warranted a priori, but the claim of a priori support carries with it no implication of certitude, incorrigibility, or being confirmed come what may.

In defending his view, Devitt (1997, 48) draws a distinction between two ways further experiential evidence should lead a person to change her mind about some statement p: (1) the evidence might bear for or against p itself; and (2) the evidence might throw light on the goodness (or badness) of her thinking about p. Quine's revisability thesis, Devitt claims, concerns only (1), i.e., the possibility of the new evidence telling against the statement itself. Devitt is right about what Quine intended, but his distinction does not salvage the Quinean argument. It is precisely p, the statement itself, which can be both warranted a priori and later empirically disconfirmed. A priori warrant does not logically exclude the possibility of empirical disconfirmation.

A different sort of argument about the a priori is empirical, although few philosophers, if any, have placed much weight on it. Let us suppose that it is intuition that allegedly justifies a priori judgments. Empirical studies have shown that intuition is often unreliable. An example is the demonstrated unreliability of relying on intuition in the interrogation of crime suspects in determining if a suspect is lying. In other cases, the problem is not the demonstrated unreliability of intuition but the fact that the intuitively accepted hypothesis has credible rivals. In evaluating psychotherapies, people often find it intuitively plausible to explain outcome results in terms of the therapy's effects even when they have no secure grounds for this conclusion. Their intuitively based belief about the cause of the therapeutic improvement may even be right, but they ignore the rival hypotheses of spontaneous remission and a placebo effect. The intuition itself in this sort of case does not count as good evidence. These sorts of empirical facts about intuition do indeed show that there is often an overreliance on intuition when empirical data are needed, but in the case of intuitive support for fundamental principles of logic, such as the principle of modus tollens, there are no studies to show that the intuitions of logicians are unreliable, nor are there credible rivals that can be brought in to discount the intuitions of logicians.

The point about the absence of empirical studies demonstrating unreliability applies just as well to the sorts of normative judgments talked about by the theory of defective desires. There is no empirical evidence that when people have the intuition that happiness is good for them, they are wrong most of the time. As to appealing to alternative hypotheses in ethics, I will try to show shortly that this may be a problem for appeals to intuition to support moral judgments but it is not a serious problem, or at least is a much less serious problem, for judgments about what is good for one's self.

Another source of skepticism about the a priori concerns the alleged obscurity of the idea of intuitive evidence. John Mackie (1977) notes that if we were aware of objective values, "it would have to be by some special faculty of moral perception or intuition, utterly different from our ordinary ways of knowing anything else" (38). While it is true that some early intuitionists in ethics did presuppose a mysterious faculty of intuition, there is no need to do this. I will not assume that there is any such faculty.

Others claim that even without a presupposition of a mysterious faculty, the idea of a priori evidence is too obscure to *explain* anything unless a satisfactory positive characterization is worked out, something, it is said, not yet done. The same point used to be made about analyticity: Unless a satisfactory reductive definition can be given, it was widely claimed, the concept has no explanatory usefulness. The latter point about analyticity may be right, but to say with good reason that there are analytic truths does not require a reductive definition or nor does it require that the concept have explanatory power, a point that Quine later recognized ("Analyticity undeniably has a place at a common-sense level, and this has made readers regard my reservations as unreasonable. My threadbare bachelor example is one of many undebatable cases" [Quine 1991, 270]). A very similar point can be made about a priori evidence. If one is merely trying to show that there is such evidence and not trying to develop an explanatory epistemological theory, a negative characterization is enough to grasp what is being said. Philosophers who talk about a priori evidence or warrant generally understand this to mean non-empirical evidence or warrant. This is not too obscure to understand, assuming that the idea of empirical evidence or warrant is itself sufficiently clear to grasp what is being said when one talks of empirical evidence.

There is a further question of what sorts of items count as a priori evidence, the answering of which moves us further in the direction of developing a full-blown theory of the a priori. Some talk of "rational insight," others speak of "intuition," and others of "self-evidence"; there are other possibilities (see some of the papers in Boghossian and Peacocke 2000). I will use the idea of intuition here, although I believe that speaking of rational insight will often do just as well.

To say that A has the intuition that P is true is just to say that *P appears to A to be true* (or, alternatively, that it seems to A that P is true). Does saying this collapse intuitions into beliefs? It does not. It is an objective fact, not logically dependent on what A believes, that P has the appearance of being true or does not have the appearance of being true. Someone, furthermore, may have the intuition that P is true without believing P, or vice versa (see Bealer 1995, 123–24 on this point).

A great deal more needs to be said about what intuition or rational insight is if one wants to develop a satisfactory theory of the a priori, but that is not the goal here. The goal is just to make the case that some value judgments of the sort talked about by the theory of defective desires can be justified a priori.

2.2 The Analytic Position

Even if it is conceded that intuitions can warrant some propositions, many philosophers have taken the position that this is possible only for analytic propositions. These include basic principles of logic and mathematics, and obvious definitional truths, such as Quine's "threadbare" example about bachelors, and nothing else. This theory about the analytic and the a priori, however, is hardly self-evident; it needs to deal with apparent counterexamples and then it needs to be demonstrated.

Many of the most discussed alleged counterexamples, such as "Nothing can be green and red all over," are of no intrinsic philosophic interest and their status as counterexamples remains contentious. Other examples from metaphysics, epistemology, and philosophy of language are more philosophically interesting and may be more compelling. Some are developed by Kripke in *Naming and Necessity* (1972). One concerns the theory of direct reference. The proposition that there is a possible world in which Richard Nixon was not president in 1972 is not analytically true and is not known on the basis of empirical evidence, but is warranted intuitively. Other examples are from metaphysics. An obvious one is "Nixon is Nixon in all possible worlds"; a less obvious, but still plausible example, is "That heat is the motion of molecules is necessarily true, if true at all."

There are also plausible examples from epistemology. One is the thesis that all confirmation is differential (Erwin and Siegel 1989). The thesis is not true by definition and yet it is warranted a priori (Erwin 1996, 47).

Even if all counterexamples can be defeated, which I deny, the thesis that only analytic propositions can be warranted a priori would still have to be proved. Probably the best known argument for the thesis is that the a priori warranting of judgments can be explained in terms of the analytic, and without this explanation, which is obviously not available for nonanalytic judgments, the idea of a priori warranting becomes hopelessly obscure. This is not a good argument; for even in cases of analytic judgments, their a priori support, if they have any, cannot be explained in terms of their analyticity (BonJour 1998, ch. 2). In addition, I have already addressed the claim that a priori evidence is too obscure to understand; my reply was not restricted to claims of a priori judgments about analytic truths.

Although a great deal more needs to be said, I will henceforth assume that there is no convincing reason for holding that intuitions have evidential value only if the judgment is analytic. It could still turn out that this thesis is true, but, as far as I can tell, it has not been proved.

2.3 The A Priori and the Ethical

Some who are skeptical about the role of intuition in ethics, however, rest their case not on general theses about intuition or a priori evidence but on specific arguments about the normative. It will be worthwhile to separate out some of these arguments:

a. *The Problem of Conflicting Intuitions*: One of the most powerful objections to relying on intuitions in ethics is that there are so many conflicting intuitions in this area. In fact, one of the most widely used arguments for moral skepticism is based on the widespread disagreement about moral matters (for a recent and particularly powerful presentation of the argument see Harman 1996).

b. *The Conditioning Objection*: Even where there is a great deal of agreement about ethical matters, this may be because of societal conditioning. People brought up in the same culture are taught the same values and are rewarded for adhering to them and are punished for not doing so.

Where this is a plausible explanation of the convergence of intuitions, the argument continues, the epistemic value of the intuitions is lost.

c. *The Cognitive Thesis*: Another rival hypothesis is cognitive: People often have the same intuitions about fundamental ethical matters because they believe the same religious, philosophical, or political theories; if the theories are false or unwarranted, the probative value of the intuitions is undermined.

These arguments, unlike the more general arguments about the a priori considered earlier, have a direct bearing on the theory of defective desires. The first thing to notice, however, is this. Because the intuitions specified by the theory are not marshaled to support any moral judgments or even any general principles about what is generally good, but merely the judgment that something is (nonmorally) good for one individual, the problem of conflicting intuitions, at least in its usual form, is not compelling. No judgment is being made that, say, capital punishment is immoral, or that happiness is intrinsically good.

A single individual is judging merely that something he or she intrinsically desires is good for himself or herself, not for other people. I intrinsically desire, say, autonomy; autonomy appears to me to be a good for me because that is what I intrinsically desire for me, and my desire for it is not defective. I could disagree with myself if I were to change my mind, but this is quite different from the sort of disagreement that has been traditionally cited to support moral skepticism. Harman's (1996) version of the argument, for example, would lose whatever force it has if it were discovered that people almost never disagree with others about moral matters, but only occasionally with themselves.

Other sorts of disagreements, however, can also arise between agents. A therapist and client can disagree about the proper goals of the therapy because they disagree about what is good for the client. In the majority of such cases, the desires of the client that are at issue are instrumental. Who is right, the client or the therapist, turns in these cases on empirical issues. Is controlled drinking a beneficial outcome for my alcoholic client? I believe that it is not; my client believes that it is. However, if the client values her preferred outcome only as a means to a goal—she likes to drink in moderation and believes that she can do this—the disagreement is hardly irresolvable. Evidence from experimental studies of controlled drinking by alcoholics may tip the balance in one way or the other (and in this case will probably tip in favor of the client's judgment).

The harder case is where the client wants something intrinsically, say, happiness, and the therapist believes that she should want something else for its own sake, say autonomy, or want it even more than happiness. Yet these sorts of disagreements are relatively rare; if moral disagreement was as rare as this, the argument from disagreement about moral matters would not be even initially plausible. In addition, there is no obvious reason to believe, unless one is just assuming what needs to be proved, namely, that no value judgments of any kind can be justified, that disputes involving competing intrinsic desires cannot be rationally resolved. If the basis for the therapist's judgment is the theory that autonomy is the only intrinsic good or that it trumps happiness as an intrinsic good, then it is unlikely that the therapist will be able to support his theory. There are too many intuitive disagreements about what is intrinsically good to rely on intuition here.

Suppose, however, that the therapist relies on no such theory. She just intrinsically desires autonomy for herself in preference to happiness. In that event, the client can rightly reply that if it is the good of the client that is at issue, then it is *her* desire, assuming that it is not defective, not the desire of the therapist, that is relevant in determining her good. Some argument might have to be given here, but when all is done, the theory of defective desires furnishes that argument. It would be question-begging to appeal to that theory now; but I am not. I am contending merely that disagreements between a therapist and client about what the client ought to intrinsically desire are neither plentiful compared to moral disagreements nor in any obvious way irresolvable on rational grounds.

The conditioning objection (the second objection) is also much less threatening here. Suppose that an individual intrinsically desires to be happy. It is not plausible on empirical grounds to argue that her desire to be happy has been maintained into adulthood because of societal conditioning (people with varied kinds of histories of reinforcement share the desire to be happy), nor is it plausible to believe that being happy seems to her to be a benefit for her because of her history of rewards and punishments. Indeed, it would be difficult to use any known conditioning technique to get most people to lose their desire to be happy. Even if, in a rare case, the conditioning thesis could be made plausible for that one case, it is not clear that this would matter epistemically. Whatever the origin or causal maintenance of a woman's desire to be happy, the fact that it seems good to her to be happy—i.e. it seems to be beneficial for her, whatever its status for other people—would still be a reason to think that she is right.

A similar argument can be given against the cognitive thesis. We do have evidence in some cases that people have intuitions about basic moral principles because they hold some unwarranted religious or philosophical theory, but there is no such evidence pertaining to judgments about what one intrinsically desires, at least for most people. People who desire to be happy, or free, or excellent in their endeavors, as far as is known, do not generally desire such things because they hold some general theory, unwarranted or otherwise; it seems to them that such things are beneficial to them because such things as happiness and freedom from pain are things they desire for their own sake, not because they hold some theory.

There are, however, exceptions to the general rule. Suppose that I desire fame for its own sake, to take an example mentioned earlier, and it seems to me to be a really important benefit for me if I can gain it, but I have the desire because of certain unwarranted beliefs about the rewards of fame. In that case, my desire is defective; it falls into the category of irrational desires. In such cases, the subject's intuition may have no probative value, but that is exactly what the theory of defective desires predicts: Where the desire is defective, the bond between the desire and the good of the person is broken.

To sum up: The argument so far goes as follows. First, I answered general objections to there being any a priori justification at all. Second, I replied to those who try to restrict a priori justification to analytic truths. Third, I tried to show that more specific problems pertaining to conflicting ethical intuitions and to the origin of ethical intuitions, whatever their force against appeals to intuition for support of moral judgments, are not a serious problem for the sorts of judgments covered by the theory of defective desires.

2.4 The Positive Case

Not everyone, it is safe to say, will be convinced by the argument so far, but rather than continue that line of discussion, I want to move to an even more difficult problem. Even if all general and specific arguments against ever allowing an evidential role for intuition in ethics can be discredited, a skeptic can still ask for a positive argument for according intuition an evidential role. This is a challenge that is extremely difficult to meet; it may prove the undoing not merely of the ultimate grounds for the theory of defective desires but of all intuitionist theories either for logic, mathematics, or ethics. Something of a positive nature can be said, but the question at the end will be: Is it enough?

The beginning of a positive argument should start with logic. Suppose that a researcher concludes that if therapy T is effective for treating disorder D, and the therapy is administered under certain conditions, then result R will be obtained. But repeated experiments show that the predicted result never occurs. Therefore, the researcher concludes, T is not effective in treating D. The premises of this argument, let us stipulate are true, and well supported, but what supports the inference? Is there an empirical way to prove that if "If p, then q; but not q" is true, then it is correct to infer that p is false? In principle, we could discover such evidence by appealing to a Confirmation Machine (Erwin 1970) to establish the truth of modus tollens, thereby justifying the inference, but there is no such evidence now, and it is unlikely that there ever will be such evidence (although, for a dissenting view that appeals to holism, see below).

If one looks at an even more fundamental principle, such as the principle of noncontradiction, it is even harder to see how we will ever likely to find such evidence: An empirical argument in its favor will have to presuppose that no proposition is both true and false and, therefore, will presuppose what it purports to prove (this problem may be overcome with the use of a Confirmation Machine, but this is at best a logical possibility).

One positive argument in favor of treating intuitions as evidence under certain conditions, then, is that if we deny this possibility, we have to throw out logic as consisting of a set of warranted principles, and if we do that, then nothing, including the skeptical thesis about the a priori, can be warranted. This argument has been made by many philosophers (for recent versions see BonJour 1998; Bealer 1995). There are, however, replies to this argument; so, a detour is needed before continuing the positive case for a priori warranting of value judgments.

Harman (2001), in a reply to BonJour, challenges the argument. He cites an alternative theory that he calls "a general foundations theory." This theory holds that all of our beliefs are prima facie justified and that no belief requires a justification in terms of other beliefs in the absence of a specific well-motivated objection to the belief. If we believe, then, that some fundamental belief in logic is true, then we are prima facie justified in believing it. No appeal need be made to intuition. If believing a proposition automatically justifies one in believing it to some minimal degree, then why not say that moral beliefs are also justified to some degree? Harman presumably does not allow such justification because he believes that the argument for diversity does present a well-motivated objection to moral beliefs being supported by intuition. There is, however, another problem with Harman's general foundations theory.

Some philosophers equate epistemic justification with basing one's belief on evidence, while others do not. On some theories, if one does one's epistemic duty, then one might be justified in believing a proposition to be true even if it is unsupported by evidence. General foundations theory resembles these nonevidential theories in that it does not require evidence for justification; if it did, it would be extremely implausible from the start. It would be extremely implausible to claim that I could obtain evidence for a proposition merely by getting myself to believe it. It is also implausible to think that every time someone believes something as a result of a guess or conjecture, in the absence of a specific well-motivated objection to the belief, the person has evidence that the belief is true. Because I find these things so implausible, I will assume that Harman is not committed to them and I will not pursue them further.

Let it be true then, as general foundations theory holds, that I have prima facie justification for any unchallenged belief that I hold. But being prima facie justified, then, cannot be equated with basing one's belief on evidence, or what BonJour calls an "epistemic reason" for belief. Many people believe all sorts of things for which they have no evidence at all, and they often admit they have no evidence, as when people say that they believe in God merely because they have faith that God exists or that they have faith in democracy but no argument or evidence to back up their belief. They may be prima facie justified (in a nonevidential sense) in holding these beliefs, but that is not the same thing as having grounds or evidence for their beliefs.

General foundations theory, then, does not explain how we can have evidence for believing fundamental truths of logic without appeal to intuition; it explains at most how we can be prima facie justified in a nonevidential sense in believing them.

Harman also points out, in opposition to BonJour, that one does not have to have rational insight into the necessity of a proposition to be justified in believing it. I think this is right even if we are talking about necessary truths. Someone might be intuitively justified in believing a principle of arithmetic and yet not understand the concept of logical necessity, or might have a philosophical theory about necessity that prevents him from grasping that the proposition is true in all possible worlds. However, BonJour's argument that the rejection of all a priori warrant leads to skepticism does not depend on the claim that all a priori warrant involves rational insight into necessity. One can speak of having intuitive evidence without speaking of the grasping of the necessity of a proposition being true. Some people who are warranted intuitively in believing truths of logic see that the proposition has to be true in all possible worlds, but others who are warranted may not grasp this fact.

I conclude that Harman has not explained how we can be warranted in believing basic truths of logic without any appeal to intuition or any sort of a priori warrant.

Another challenge to the thesis that a priori evidence is indispensable comes from naturalists who explain how basic principles of logic are warranted empirically by appealing to Quine's holistic views about the web of belief. In what follows, I will not assume that anyone is committed to all of the following theses, although Quine appears to have accepted all or most of them before he changed his mind.

2.5 The Myth of the Web of Belief

Many myths contain some true elements. One element in the myth of the web of belief that is both true and uncontroversial is:

Moderate Holism: "Moderate holism . . . says that a scientific sentence cannot in general be expected to imply empirical consequences by itself. A bigger cluster is usually needed." (Quine 1991, 272)

As Quine acknowledges (272), the doctrine he is seconding can be found in the writings of Duhem, who in a particularly nice example points to the auxiliary hypotheses presupposed in deriving an observational prediction from Newton's emission theory of optical phenomena. In the experiments conducted by Arago and Foucault, there was an experimental disconfirmation, Duhem notes, but not of Newton's theory. What the experiment declares "stained with error" is the whole group of propositions needed to derive the experimental prediction: the experimental results by themselves do not tell us where the error lies (Duhem 1998 [1954, 263]).

The Duhemian point is very well known; yet it is worth pointing out that it concerns propositions, or, as Quine would say, sentences. It says nothing at all about beliefs. A scientist who tentatively accepts a hypothesis may try to derive an observational prediction without even being aware of all of the auxiliary hypotheses required to make the derivation succeed. There may be a cluster of propositions logically related to each other, but the experimenter need not believe all of them. Because moderate holism entails nothing about beliefs, it lends no support to the idea that a web of belief even exists. The next thesis, however, does concern beliefs.

Cluster Thesis: Belief clusters are often tied together by logical relations.

By the time Quine abandoned, or at least apparently abandoned, some of the key elements of the myth of the web of belief (see his 1991, 268 and 272), he had invoked in his later writings not the whole of science but chunks of it—"clusters of sentences just inclusive enough to have critical semantic mass. By this I mean a cluster sufficient to imply an observable effect of an observable experimental condition" (268). Assuming that such clusters are often believed to be true, the cluster thesis is also true and is presumably noncontroversial. Neither of these judgments can be reasonably made about the rest of the myth.

Web of Belief Thesis: All of our beliefs are logically joined together in a single, interlocking seamless web.

In the title of one of his books, Quine speaks of the "The Web of Belief" (Quine and Ullian 1978 [1970]), but elsewhere he talks of our belief system as a "corporate body" (1998 [1951], 295) or simply as "The totality of our so-called knowledge or beliefs" (296) or as "the total system" (296). Regardless of the terminology, the idea is the same: Our beliefs are locked together through logical relations in a single seamless system. This thesis is crucial for another element in the myth: that, with the exception of certain observational beliefs, our beliefs face the tribunal of experience not singly but in a body (Quine and Ullian 1978 [1970], 22). But what is to be said for the web of belief thesis itself? It cannot be justified a priori, and even if it could, philosophers who want to avoid all appeals to a priori justification—the target of the discussion here—would not want to make such an appeal.

The hypothesis appears to be a very general empirical hypothesis about all human minds. But what observational evidence supports it? None, as far as I can tell. Perhaps we could do an experiment of some kind. What kind? It is hard to envisage what sort of experiment could be done.

Perhaps we can appeal to introspection to confirm the hypothesis. When I give the matter some thought, I can sometimes find logical relations between clusters of propositions I believe which I had thought to be unrelated. Yet I can not do the same for all of my beliefs for an obvious reason: I cannot through introspection identify each and every belief I hold. I cannot even tell how many beliefs I have. Introspection is not going to settle the issue.

It is hard to tell whether Quine, in "Two Dogmas," believed he had an argument for the web of belief thesis, especially since his key point in speaking of the totality of belief, apart from rejecting reductionism, was to support the revisability thesis, to show that no statement is immune from revision; conversely, the point was also to show that any statement can be held true in the face of recalcitrant experience (1998 [1951], 296–97). If he did think that he had an argument, it appears to be this. When faced with a recalcitrant experience, for example, failing to see any brick house on Elm Street after walking up and down the entire street, I can continue to believe that there are such houses on Elm Street if I choose to believe, say, that I am now hallucinating or if I revise one of my other beliefs providing that it is of the right sort. I can even give up my belief in certain laws of logic if I make certain other radical adjustments in what I believe and thus manage to hold on to my belief about brick houses.

This argument may be a good one for the revisability thesis, and perhaps that is all that Quine intended, but taken as an argument for the web of belief thesis, it is no good. The proposition that I can give up, even rationally give up, any belief I hold by changing some of my other beliefs does not entail or make likely the proposition that my belief system consists of a single web of logically interlocking beliefs. All that is required to make the "no belief is immune from revision" argument work is the existence of small clusters of beliefs (for an argument along these lines that does not require the web of belief thesis see Erwin 1970).

The next thesis presupposes the web of belief thesis; so, it is in trouble right away if the former thesis is false:

The Experiential Thesis: Our beliefs face the tribunal of experience not singly but as a corporate body.

Sometimes referred to as "holism," the thesis implies something about the testing of our beliefs: Whenever we put what appears to be one of our beliefs to the test, say that there are brick houses on Elm Street, we are really testing our entire web of beliefs. As with the web of belief thesis, Quine may have thought that his belief revision argument also supports this thesis. After all, when I check my belief about brick houses on Elm Street and find no houses, logic alone does not force me to give up my belief. I have many other choices, even if they are foolish ones. Am I not, then, testing the entire set of beliefs that I may revise in order to avoid agreeing that my belief about brick houses on Elm Street has been refuted? No, I am not: The argument, which may or may not be due to Quine, is not cogent.

In the Duhem sort of case, it is not unreasonable to say that in testing a single hypothesis by first deriving an observational prediction and then experimenting to determine if the prediction is true, I am, whether I realize it or not, testing the collection of propositions needed to derive the prediction. However, to test my belief that there are brick houses on Elm Street, I need not test it in combination with my belief that I am not now hallucinating. I may later deny the latter belief to avoid admitting being wrong, but the belief about not hallucinating was not part of the set of auxiliary propositions needed to derive the prediction that if I walk up and down Elm Street in the middle of the day, and look around carefully, I will see some brick houses.

Even if all of the theses discussed so far were true, there is still one final thesis crucial to the web of belief argument for saying that no belief is supported by a priori evidence or reasons:

Evidential Support Thesis: Each of our beliefs that has support, including fundamental logical beliefs, get its support indirectly through empirical support for our entire web of beliefs.

Suppose we take one more look at Duhem's example of the Arago and Foucault experiments concerning Newton's emission theory. Duhem takes the fundamental hypothesis being tested to be the thesis that light consists in projectiles thrown out with great speed by luminous bodies. He makes the now familiar point that the negative results of the experiments falsify only the combination of the fundamental hypothesis with the auxiliary assumptions. Suppose, however, that the results had been positive and that the Arago-Foucault experiments were well designed. The positive results might then have provided some support for the fundamental hypothesis being tested, but it does not follow that the same results would also have confirmed to any degree each auxiliary assumption. Suppose two psychologists do an experiment to test the claim that the use of the subliminal message "Mommy and I are one" reduces pathology in schizophrenics (Silverman and Weinberger 1985) and assume as an auxiliary assumption that the Rorschach test is a valid measure of schizophrenia. A positive result, assuming no design flaws, might well confirm the research hypothesis, but it would give us no additional reason to believe the hypothesis about the validity of the Rorschach test, assuming there was supporting evidence prior to the experiment.

Although this would be an odd thing to do, suppose, further, that the experimenters were to conjoin with the research hypothesis and the needed auxiliary assumptions additional propositions they believe but which play no role in the derivation of the experimental prediction, say the principles of noncontradiction and modus tollens. Even with experimental support for the research hypothesis, no reason would have been provided by the experimental results for believing any of these additional hypotheses. Part of the belief cluster would have been confirmed but not each and every proposition that makes up the cluster. Even if Silverman and Weinberger (1985) could, contrary to fact, increase the size of the belief cluster so that it were identical to their entire belief system, the result would be the same: All that would be confirmed would be the research hypothesis.

In other cases, empirical findings might unwittingly confirm additional beliefs of the experimenters that were not being put to the test, and which played no role at all in the experiment, but in no case would the results warrant all of their beliefs. They would not even warrant all of the beliefs in the small cluster of propositions needed to derive the experimental prediction. The evidential support thesis, then, appears to be not just unsupported but false.

I conclude that the first two elements of the myth of the web of belief, moderate holism and the cluster thesis, are true, but the remaining elements—the web of belief, the Experiential, and evidential support theses—are all unsupported or false.

Those who believe in some form of Quinean epistemic holism might do what he did: Stop appealing to a doctrine about the whole of science and be content to talk about small clusters of beliefs or sentences: "clusters of sentences just inclusive enough to imply an observable effect of an observable experimental condition" (Quine 1991, 268). In short, retreat to moderate holism and the cluster thesis. This retreat, however, would also force a retreat from the Quinean argument that appealing to the web of belief can explain how basic logical beliefs are warranted as of now, as opposed to being warranted in principle, by empirical factors. Saying that, in general, scientific sentences by themselves cannot be expected to imply empirical consequences and that clusters of logically connected propositions exist does nothing to explain how basic principles of logic can be justified a priori.

A holist might try to add to moderate holism and the cluster principle additional holistic principles that are more plausible than the three unfounded principles in the myth of the web of belief. But what would they be? Without some specification and defense of these additional principles, the verdict should be: As of now, the appeal to holism does not explain how basic principles of logic are warranted by empirical evidence.

The argument can now continue. Assuming that intuitions can sometimes count as evidence in logic and mathematics, and that the arguments for drawing the boundaries around those areas and not permitting a similar appeal in ethics, are all unconvincing, there is a positive reason for granting intuitions evidential status for moral claims: It is the same sort of evidence that is sometimes satisfactory in logic and mathematics, and most likely in metaphysics, epistemology, and other areas of philosophy.

Some skeptics about the probative value of intuitions will not be convinced. They are likely to ask: What positive reason is there for believing that intuitive evidence in ethics is "truth conducive," i. e, when we base our beliefs on it, we are right more than 50 percent of the time?

The requirement that evidence be proven truth-conducive presupposes that it must be truth-conducive in the first place, a claim widely accepted but not obviously correct. As several philosophers have pointed out, it is logically possible that a world exists where people have the same perceptual evidence that we have. They seem to see trees, dogs, people, and mountains, and consequently believe that these things exist. Yet, let us imagine, that God or a competent evil demon causes their beliefs to be wrong more than 50 percent of the time, but these people never learn this fact. If the evidence they have for believing that neutrinos or stars exist is the same evidence that we have, then their beliefs about the existence of neutrinos and stars are well grounded despite their evidence not being truth-conducive. But not everyone agrees. Philosophers have different intuitions about what to say about so-called "demon worlds," but at least it is not beyond dispute that truth-conduciveness is necessary for having a good epistemic reason.

The next problem, however, is the more serious one for the skeptic's position. Even if intuitions must be truth-conducive to count as sound evidence, do we have to be able to prove that they are in order for them to qualify as good evidence? Even if it cannot be proven that intuitions in ethics are ever truth-conducive, neither can we prove it about fundamental principles of logic. In fact, it is hard to see how even perceptual evidence can meet a skeptical challenge about truth-conduciveness. I seem to see a tree right in front of me under normal lighting conditions. Can anyone prove that this sort of perceptual evidence is truth conducive? We might try by pointing to numerous cases where people relied on such evidence and were proven right. But what proved them right if it was not more perceptual evidence, the very sort of evidence that we are questioning?

The answer, then, to the moral skeptic is this: We cannot prove the truth conduciveness of moral intuitions, but neither can we prove the truth conduciveness of logical intuitions or perceptual evidence; the fact that we cannot demonstrate that a certain type of basic evidence is truth conducive does not mean it is not good evidence (for additional discussion of these issues, see Veber 2002 (189–97).

Without repeating all of the steps, a case can be made, then, for intuitions supporting some normative judgments by arguing, first, that intuitions count as evidence for fundamental principles of logic; second, that it is plausible to think that if intuitions count as evidence in logic, then it is plausible to think that they can count as evidence in ethics, unless there is a compelling reason not to believe this; third, that there is no compelling reason not to believe this (the general and specific arguments for saying the same sort of evidence cannot be used in ethics all fail), and fourth, that the demand for a positive proof of truth-conduciveness for ethical intuitions is too stringent and cannot be met in logic either. In saying all of this, however, I intend to support only a modest proposal: that intuitions that someone has about the benefit to him of obtaining what he intrinsically and nondefectively desires is some reason to think that his judgment is correct. If he (nondefectively) intrinsically desires that he do excellent work in his chosen field, or that he be free from excruciating pain, or that he not be depressed, and it seems to him that his judgments about these matters is true, then his intuition in these circumstances count as evidence for his judgment.

Perhaps this case is not solid enough; if it is not and no better case can be made, then we would need to explore other options if the goal of working out an evidence-based science of psychotherapy is to be retained.

REFERENCES

Bealer, G. 1995. A Priori Knowledge and the Scope of Philosophy. *Philosophical Studies* 81: 121–42.

Boghossian, P., and Peacocke, C. 2000. *New Essays on the A Priori*. New York: Oxford University Press.

BonJour, L. 1998. *In Defense of Pure Reason*. New York: Cambridge University Press.
Brandt, R. 1979. *A Theory of the Good and the Right*. Oxford: Oxford University Press.
———. 1996. *Facts, Values, and Morality*. New York: Cambridge University Press.
Devitt, M. 1997. Naturalism and the A Priori. *Philosophical Studies* 92: 45–65.
Dryden, W. 1991. *A Dialogue with Albert Ellis: Against Dogma*. Philadelphia: Open University Press.
Duhem, P. 1998 [1954]. Physical Theory and Experiment. In *Philosophy of Science: The Central Issues*, ed. M. Curd and J. Cover, 257–79. New York: W. W. Norton & Company.
Erwin, E. 1970. The Confirmation Machine. In *Boston Studies in the Philosophy of Science*, vol. 8, ed. R. Buck and R. Cohen, 306–21. New York: Humanities Press.
———. 1978. Quantum Logic and the Status of Classical Logic. *Logique et Analyse* 82-83: 279–92.
———. 1996. *A Final Accounting: Philosophical and Empirical Issues in Freudian Psychology*. Cambridge, MA: MIT Press.
———. 1997. *Philosophy and Psychotherapy: Razing the Troubles of the Brain*. London: Sage.
———. 2010. An Evidence-Based Science of Psychotherapy: Foundational Issues. Unpublished Manuscript.
Erwin, E. and Siegel, H. 1989. Is Confirmation Differential? *British Journal for the Philosophy of Science* 40: 105–19.
Garfield, S., and Bergin, A. 1986. Introduction and Historical Overview. In *Handbook of Psychotherapy and Behavioral Change*, ed. S. Garfield and A. Bergin, 3–22. New York: John Wiley & Sons.
Harman, G. 1996. Moral Relativism. In *Moral Relativism and Moral Objectivity*, ed. G. Harman and J. Thomson, 3–64. Cambridge, MA: Blackwell Publishers.
———. 2001. General Foundations versus Rational Insight. *Philosophy and Phenomenological Research* 63: 657–63.
Heathwood, C. 2005. Defective Desires. *Australasian Journal of Philosophy* 83: 487–504.
Holmes, J., and Lindley, R. 1989. *The Values of Psychotherapy*. Oxford: Oxford University Press.
Kovel, J. 1978. *A Complete Guide to Therapy: From Psychoanalysis to Behaviour Modification*. Harmondsworth, England: Penguin.
Kripke, S. 1972. *Naming and Necessity*. Cambridge, MA: Harvard University Press.
Loewenthal, D., and Snell, R. 2001. Psychotherapy as the Practice of Ethics. In *Values and Ethics in the Practice of Psychotherapy and Counselling*, ed. F. Barnes and L. Murdin, 23–31. Philadelphia: Open University Press.
Mackie, J. 1977. *Ethics: Inventing Right and Wrong*. Harmondsworth, England: Penguin.
Miller, R. 2004. *Facing Human Suffering: Psychology and Psychotherapy as Moral Engagement*. Washington D.C.: American Psychological Association.

Putnam, H. 1983. "Two Dogmas" Revisited. In *Realism and Reason, Philosophical Papers*, vol. 3, 87–97. New York: Cambridge University Press.
Quine, W. 1991 [1951]. Two Dogmas of Empiricism. In *Philosophy of Science: The Central Issues*, ed. M. Curd and J. Cover, 280–301. New York: W. W. Norton & Company.
Quine, W., and J. S. Ullian. 1978 [1970]. *The Web of Belief*. New York: Random House.
Rey, G. 1997. A Naturalistic A Priori. *Philosophical Studies* 92: 25–43.
Silverman, L., and Weinberger, J. 1985. Mommy and I Are One: Implications for Psychotherapy. *American Psychologist* 40: 1296–1308.
Scriven, M. 1994. The Exact Role of Value Judgments in Science. In *Ethical Issues in Scientific Research: An Anthology*, ed. E. Erwin, L. Kleiman, and S. Gendin, 29–50. New York: Garland Publishing Inc.
Sumner, L., and Woods, J. 1969. Introduction. In *Necessary Truth*, ed. L. Sumner and J. Woods, Dordrecht, Holland: D. Reidel.
Thompson, A. 1990. *Guide to Ethical Practice in Psychotherapy*. New York: John Wiley & Sons.
Tjeltveit, A. 1999. *Ethics and Values in Psychotherapy*. New York: Routledge.
Veber, M. 2002. Recent Rationalism: A Survey and Evaluation of Contemporary Theories of the A Priori. PhD diss., University of Miami.
Wolpe, J. 1993. Commentary: The Cognitivist Oversell and Comments on Symposium Contributions. *Journal of Behavioral Therapy and Experimental Psychiatry* 24: 41–51.
Woolfolk, R. 1998. *The Cure of Souls: Science, Values, and Psychotherapy*. San Francisco: Josey-Bass.

[3]

The Philosophical Insignificance of A Priori Knowledge

DAVID PAPINEAU

1. Introduction

According to some philosophers, a defining characteristic of naturalism is its rejection of a priori knowledge. Thus Michael Friedman (1997) says,

> "philosophical naturalism" is characterized by . . . the rejection of any special status for types of knowledge traditionally thought to be a priori . . . in that all knowledge whatsoever is now conceived of as having fundamentally the same status as that found in the empirical natural sciences.

And Michael Devitt (2005) asserts that,

> It is overwhelmingly plausible that *some* knowledge is empirical, justified by experience. The attractive thesis of naturalism is that *all* knowledge is; there is only one way of knowing.

I do not accept this characterization of naturalism. I take myself to be a fully paid-up naturalist. But I see no reason to deny that a priori knowledge is possible. My view is rather that a priori knowledge is unimportant. In particular, it is unimportant to philosophy.

I shall take it as given throughout this essay that, if there is any a priori knowledge, it is analytic—that is, guaranteed to be true by the structure of our concepts. But any such analytic knowledge will be empty. It will fail to tell us anything substantial about the world. Here I am in agreement with Locke, who saw clearly that conceptually guaranteed truths are always uninformative. Locke claims that, "[H]e trifles with words who makes such a proposition, which, when it is made, contains no more than one of the terms does, and which a man was supposed to know before: v.g. 'A triangle has three sides', or 'Saffron is yellow'," And "[T]hose trifling propositions that have a certainty in them, but 'tis but a *verbal certainty*, but not instructive" (Locke 1690, book IV, ch. VIII).

It is widely supposed that a priori conceptual analysis is central to philosophical investigation. I disagree. Insofar as philosophers do engage in conceptual analysis, they have nothing important to contribute. I would say that all worthwhile philosophy consists of synthetic theorizing, evaluated against experience.

To this extent then, I am agreement with Devitt and Friedman. A priori conceptual analysis may be possible, but it is of no philosophical significance. Philosophy needs only the empirical way of knowing. Insofar as philosophy is important, it contributes nothing but "knowledge [that] is empirical, justified by experience," "knowledge . . . having fundamentally the same status as that found in the natural sciences."

In the next two sections I shall flesh out the idea that philosophy consists of synthetic theories. In section 4 I shall qualify this thesis to accommodate the normative and mathematical elements in philosophy. Section 5 will explain how a priori knowledge is at least possible. Sections 6 and 7 will then consider whether there is a real difference between my view that philosophy articulates theoretical assumptions and the view that it engages in conceptual analysis. I conclude by allowing that some apparently serious philosophical issues are nonempirical—however, these issues turn out to reflect indeterminacy in our concepts, rather than any nonempirical subject matter for philosophy.

2. Philosophy as Science

I say that philosophy aims to construct synthetic theories that are consistent with the empirical evidence, just like the empirical sciences. The obvious objection is that philosophy does not look like empirical science. For one thing, philosophers do not generate empirical data in the way that scientists do. Philosophers do not engage in systematic observation and experiment. By contrast, nearly all scientists regard the production of new empirical data as essential to their enterprise.

My response is to admit this difference, but to insist that it is superficial. Maybe philosophers do not play an active role in gathering data, but leave that to the scientists—who after all are professionally trained in such matters. Still, gathering data is only the initial stage of science, a preliminary to the construction and development of theories that will account for those data. The empirically-minded philosopher can argue that, after the initial data-gathering stage, philosophy proceeds in just the same way as science, aiming to construct cogent theories of the natural world that are supported by the empirical data. Philosophers might not gather the data themselves, but their theories can still answer to the data gathered by others.

At first sight, even this claim might seem to be belied by the subject matter of philosophy. Do philosophers and scientists not study quite different topics? Maybe there are a few areas where philosophy and science share interests. When philosophers of biology discuss the units of natural selection, or philosophers of cognitive science assess the empirical plausibility of connectionism, they do indeed seem to be discussing the same topics as scientists. But this does not seem true of much other philosophy. Philosophers are also interested in knowledge, truth, moral value, possible worlds, persistence and change, free will, and the existence of numbers. This is not the stuff of normal scientific theorizing.

I say that this difference too is relatively superficial. Of course, there are systematic differences between philosophical and scientific subject matters. The things discussed in philosophy textbooks overlap very little with those discussed in science textbooks. But this does not mean that philosophers are not still constructing theories of the natural world that answer to the empirical data.

We can distinguish two characteristics that differentiate philosophical problems from scientific ones. As it happens, both of these characteristics mean that solutions to philosophical problems will not normally derive from the availability of new empirical data. This is no doubt why scientists do not regard philosophical problems as scientific. But this does not mean that philosophical theses are not empirical theories—just that they are not empirical theories whose acceptability depends on new empirical data.

The first way in which philosophy can differ from science is in terms of the *generality* of the categories it deals with. Where scientists think about viruses, electrons, or stars, philosophers think about spatiotemporal continuants, universals, and identity. These latter categories do not relate to specific branches of science, but structure all our thinking about the natural world. This makes it unlikely that any specific empirical data will ever decide between competing theories of these fundamental categories. Their extreme generality gives them room to account for an open-ended range of empirical findings. But the same is true of many fundamental scientific theories. For example, no specific body of data can by themselves discredit Newton's laws of motion. Nevertheless, the warrant for such extremely general theories can still depend on their providing the best overall fit with the empirical data.

The second way in which philosophy differs from science cuts across the first. Not all philosophical issues are of great generality. Think of topics like weakness of will, the importance of originality in art, or the semantics of fiction. What seems to make these topics philosophical, despite their lack of generality, is that our thinking is in some kind of *theoretical tangle*, supporting different lines of thought that lead to conflicting conclusions. Progress towards a satisfactory theory thus requires an unravelling of premises, including perhaps an unearthing of implicit assumptions that we did not realize we had, and leading to a search for alternative positions that do not generate further contradictions. Here too we can see why philosophical progress will not normally derive from new empirical data, but rather from a creative restructuring of assumptions. But again there is no reason to deny that the results of such restructuring will amount to substantial empirical theories

3. Intuitions and Philosophy

The view that a priori conceptual analysis plays no important role in philosophy might seem to be belied by the importance that philosophers attach to *intuitions*. Philosophical debate often proceeds by testing general claims against intuitions about possible scenarios. Consider, for example, the descriptive theory of names, or the tripartite analysis of knowledge. These views have been refuted by appeal to intuitions about counterexamples. Thus Kripke (1980) constructed imaginary cases where intuition clearly distinguishes the bearer of some name from the individual that satisfies the descriptions associated with it. And Gettier (1963) has similarly produced imaginary cases of people who have true justified beliefs but intuitively lack knowledge.

Such examples are standardly taken to support the view that conceptual analysis is central to philosophy (cf. Jackson 1998). To see whether this view is justified, it will help to schematize the structure of such philosophical appeals to intuition. Let us assume that the relevant examples involve some modal philosophical claim that $\Box(x)(Ax > Bx)$ (for example, necessarily, if x has a true justified belief, then x knows). We then imagine some specific possible case of A (someone with a justified but accidentally true belief) and intuitively judge that it would not be B (such a person will not know). To the extent that intuition here shows us that this case is possible—$\Diamond(\exists x)(Ax \ \& \ -Bx)$—then the original thesis is disproved.

Whether this kind of procedure requires a view of philosophy as conceptual analysis depends on the status of the relevant intuitions. Suppose first that the intuitions merely show what is *conceptually* possible: our thought-experiments serve only to show that certain kinds of cases are not ruled out by our concepts. If this is the import of the intuitions, then they are only sure to refute the relevant philosophical theses if these theses are themselves conceptual necessities—after all, the mere conceptual possibility of A without B does not rule it out that that A naturally or metaphysically necessitates B.[1] The assumption that philosophical intuitions deliver

---

[1] Advocates of the "two-dimensional argument against materialism" (Jackson 1993, Chalmers 1996) hold that conceptual difference does indeed imply metaphysical difference in

conceptual possibilities thus goes hand in hand with the view that philosophy is in the business of articulating conceptual theses.

Some of those who ally philosophy with science accept this account of intuitions, and in consequence reject the method of intuitive counterexamples. Since philosophical theses are substantial synthetic claims, so this line of thought goes, merely conceptual possibilities cannot discredit them. Rather philosophical theories need to be tested against real empirical evidence derived from active observation and experiment. They cannot be decided merely on the basis of armchair reflection.

However, it is important that this is not the only response to the method of intuitive counterexamples open to those who think of philosophy as aiming at synthetic theories. Instead they can allow that the method is often sound, but say that this is because philosophical intuitions normally embody more that conceptual information alone. In many cases, the relevant intuitions convey substantial information about the world, not just analytic consequences of concepts alone. Accordingly, they are capable of discrediting the kind of synthetic theses that I take philosophy to involve (cf. Williamson 2005).

In support of this alternative, note that intuition arguably plays a role in science as well as philosophy, in the form of scientific thought-experiments, like Galileo's analysis of free fall, or Newton's bucket experiment. Here too the scientist imagines some possible situation, and then makes an intuitive judgement about what would happen. But here the theory at issue is not some conceptual claim, but rather a thesis of natural necessity (say, that heavier bodies fall faster). If intuition is to falsify this, it needs to tell us that there is a naturally and not just a conceptually possible situation that violates this thesis (for example, if a big and small body are tied together, they will be heavier than the big one, but will not fall faster). This thought is clearly not guaranteed by concepts alone, but by empirical assumptions about the way the world works. When Galileo moves from his initial description of the imaginary scenario to his judgment about what will happen next, his inference is not underpinned by the structure of concepts alone, but by some substantial assumption about the empirical world (tying a small body to a big one does not speed them up).

Naturalists can allow a corresponding use for thought-experiments in philosophy. Intuitions play an important role, but only because they embody substantial information about the world. Recall a point made in the last section. Even if philosophical claims are substantial synthetic theories, a common cause of philosophical uncertainty is not that we are short

---

the special case of concepts whose "primary intension" does not differ from their "secondary intension." I am not persuaded by even this limited connection between conceptual and metaphysical possibility (cf. Papineau 2006, sec. 4.3).

of empirical evidence, but rather that we are in some kind of theoretical tangle. Unravelling this tangle requires that we lay out different theoretical commitments and see what might be rejected or modified. A useful heuristic for this purpose may well be to use intuitions about imaginary cases to uncover the implicit assumptions that are shaping our thinking. The assumptions so uncovered can well be straightforwardly substantial theses about the working of the empirical world. These assumptions may not derive from new empirical evidence—as I said, philosophical problems do not normally call for new empirical evidence—but they can be substantial synthetic claims for all that. From this naturalist perspective, then, armchair appeals to intuitions about imagined cases can play a central role in philosophy after all. But these intuitions will not manifest conceptual information, but rather empirical information about the way the world works, albeit empirical information that is part of preexisting thought, as opposed to information prompted by novel evidence. (From this perspective, then, Kripke and Gettier were appealing to familiar empirical information about names and knowledge respectively, rather than to purely conceptual intuitions.)

Note that intuitions understood in this way are by no means guaranteed to be authoritative. Maybe conceptually-based intuitions cannot be mistaken. But the same is clearly not true for every synthetic assumption that is embedded in accepted thought. This is why scientific thought experiments sometimes misfire. For example, consider the widely accepted sixteenth-century "tower argument" against the Copernican claim that the earth moves: the earth can't be moving, because a stone released from a tower will fall "straight down" to the foot of the tower, and not land some distance to the west as apparently required by Copernicus. However, the operative intuition here is flawed, since the stone, which shares the motion of the earth, will not fall "straight down" in the relevant reference frame. The contrary intuition is an implicit product of the geocentrism that Copernicus was disputing, and so is no good as a basis for rejecting Copernicus's theory.

The same point applies in philosophy. To the extent that intuitions hinge on synthetic prior commitments, they are not automatically authoritative in philosophical argument. True, many intuitions will reflect some well-grounded theoretical principle, and to that extent should be respected. But other intuitions can be misbegotten, resting on unsubstantiated assumptions, or some natural but fallible modes of thought, and in such cases it will be legitimate to reject them. For example, materialists about the mind will allow that it is highly counterintuitive to identify the conscious mind with the brain, but respond that it is intuition rather than their theory that is here at fault. In general, then, naturalists will view conflicts between philosophical proposals and intuitive counterexamples as simply special cases of conflicting empirical theses, to be decided, as with all such conflicts, on the basis of overall fit with the evidence (cf. Weatherson 2003).

4. Morality and Mathematics

In this section I want to qualify my thesis that philosophy, like science, is concerned with the construction of synthetic theories that gain their ultimate support from empirical evidence. I recognize that there are elements in philosophy that do not fit this characterization. In particular, I have in mind the normative and mathematical elements in philosophy. Here I want to mark these exceptions, and qualify my general thesis accordingly.

Let me begin with the normative issue. Some parts of philosophy—ethics, political philosophy, aesthetics—deal centrally with normative matters. By contrast, the first task of empirical science is always to establish descriptive findings (even if those findings will themselves sometimes have normative implications). Given this, it seems unlikely that the normative areas of philosophy will yield the same kind of knowledge as the empirical sciences.

An initial counter to this objection would be that metaethics (and metanormativity more generally) is in effect a branch of metaphysics, and to that extent does arguably depend on synthetic theorizing. When philosophers consider the nature of moral or aesthetic value, and analyze the structure of moral or aesthetic discourse, they aim to figure out what kinds of facts the world contains and how humans interact with those facts. If metaphysical investigation in general can be understood as depending on a posteriori scientific methods, there seems no reason why metanormative philosophy should not be similarly understood.

Still, this response only takes us so far. Metanormative investigations form part of the normative areas of philosophy, but it is implausible to argue that they exhaust these areas. Philosophers also engage in first-order normative theorizing. Moral philosophers debate the permissibility of abortion, the acceptability of the death penalty, and so on. Political philosophers ask when outside powers can invade sovereign states and whether liberal values are universal. Aestheticians debate the significance of originality and the worth of conceptual art. If normative philosophy were restricted to metanormative issues, it would be far less interesting and important.

There is no question of here entering into any serious discussion of the sources of normative judgment. But it seems hard to deny that such judgments are formed in ways that have no parallel in scientific investigation. At some level, normative judgments are grounded in characteristic human responses of an emotional and motivating kind. Reactions of this kind play no obvious role in science. This then looks like one place where we must admit that philosophy uses different techniques from science.

It might seem as if I am here presuming some noncognitivist account of normative judgment. But in fact the point applies more generally. The idea that normative judgments must be grounded in characteristic human responses is not peculiar to noncognitivist theories. True, noncognitivism builds the reactive grounding directly into the content of normative judgments, whereas realist and other cognitivist theories present normative judgments as answering to contents that are metaphysically independent of subjective human responses. Still, at an epistemological level, even cognitivist theories of normativity are likely to appeal to something like natural human responses—no doubt refined by education and reason—to explain how we identify the putatively independent normative facts. And, as I said, this looks like something that has no parallel in science.

Having made this point, it is worth observing that this does not necessarily mean that philosophy is here relying on a priori analysis. It is one thing to point out that first-order normative judgments rest on something other than ordinary empirical evidence. It would be quite another to show that such judgments are a priori. The issues here are complex and deserve extended discussion, but this is not the place. For what it is worth, my view is that the grounding of normative claims in emotional and motivating responses makes them more akin to empirical than a priori judgments. The appropriateness of such responses to given situations does not seem like an analytic matter.

Still, the aim of this paper is not just to defend the negative claim that philosophy is not an a priori discipline, but also to develop the positive thesis that philosophy, like science, aims to construct empirically supported synthetic theories. And first-order normative claims will not fit this thesis if their evidential basis lies in something other than empirical evidence, even if they are not priori. So from now on I would like my overall thesis about the similarity between philosophy and empirical science to be understood as making an exception for the first-order normative element in philosophy.

I turn now from morality to mathematics. Many mathematical results are of great philosophical interest, not only within the philosophy of mathematics, but more generally. We need only think of the independence of Euclid's fifth postulate, or the inconsistency of naïve set theory, or the non-denumerability of the reals. Yet mathematical claims do not seem to rest on the kind of empirical evidence that backs normal scientific theories about the empirical world. To the extent that philosophy is concerned with mathematics, then, it seems once more that it diverges from the construction of synthetic theories.

Some empirically-minded philosophers will no doubt respond that mathematical theories are not in fact significantly different from synthetic scientific theories, and provide no reason to question philosophy's status as a synthetic discipline. According to this line of thought, our best empirical theories of the world commit us to mathematical claims, and in consequence those mathematical claims are empirically supported by the evidence for those empirical theories.

I myself do not accept this picture of the epistemology of mathematics. Our empirically best-supported theories may commit us to certain abstract mathematical entities. But this does not necessarily mean that this is what *justifies* our commitment to those entities. Showing *that* we are committed does not automatically explain *why* we should be. It may be that mathematical claims are inseparable from our best empirical theories, but that even so those claims are established by some distinctive mathematical route.

Perhaps the thesis that mathematics gains empirical support from its role in science would follow if we adopted a strong Quinean confirmational holism according to which all parts of a theory are equally empirically confirmed, if any are. But this Quinean holism is difficult to defend (Glymour 1980). (What is more, it is not to be taken for granted that our best-supported empirical theories do commit us to mathematical claims. This is denied by various philosophies of mathematics.)

Just as with morality, the fact that mathematics does not gain its support from normal empirical evidence does not automatically mean that it is a priori. Again, it would take us to far afield to discuss this issue properly here. For what it is worth, my own view is that branches of mathematics that commit us to abstract objects are best viewed as useful fictions (cf. Field 1980). Insofar as we do have genuine knowledge in the mathematical realm, it is logical knowledge that is free of ontological commitment. This leaves us with the issue of the epistemological status of logical knowledge. I accept that logical knowledge is epistemologically peculiar, quite different from empirical scientific knowledge. But I am doubtful that it is grounded in conceptual analysis. I would say that it is sui generis, but not a priori.

Still, as before, it is not enough for my positive thesis that mathematics should fail to be a priori. My positive claim is that philosophy aims to construct empirically supported synthetic theories, and for the reasons given I do not think that mathematics fits this requirement. So, to the extent that mathematical knowledge is part of philosophy, I need once more to qualify my positive thesis.

So from now on I intend to assert an affinity between philosophy and empirical science only insofar as the mathematical and first-order normative branches of philosophy are excluded. I shall not tire the reader by inserting this qualification every time I mention my positive views, but that is how I should be understood from now on.

5. A Priori Knowledge Is Possible

I now want briefly to argue that a priori knowledge is at least possible. As I have said, I do not think that such knowledge is of any philosophical significance. But I do not go so far as to say that such knowledge is impossible, and it will be helpful for what follows to see how it might arise.

Suppose you and I agree that we are going to use 'Eve' to refer to the most recent common matrilineal ancestor of all extant humans. Then surely we know a priori that, unless general evolutionary assumptions are completely wrong, that all contemporary humans are descended from Eve.

It is true, as Quine observed, that stipulations fade. After a while, the use of the term 'Eve' might pass into general currency, and cease to be grounded explicitly in the above stipulation. Still, this does not alter the basic point at issue, which is whether a priori knowledge is so much as possible. Even if stipulation-based a priori knowledge is short-lived, that does not mean it is not real.

In any case, it is unclear that explicit stipulation is the crucial issue here. Suppose some thinker's concepts are structured in just the way that would result from linguistic stipulation, even in the absence of any explicit proclamation. (Your concept <Eve> is constituted by its tie to the actualized description <the actual most recent common matrilineal ancestor of all extant humans>. Why should this not work just as well? The relevant issue is not how the term is introduced, but rather that its reference is fixed in such a way that certain judgments (*if standard evolutionary assumptions are sound, all contemporary humans are descended from Eve*) will come out true whatever the actual facts. This reference-fixing feature is what allows explicit stipulation to yield a priori knowledge. As long as it is present, it would seem to make room for a priori knowledge, even in the absence of stipulation.

Of course, there are serious questions about the analytic-synthetic distinction implicit in the idea of a priori knowledge without explicit stipulation. What distinguishes those assumptions that play a role in fixing the reference of a given concept (<the actual most recent common matrilineal ancestor of all extant humans>) and those that do not (<lived in Africa>)? As it happens, I myself do not think that these questions are as unanswerable as is often supposed. I shall return to this issue at various points below.

There are also serious questions about the epistemological route from reference-fixing facts to a priori knowledge. It is one thing for the reference of my concepts to be fixed in such a way that certain claims are sure to true. It is another thing for me to have knowledge of those claims. Still, it is not hard to imagine cognitive mechanisms take that us from one to the other. One possibility is to suppose that thinkers reason metarepresentationally from the reference-fixing facts to the truth of the relevant claim. But this credits thinkers with a significant amount of metarepresentational knowledge, and moreover does not seem a very happy account of a priori knowledge, since it will hinge on detailed empirical information about the concepts thinkers possess. What seems to be needed is rather some subpersonal mechanism that takes the reference-fixing facts as input and therewith delivers the consequently guaranteed claims as output.

I do not propose to investigate the possibility of a priori knowledge any further at this stage. No doubt there is more to say. But I have no need of a detailed model of a priori knowledge. After all, I shall be arguing that such knowledge is philosophically insignificant. So it will not matter for my purposes exactly how it works.

6. Theories and Concepts

My thesis is that philosophy aims to construct theories in the same way as science does. Some readers may wonder whether this picture of philosophy is significantly different from the idea that philosophy engages in a priori conceptual analysis.

After all, many concepts are arguably constituted by the roles they play in our theories. Quine may have argued that our theoretical net does not divide neatly into analytic white and synthetic black threads. But, still, are not the assumptions at the center at least very light grey, and to this extent is not the philosophical articulation of the assumptions central to our theoretical view of the world effectively the same conceptual analysis?

I say not. Theories are one thing, concepts another. Philosophy is interested in central theoretical assumptions, but this does not make it interested in concepts.

As will become clear, my view here is not that the lack of a clear analytic-synthetic distinction makes everything empirical. Even if there were a clear analytic-synthetic distinction, this would not make philosophy's interest in central theoretical assumptions a conceptual matter. Articulating theories and analyzing concepts would still be quite different.

There are different ways of thinking about the relationship between concepts and theories. For much of the last century, most philosophers thought of this relationship in a verificationist way. However, verificationism thinking has now quite rightly fallen out of favor, and the connection between concepts and theories is now generally conceived in different terms. Let me consider these two approaches in turn.

If you think of representation in a generally verificationist manner, then you will hold that the nature of a community's concepts is bound up with the theories that the community *accepts*. For such accepted theories will determine which *inferences* govern the use of concepts, and therewith which situations will be taken to verify the application of concepts. If concepts are related to theories in this way, then analyzing concepts will be a matter of articulating the relevant theories. On this account, moreover, concepts can be *criticized*, by showing that the theories that constitute them are defective. (For a particularly clear version of this picture of conceptual analysis see Brandom 2001.)

The first thing to say about this picture of conceptual analysis is that it seems perfectly consistent with my account of philosophical method. According to this account of conceptual analysis, the job of philosophy is to articulate theories and criticize those that fail to pass muster. I agree wholeheartedly.

If I do have an objection to this account, it will be that it betrays an odd account of concepts. Note how this view depends crucially on the verificationist underpinning. It is uncontentious that which theories you accept dictates how you *apply* your concepts (at least your nonobservational concepts) in response to sensory evidence. But some kind of verificationism is needed to move from this to the conclusion that your *concepts* themselves depend on which theories you accept.

The difficulties that arise for this verificationist account of concepts are familiar. For one thing, it implies that thinkers will not share concepts with adherents of theories they reject. So those who reject the phlogiston theory of combustion, or the psychoanalytic theory of the self, will not possess the same concepts of <phlogiston> or <superego> as adherents of those theories, and so will be unable to deny what those theories assert by saying *there is no phlogiston* or *there is no superego*.

Other difficulties relate to the analytic synthetic-distinction. If concepts are constituted by their possessors' dispositions to apply them, then it is hard to see how there can be any difference between analytic assumptions that are constitutive of concepts and those that are synthetic. For all parts of a theory will affect dispositions to apply concepts equally.

All in all, verificationist assumptions seem to generate a strange account of the relationship between concepts and theories. Still, as I said, I do not object to the positive conception of philosophy that goes with this view of concepts, as opposed to the view of concepts itself. I agree that the main business of philosophy is articulating and assessing substantial theories, and simply demur from the idea that this amounts to analyzing concepts.

Let me now turn to the alternative nonverificationist way of thinking about the relationship between concepts and theories. Note first that without verificationism there is no compulsion to suppose that concepts are affected by theoretical commitments. What theories we accept may affect our dispositions to apply concepts, but nonverificationists can hold that the nature and referential powers of our concepts is determined quite independently of these dispositions, by causal history, or teleosemantic function, or some such. From a nonverificationist point of view, then, there is no general reason to think of our disposition to apply concepts as making any difference to the nature of those concepts.

Still, are there not at least *some* concepts that are constituted by the role they play in theories? This certainly seems arguable for scientific concepts of entities initially postulated on purely theoretical grounds, like black holes, or quarks—given that these concepts have no nontheoretical connection to their referents, there seems no alternative to supposing that these concepts constitutively refer to whichever entities play such-and-such a theoretical role. And perhaps the same model applies a range of philosophically concepts, like free will, knowledge, or moral value. It is not implausible to suppose that the reference of these terms is fixed by the structure of theoretical assumptions in which they are embedded.

Still, even if many important concepts are so constituted by their theoretical roles, nonverificationists will deny that they depend on which theories are *accepted*. To see the point here, we need to distinguish between Ramsey-sentences and Carnap-sentences. Suppose we represent the theory which defines some term 'F' as T(F). Then the Ramsey sentence of that theory is '$(\exists!\Phi)(T(\Phi))$'.[2] For example, if the theory is that phlogiston is given off in combustion and can saturate the surrounding air, then the Ramsey sentence will say *that there is some unique substance* that is given off in combustion and can saturate the surrounding air. Plausibly, the Ramsey sentences of theories have the same empirical content as the original theories, but say it without employing theoretically defined terms.

More generally, the Ramsey construction shows us how to eliminate theoretical terms from any claims. For example, suppose we want to say 'phlogiston has negative mass'. Using the Ramsey approach, we can replace this by 'there is some substance that is given off in combustion and can saturate the surrounding air, and it has negative mass'. Again, the Ramsey rewriting looks as if it makes the same claim as the original sentence, but without using 'phlogiston'.

The Carnap sentence of a theory is 'If $(\exists!\Phi)(T(\Phi))$, then T(F)'. (For example: 'if there is some unique substance that is given off in combustion and can saturate the surrounding air, then that substance is phlogiston.') For a theoretically defined term 'F', the Carnap sentence can be viewed as a stipulation fixing the meaning of 'F'. Thus: let us understand 'F' in such

---

[2] '$(\exists!\Phi)(T(\Phi))$' abbreviates '$(\exists\Phi)(T(\Phi)\ \&\ (\psi)(T(\psi) \rightarrow (\psi = \Phi)))$'.

a way as to make 'If $(\exists!\Phi)(T(\Phi))$, then $T(F)$' come out true. So viewed, the Carnap sentence does not say anything about the world. It just gives us a shorthand for making theoretical claims. We do not *have* to use the complicated 'there is some substance that is given off in combustion and can saturate the surrounding air, and it has negative mass'. We can simply say 'phlogiston has negative mass'. And in general we can replace the clumsy '$(\exists!\Phi)(T(\Phi))$ & $G(\Phi)$)' by the simple '$G(F)$'.

Note now how this account of theoretically defined terms avoids the debilitating consequences of the verificationist account. Since theoretically defined concepts are constituted by Carnap sentences rather than Ramsey sentences, possessing such concepts does not depend on your accepting some substantial theory, but simply on your accepting a conditional Carnap sentence. My possessing the concept of <phlogiston> does not require me to accept the phlogiston theory itself, but simply to recognize that *if* there is a substance given off in combustion that can saturate the surrounding air, then it is phlogiston. Since I accept that conditional claim, even though I reject the phlogiston theory itself, there is happily no barrier, as there was on the verificationist account, to my expressing that rejection of the phlogiston theory simply by saying 'There is no phlogiston'.

This works because the Ramsey-Carnap account of theoretically defined terms involves no commitment to verificationism. Your dispositions to apply the term 'phlogiston' in response to sensory information of course hinge crucially on whether or not you *accept* the phlogiston theory. But, on the Ramsey-Carnap account, your acceptance of this theory is irrelevant to whether or not you possess the concept phlogiston. That account requires only that you appreciate that this concept has its reference fixed via a certain description ('the substance if any which is given off in combustion and which can saturate the surrounding air'), and you can appreciate this whether or not you accept the phlogiston theory.

Relatedly, the analytic-synthetic distinction is far less problematic within the Ramsey-Carnap framework than on verificationist assumptions. The issue here is which assumptions embraced by some community actually play a role in defining their concepts—which assumptions go into the theory that appears in the Carnap sentence that defines some term 'F'? The obvious way to decide this is to ask the relevant community what they would say if, contrary to their opinion, it turns out that there is no scientific kind that uniquely satisfies some putative definition T. Would they say that there are no Fs, or would they simply say that they had previously been mistaken to think that the whole of T was true of Fs? The former answer would imply that T is indeed criterial for 'F', in that by definition the kind F must satisfy all of T. By contrast, the latter answer would indicate that T includes assumptions that play no role in defining 'F'.

Note how this strategy hinges crucially on the rejection of verificationism. On the verificationist story, the fact that people would continue to say 'there are Fs' if they came to reject T provides no strong reason to suppose that T was not previously criterial for 'F'. For, on the verificationist story, if T *were* originally criterial for 'F', then rejecting T would inevitably occasion *some* change in the meaning of 'F'. Either speakers would cease to apply 'F' altogether, or they would apply it to a modified range of situations—but, either way, by verificationist lights they would no longer be using it with the old meaning. So, as Quine insisted, conditional facts about how they would come to use 'F' *if* they rejected T cannot automatically be taken to reflect the original meaning of 'F'. In particular, the fact that would continue to say 'there are Fs' does not show that all of T was not *previously* criterial for 'F'. (Even if it had been criterial, rejecting T would have required them to change the meaning of 'F' somehow, so why should they not have changed it so as to keep saying 'there are Fs'?)

None of this applies on the Ramsey-Carnap approach. If meaning does not depend on what theory is accepted, rejecting a meaning-constituting theory applies no pressure whatsoever to change meanings. Correspondingly, if you would continue to maintain that 'there are Fs' even if you came to reject T, the obvious inference to draw is that T is not criterial for Fs. True, this inference is defeasible. Even on the Ramsey-Carnap view, speakers *could* in principle change the meaning of 'F' if they came to reject some criterial T, and so end up saying 'there are Fs' even if Fs had previously by definition required T. But in general there is no reason why they should change 'F''s meaning in this way, just because they cease to believe T, and so such a diagnosis would call for special evidence, by contrast with the default assumption that their hypothetical judgments are simply dictated by the current meaning of 'F'.

Having made this point about the analytic-synthetic distinction, I should also say that I do not think that questions about which assumptions enter into the meanings of theoretically defined terms are always clear-cut. This is because there is no reason why speakers should always be sure about what they would say if some theoretical assumption turned out to be false. I think this is the real insight behind Quine's attack on the analytic-synthetic distinction. Would there still be *plants* if it turns out that there is no photosynthesis? Would there still be *comets* if it turns out those eccentrically orbiting bodies are all alien spacecraft? Would there still be *beliefs* if it turns out that no cognitive states have causally significant compositional structure? There is no reason why speakers should have definite answers to these questions. To the extent that they do not, the relevant concepts will embody a certain kind of indeterminacy, albeit an indeterminacy that is normally perfectly benign. I shall return to these issues in the section after next.

From now on I shall assume that theoretically defined terms should be understood on the Ramsey-Carnap model. This model detaches the possession of concepts from *commitment* to theories. Correspondingly, analyzing our concepts will not, as on the verificationist picture, amount to articulating our substantial synthetic theories, but will simply analytically outline what it takes for our concepts to be satisfied. This is why I hold that conceptual analysis is generally of no philosophical significance. Conceptual analysis does not yield substantial information about the actual world, but only such hypothetical information as falls out of the structure of our concepts.

7. The Canberra Plan

There is an influential contemporary school of thought, led by David Lewis and Frank Jackson, and widely know as 'The Canberra Plan', that views philosophical concepts in the Ramsey-Carnap manner, yet nevertheless holds that conceptual analysis does play a central role in philosophy.

Jackson (1998) argues that 'serious metaphysics' accords a central role to conceptual analysis. As Jackson sees it, serious metaphysics aims to demonstrate how a limited number of ingredients (for example, physical ingredients) might metaphysically determine all the different things that everyday thought supposes to be found in the world. Given some everyday category—like belief, or free will, or moral value, or knowledge—Jackson takes it that such a demonstration will proceed in two stages. First, the ordinary folk conception of that category will be analyzed: this will show how our commonsense thinking fixes the relevant subject matter as that category which plays a certain folk-theoretical role. Second, we will then look to our preferred account of reality to ascertain which fundamental ingredients, if any, actually play that folk-theoretical role. This second stage is likely to appeal to a posteriori scientific knowledge about the fundamental nature of reality. But the purely conceptual first stage, argues Jackson, also plays an essential part in reaching the overall metaphysical conclusion.

Jackson explicitly presents this account of 'armchair metaphysics' as opposed to the view that conceptual analysis plays no significant philosophical role.[3] I am not persuaded. For a start, we can query whether all

---

[3] Moreover, Jackson distinguishes between the 'extreme naturalist' who denies that conceptual analysis is so much as possible, and the 'moderate naturalist' who insists only that it is unimportant to philosophy. He aims to discredit moderate naturalism along with extreme naturalism (1998, 154–55).

philosophically interesting concepts admit of an analysis in terms of folk thinking. Jackson assumes that all philosophically interesting concepts (along with all other concepts) can be analysed as equivalent to 'the kind that plays such-and-such a folk-theoretical role'. But it is not uncontroversial that all philosophical relevant concepts are so constituted, as opposed to having their identities fixed by observational, causal or historical relations to their referents.[4]

Still, let us suppose, for the sake of the argument, that *some* philosophically interesting concepts (<free will>, say, or <knowledge>) do admit of folk conceptual analyses in the way Jackson envisages. Even in such cases naturalists can resist his contention that such conceptual analyses are philosophically important. According to Jackson, it is conceptual analysis that sets the agenda for serious metaphysical investigation. But a naturalist can deny that it is the analytic Carnap sentence of the relevant folk theory that sets the agenda, as opposed to the underlying synthetic Ramsey sentence. Imagine that the folk theory that constitutes the concept of belief is that beliefs respond to evidence, that beliefs have a compositional structure, and that belief combine with desires to generate actions—'T(Belief)', for short. Recall now how 'T(Belief)' decomposes into the synthetic Ramsey sentence '(∃!Φ)(T(Φ))' and the analytic Carnap sentence '(∃!Φ)(T(Φ)) then T(Belief)'. Given this decomposition, a naturalist can plausibly maintain that it is the synthetic Ramsey sentence that poses the substantial metaphysical question, not the analytic Carnap sentence. We will want to know about the fundamental nature of belief as soon as we suppose that *there is* a kind of state that responds to evidence, has a compositional structure, and combines with desires to generate actions—this much is already motivation for figuring how the fundamental components of reality constitute this state. All that the Carnap sentence adds is an alternative but inessential shorthand for naming this state. It is hard to see how any

---

[4] In support of his theory-dependent view of concepts, Jackson has argued (2003, 254–55) that we would have no basis for identifying some folk kind with some fundamental kind (temperature with mean kinetic energy, say) in the absence of initial conceptual information about the causal role of the folk kind (heat sources raise the temperature of bodies, temperature in gases goes up with pressure, etc.). His thought is that this conceptual information is essential to our deriving the conclusion that temperature = mean kinetic energy from the empirical discovery that mean kinetic energy plays the same role. However, this is quite unconvincing. Jackson is, of course, right that we need to know that heat sources raise the temperature of bodies, that temperature in gases goes up with pressure, etc., if we are to conclude that temperature = mean kinetic energy from empirical knowledge that mean kinetic energy plays the same causal role. But I can see no reason at all why the derivation should not work quite as well if our knowledge of the causal role of temperature is inductive knowledge derived from a posteriori observational investigation of the temperatures of bodies and gases, rather than a priori knowledge built into the very concept of temperature.

important metaphysical issues could hang on the availability of this shorthand.[5]

To bring out the point, consider the everyday concept of <soul>, understood something that is present in conscious beings and survives death. This concept of a soul can be captured by the analytic Carnap sentence: 'If $(\exists!\Phi)(\Phi$s are in conscious beings and survive death), then souls are in conscious beings and survive death)'. Now, as above, this Carnap sentence will be agreed by everybody who has the concept of soul, whether or not they believe in souls. Yet this Carnap sentence in itself will not raise any interesting metaphysical questions for anybody who denies the existence of souls. They will not start wondering how the fundamental constituents of reality realize souls, given they do not believe in them. It is only those who accept the corresponding Ramsey sentence ('There *are* parts of conscious beings that survive death') who will see a metaphysical issue here. Moreover, the Ramsey sentence will pose this metaphysical issue whether or not it is accompanied by some analytic Carnap sentence to provide some shorthand alternative terminology. In short, the methodological naturalist can insist that anybody interested in 'serious metaphysics' should start by articulating the substantial existential commitments of our folk theories, as articulated in their synthetic Ramsey sentences. Any further analytic conceptual commitments, of the kind that might be articulated a priori, add nothing of philosophical significance.[6]

---

[5] Jackson (1998, 31) urges that interesting philosophical questions hinge on the existence and nature of certain kinds (free will, belief) "according to our ordinary conception." Well, we can agree that philosophical interest often attaches to the putative kinds that are picked out by our ordinary concepts. But this is not to say that there is anything philosophically interesting in these kinds being so picked out, as opposed to their existence and nature.

[6] Might somebody not start with the concept of a soul, and then seek to demonstrate a priori that nothing can satisfy it, because it imposes contradictory requirements (souls have mental states, mental states imply bodily behavior, souls are sometimes disembodied)? Or, to take another example, might somebody not aim to show that the concept of change is unsatisfiable, because it requires specific times to have both of the contradictory properties of presentness and pastness? I respond that there is no cause to think of such demonstrations as aiming to showing the *unsatisfiability of concepts*, as opposed to the *falsity of theories* (that there are so-defined souls, that there is so-defined change). After all, why would it be interesting that certain concepts are unsatisfiable, except against a background where we attach some credence to their instantiation? There remains the point that the theories here are shown false without any appeal to contrary empirical evidence. However, this is to do with logic, rather than concepts. After all, we can as easily use logic to demonstrate that the relevant concept-free Ramsey sentences are inconsistent, as that the Carnap-defined concepts are unsatisfiable.

8. Conceptual Indeterminacy

So far in this essay I have argued that (most) philosophy is no different from science. Just like science, it aims to construct synthetic theories that are supported by the empirical evidence.

One possible objection to this thesis is that some philosophical problems seem manifestly nonempirical. For example, consider the problem of free will. If determinism is true, can any actions be free?[7] Compatibilists say yes, incompatibilists say no. But it seems highly implausible that this issue can be settled in some a posteriori way. Surely all the evidence is already in, and the alternative views are clearly articulated and understood. It looks as if any resolution of this issue is going to need something more than principles of scientific theory-choice.

I agree that this and a range of similar philosophical questions cannot be resolved by a posteriori means. But it does not follow that they can be resolved in some other way. Maybe they cannot be resolved at all, because some crucial concept (for example, <free will>) is *indeterminate*.

Suppose that the concept of free will is a theoretically defined concept. If so, which theory defines this concept? It could be the theory that free actions are those that spring from the agent's motives. Or it could be the theory that free actions are those that spring from the agent's motives *and* are undetermined.

Note now that a community will see no need to decide between the two options if they think that any actions that spring from motives are also undetermined. In their view just the same category of actions will be picked out whether we define <free will> as (a) the type of actions that spring from motives or as (b) the type of actions that spring from motives and are undetermined. (Who cares which way we define <free will>, given that we'll be talking about the same category either way?)

I would like to suggest that this is the reason why the issue of free will can seem so intractable. We have inherited our concept of free will from an intellectual tradition that took it for granted that motivated actions are undetermined. Given this, the tradition was happy to leave it open whether lack of determination should be added into the definition of free will. It would not make any difference either way, if all motivated actions are undetermined.

But, of course, this choice does make a difference if you come to believe, say, that everything is determined, including actions. Then the

---

[7] As is well known, the threat to free will is not determinism as such, but the hegemony of natural law, whether determininstic or indeterministic. Still, I shall ignore this point in the interests of expository simplicity.

weaker definition (free actions = those stemming from motives) will imply there is still plenty of free will around, while the stronger definition (free actions = stemming from motives *and* undetermined) will imply that there is no free will.

Of course, viewed from this perspective, this is not a substantial issue. It is simply a question of how to refine the definition of the term 'free will', once we realize that an indeterminacy in the notion, which was previously thought not to matter, makes a difference to how we describe the world.

This kind of indeterminacy is to be expected whenever concepts are theoretically defined. Recall a point made in the section before last. I said that Quine's real insight was that speakers will often be unsure about what they would say if some theoretical assumption turns out to be false. (Would there still be *plants* if it turns out that there is no photosynthesis? Would there still be *comets* if it turns out those eccentrically orbiting bodies are all alien spacecraft? Would there still be *beliefs* if it turns out that no cognitive states have causally significant compositional structure?) We can now see why this should be so. When some term is theoretically defined, there will in principle be a choice about how much to pack into the defining theory. We could include a lot of what we believe about Fs, thus using a strong theory (T_S) in the relevant Carnap sentence (If '$(\exists!X)(T_S(X))$, then $T_S(F)$)'. Or we could include relatively little, using a weak theory (T_W) for the same purpose. Or we could use any of the theories in between. As long as we are confident that T_W is strong enough to pick out a unique kind, and that T_S does not include so much detail that nothing in fact satisfies it, we will regard the choice between these options as unimportant. For we will be confident that the same kind will be picked out whichever choice we make. And, insofar as this confidence is justified, the resulting indeterminacy in our definition will not matter. The actual-world referent of the relevant term 'F' will be unaffected by the indeterminacy, as will the truth of any sentences involving 'F'.[8]

Still, there are occasions where it turns out that such confidence is misplaced, and that what we include in our defining theory does indeed matter to the actual-world reference. In the typical such case, we realize that the entity that satisfies most of the defining assumptions does not after all satisfy some further assumption A, which previously played an indeterminate definitional role. For example, we realize that the entity that provides the medium for electromagnetic radiation is not at rest in absolute space;

---

[8] One qualification: if we regard Carnap sentences as Russellian devices for reparsing theoretical sentences as quantificational constructions, rather than as a way of introducing genuine terms, then the truth of some wide-scope modal sentences will be sensitive to whether the Carnap sentences involve stronger or weaker theories. For this and further points about the indeterminacy of theoretically defined terms, see Papineau 1996.

or, again, we realize that the quantity that is responsible for changes in temperature and is convertible into other forms of energy is not a fluid. And then we face a choice. Should we say 'there is no ether' or simply that we were previously mistaken to hold 'the ether is at absolute rest'? Should we say 'there is no caloric' or simply that we were previously mistaken to hold 'caloric is a fluid'?

Nothing of such substance hangs on such choices. It's simply a matter of tidying up our terminology once it becomes clear that this is needed. As it happens, in both of the above examples our tradition decided to include the relevant A in the definition, and so concluded that 'there is no ether/caloric'. But it could as easily have gone the other way. We need only consider the example of 'electricity', which in most respects closely parallels 'caloric', except that here we retained the term even after it turned out that the relevant quantity was not a fluid. (If there are definite reasons for a given option in such cases, they are likely to be sociological rather than rational. If the advocates of the new view want to present themselves as substantially diverging from previous theory, they will speak eliminatively—'there is no caloric'. But if they want to present themselves as continuing previous work, they will speak conservatively— 'electricity exists, though not as a fluid').

This then is my model for the apparent intractability of the free will debate. It is a standard case of imprecise theoretical definition. Originally the imprecision is thought to be of no consequence. But then some later discovery shows that the imprecision needs to be removed, while leaving it open how this should be done. More generally, I would like to suggest that a range of apparently intractable philosophical issues can be usefully viewed in the same way. Does personal identity hinge on psychological or bodily continuity? Must intentionality be conscious, or is there such a thing as unconscious intentionality? And so on. Maybe the reason that philosophy finds it so hard to find an agreed answer in such cases is that these are at bottom matters of arbitrary terminological decision.

Of course, I do not want to say that terminology is the only thing at issue in these philosophical areas. Serious and substantial issues are also be bound up with the terminological matters. To take the free will debate once more, there remains the weighty issue of whether people should be praised and blamed, rewarded and punished, if their actions are all determined. This is the real meat of the free will debate, and certainly is not a terminological issue. But note how this question can be raised without using the term 'free will' (I have just done so). Moreover, either answer to the substantial question is compatible with either way of resolving the terminological issue. (For example, you could hold that determined people can still be 'free' yet that they should not be blamed for their transgressions).

So my view is not that all philosophical debate is terminological. Far from it. I think that most philosophical issues are nothing to do with concepts, and hinge on substantial synthetic matters. I have brought in the question of indefiniteness in theoretically defined terms only by way of explanation of why *some* philosophical puzzles seem incapable of resolution by appeal to principles of empirical theory-choice. It is not that these puzzles are resoluble in some *non*-empirical way. Rather, they are not capable of resolution at all, because they are essentially terminological disputes that have no rational answer.

9. Conclusions

Let me briefly summarize the main points of this essay. Even naturalists should agree that a priori knowledge is possible. But a priori knowledge is not important for philosophy. Philosophy does not consist of conceptual analysis, but of abstract scientific theorizing.

There are connections between theories and concepts. But once we understand this on the Ramsey-Carnap model, rather than in verificationist terms, it becomes clear that it is the underlying (Ramsey) synthetic theories that are philosophically interesting, not the (Carnap) definitions of our concepts.

True, there are some apparently serious philosophical issues that seem to transcend any possible a posteriori theorizing. But these issues are not really serious. They are just terminological disputes that arise from indeterminate theoretical definitions.

REFERENCES

Brandom, R. 2001. Reason, Expression, and the Philosophical Enterprise. In *What Is Philosophy?*, ed. C. Ragland and S. Heidt, 74–95. New Haven, CT: Yale University Press.

Chalmers, D. 1996. *The Conscious Mind*. Oxford: Oxford University Press.

Devitt, M. 2005. There is No A Priori. In *Contemporary Debates in Epsitemology*, ed. E. Sosa and M. Steup, 105–15. Cambridge, MA: Blackwell.

Field, H. 1980. *Science without Numbers*. Oxford: Blackwell.

Friedman, M. 1997. Philosophical Naturalism. *Proceedings and Addresses of the American Philosophical Association* 71: 7–21.

Gettier, E. 1963. Is Justified True Belief Knowledge? *Analysis* 23: 121–23.

Glymour, C. 1980. *Theory and Evidence*. Princeton: Princeton University Press.

Jackson, F. 1993. Armchair Metaphysics. In *Philosophy in Mind*, ed. J. O'Leary-Hawthorne and M. Michael, 23–42. Dordrecht: Kluwer.

———. 1998. *From Metaphysics to Ethics*. Oxford: Clarendon Press.

Kripke, S. 1980. *Naming and Necessity*. Oxford: Blackwell.
Locke, J. 1690. *An Essay Concerning Human Understanding* London: T. Basset.
Papineau, D. 1996. Theory-Dependent Terms. *Philosophy of Science* 63: 1–20.
———. 2006. Phenomenal and Perceptual Concepts. In *Phenomenal Concepts and Phenomenal Knowledge: New Essays on Consciousness and Physicalism*, ed. T. Alter and S. Walter, 111–45. Oxford: Oxford University Press.
Weatherson, B. 2003. What Good Are Counterexamples? *Philosophical Studies* 115: 1–31.
Williamson, T. 2005. Armchair Philosophy, Metaphysical Modality and Counterfactual Thinking. *Proceedings of the Aristotelian Society* 105: 1–23.

[4]

Albert Casullo's *A Priori Justification*
ANTHONY BRUECKNER

Albert Casullo's *A Priori Justification* is a rich, intricate, innovative, and comprehensive investigation of the a priori.[1] One of the book's central questions is this: Do any of our beliefs have a priori justification (hereafter APJ)? According to Casullo, in order to answer that *existential* question, we must first answer a *conceptual* question: What is the correct analysis of the *concept* of APJ? We need to answer the conceptual question, says Casullo, before we can try to determine whether the concept in question has any instances in the world.

Accordingly, Casullo considers and rejects various candidate conceptual analyses. For example, Laurence BonJour holds that S has APJ for believing P iff S can see, or apprehend, that P is necessarily true. Never mind for now about the nature of the seeing or apprehending. Casullo puts forward several reasons for rejecting BonJour's analysis that center around the element of necessity. Here is one: people who lack the concept of necessity can nevertheless have APJ for believing that $2 + 3 = 5$.

It does not seem quite right to view Casullo's criticism as exposing a failed conceptual analysis. It is not as if there is a concept of APJ that is a part of our shared conceptual repertoire (or maybe the shared conceptual repertoire of philosophers). The concepts of knowledge and freedom, for example, *are* elements in our ordinary conceptual framework, and so it does make sense to try to engage in conceptual analysis in these cases. But the situation with APJ seems different to me. My rough picture of the situation is as follows. There are some cases of knowledge that seem to many philosophers (call them *the apriorists*) to be special, different from cases of ordinary knowledge of physical objects and their properties. Knowledge about mathematics and knowledge about logic are paradigm examples of

---

[1] Casullo 2003. All quotations in the text are from this work.

such special cases. These special cases of knowledge are in some sense "independent of experience." Let us call the special form of justification that seems to the apriorists to be present in the special cases "a priori justification." The apriorists look carefully at the special cases and try to discern what is going on in them. Different apriorists come up with different conclusions about what is going on in the special cases, about what is the nature of the special justification that seems to them to be present. BonJour claims to discern an element of necessity, for example. Casullo holds that this element is not present in *all* the special cases (e.g., a child who believes that 2 + 3 = 5). Casullo seems right on this score, but not because BonJour has misunderstood our shared concept of APJ. BonJour is wrong because he has made a mistake about what is going on in some of the special cases.

Thinking in terms of conceptual analysis, Casullo maintains that the two leading candidates are what I will call the Pure Analysis and the Mixed Analysis. Pure is minimal: it says that S's belief that P has APJ iff S's belief is nonexperientially justified. Mixed adds a second condition: S's belief cannot be defeated by experience. Casullo holds that Pure is the correct analysis. My earlier doubts lead me to put the dispute as follows: in the special cases, in which one's justification seems to be nonexperiential, is one's belief nevertheless defeasible by experience? This question cannot be answered by analyzing some shared concept. Rather, it is a substantive philosophical question: it is the question whether extensive, wildly recalcitrant experience could defeat the nonexperiential justification I have for believing, say, that 2 + 3 = 5. Radical Empiricists will obviously say yes, but what should the apriorists say? The drift of Casullo's discussion is that nothing precludes the apriorists from agreeing with the Radical Empiricist on this score.

Let me note one peculiarity of Casullo's discussion of Pure versus Mixed. He says that the two analyses agree that "rational intuition," whatever it exactly is, yields nonexperiential justification, but they disagree on the question whether nonexperiential justification is sufficient for APJ. Mixed says no, because the nondefeasability condition must also be met. It seems to me that the mixed theorist should *not* say that rational intuition yields nonexperiential *justification* that may or may not be accompanied by properties that insure indefeasibility. He should hold instead that rational intuition yields nonexperiential justification *only if* that justification is indefeasible.

Let us now turn to the existential question. Casullo maintains that the apriorists can make a case for the existence of APJ only if they can put forward a coherent notion of experience. This is because, for Casullo, the question of whether there is APJ is just the question of whether there is *non*-experiential justification. So the apriorists must be able to draw the experiential/nonexperiential distinction. This might seem easy, but it is not. Obviously, we cannot count just any mental state as experience, for rational intuition is itself a mental state. Equally obviously, sense experience is experience. But what about memory, introspection, and the reception of testimony?

Casullo thinks that trying to carve out the category of experience in an enumerative way will not work. There will be disagreements about what gets on the list, and there is the danger that new forms of experience will be overlooked. The other natural way of proceeding is to try to provide a general characterization of what counts as experience. Casullo considers several ways of doing this and argues that they all fail. First, do it in terms of phenomenology. But there is too much heterogeneity. Second, do it in terms of the contents of the beliefs that experiences justify: the contents concern just the actual world. But experiences apparently can help to justify beliefs with necessary contents, such as that $2 + 3 = 5$. Third, do it in terms of the objects of experiences: they are concreta, not abstracta. But experience can help to justify beliefs about abstracta as well as beliefs about concreta. Fourth, do it in terms of a causal relation between experientially justified beliefs and their subject matter. But experience can help to justify beliefs about abstracta, with which we have no causal contact, such as my belief that $2 + 3 = 5$.

Casullo has a way out of these difficulties in carving out a coherent category of experience. He holds that experience is a *natural kind term* like 'water', with a Putnam-style semantics. There are local paradigms associated with the term 'water', which share a set of surface properties, such as being clear, being a liquid, being thirst-quenching, and so on. The extension of the term is not fixed by these surface properties but rather by their underlying nature. This nature is revealed by empirical investigation. Sixteenth-century speakers of English were ignorant of the underlying nature in question, and it was not until the construction of chemical theory that we came to know that the underlying nature of the paradigms is their being composed of H_2O.

Casullo thinks that the term 'experience' is like the term 'water'. We are at present like the sixteenth-century speakers: we do not yet know the common underlying nature (if such there be) of the local paradigms associated with our term 'experience'. Empirical investigation of our cognitive system is required for revealing the common underlying nature of the local paradigms (if such there be). The enumerative approach to our problem failed because it tried to fix the extension of our term 'experience' in advance of the required investigation of the underlying nature of the paradigms. The general characterization approach failed because it took the relevant surface properties to be necessary and sufficient for something to count as experience. That error is on a par with taking the surface properties associated with the term 'water' to fix the term's extension.

There is a problem with Casullo's account that is highlighted by his remark that all we know a priori about our term 'experience' is the *associated semantic rule* that delivers the paradigms. But what is the semantic rule? In the case of 'water', we use the associated surface properties to "round up" the right paradigms (the clear, thirst-quenching, etc. liquids) for eventual empirical investigation of underlying structure. So presumably there will be an analogous "rounding up" rule associated with our term 'experience', which rule we know a priori. We need a "rounding up" rule to gather the right local paradigms for empirical study of underlying structure. But what is the "rounding up" rule for our term 'experience'? As we saw, Casullo argued that all the general characterizations he considered fail. These were the likely candidates for a "rounding up" rule that specified surface properties associated with our term 'experience'. In the absence of a "rounding up" rule, the empirical investigation that Casullo recommends cannot get started.

Suppose that we *could* succeed in carving out the category of experience. This would not answer the existential question, because we would still need to know whether there exist nonexperiential sources of justification—we would still need to know whether there is APJ in the world. One of the themes of the middle part of Casullo's book is that the extant attempts to answer the existential question on a priori grounds are all failures. So he thinks that the apriorist needs to use *empirical* considerations in essaying a positive answer to the existential question. Not only is this the only feasible way of going, according to Casullo, but it is a dialectically crafty procedure for the apriorist in his clash with the Radical Empiricist: how could he cavil about an appeal to empirical considerations?

Before discussing what he calls the "Empirical Project," aimed at answering the existential question, Casullo wants to undertake what he calls the "Articulation Project." This seems to be a kind of philosophical, nonempirical regimenting and ground-clearing project that will pave the way for an empirical defense of the a priori. One part of the Articulation Project is the provision of a generally accepted description of the cognitive states that, according to the apriorist, noninferentially justify beliefs in an a priori manner. Radical Empiricists hold that such putative states are utterly mysterious, and apriorists reply that they are utterly familiar. Casullo canvasses a plethora of descriptions of the putative justifying cognitive states. Butchvarov and Plantinga speak of seeing or intuiting that P is true, but it turns out that the cognitive states they highlight are doxastic in nature: finding it unthinkable that one is mistaken about P, or being convinced that P is true and necessary. BonJour speaks of seeing that P is necessary, where this sort of nondoxastic state is completely unlike seeing an apple, though it apparently entails a belief about necessity. Bealer speaks of intellectual seemings, which do not carry a doxastic component. Frege's comprehension principle *intellectually seems* to be true, but one does not *believe* the principle in the light of one's knowledge of the contradiction that it entails. Sosa speaks of a disposition to believe P solely on the basis of understanding P, which is structurally just like a perceptual seeming, in which one is disposed to believe P solely on the basis of perception.

The apriorist faces a dilemma, according to Casullo. Either (1) we have direct introspective access to the states that supposedly provide noninferential APJ, or (2) we do not have such access. If the former, then why is there such variation in how apriorists characterize the states? So it seems that we do *not* have direct introspective access to the states in question. But in that case, we cannot make plausible a positive answer to the existential question by pointing to introspective, phenomenological evidence. So empirical investigation is called for.

Here is another difficult part of the Articulation Project. We need to get clear on the *scope* of APJ. All apriorists agree that mathematics and logic constitute paradigmatic subject matters about which we can have a priori justification in our beliefs. But what about philosophy? What about modality? What about morality? Can we come to have a priori justification for beliefs about these subject matters? Apriorists disagree on these questions.

Now let us turn to the Empirical Project of seeking to gain empirical evidence for the existence of APJ. According to Casullo, we need to acquire evidence for several key theses. The first is this: "the cognitive states identified at the phenomenological level are associated with processes of a single type or relevantly similar types."[2] If empirical investigation yielded the result that there is no common belief-forming process that is triggered by the cognitive states that we take to be a priori, nonexperiential justifiers, then this would be a blow to the apriorist and a boon to the Radical Empiricist.

But in light of Casullo's discussion of the Articulation Project, I do not see how this part of the Empirical Project can get off the ground. One of the striking results of Casullo's canvassing of the literature was that sophisticated theorists' appeals to phenomenology fail to reveal any distinctive, agreed-upon cognitive state that constitutes a nonexperiential justifier. We have a problem here that is similar to the "rounding up" problem that plagued Casullo's natural kind account of our term 'experience'. Phenomenology does not enable us to "round up" the special cognitive states we are looking for. Further, we cannot easily work backwards from the subject matters of the beliefs that the states produce, since it is unclear which are the right subject matters. But if we cannot "round up" the special cognitive states, then we cannot get going on the Empirical Project of

---

[2] See the discussion in section 6.3.

investigating the belief-forming processes that are triggered by the states, in an attempt to determine whether there is a type of process that is common to all the special states.

Let me turn to a couple of other parts of Casullo's Empirical Project that seem problematic. Apriorists will agree that if APJ exists, then APJ is truth-conducive. This is because justification is in general truth-conducive. Casullo holds that the claim that APJ is truth-conducive is a contingent claim that can only be supported by empirical investigation. But consider the practice of psychologists such as Kahneman and Tversky who investigate the limitations of the logical and probabilistic reasoning powers of their subjects. The psychologists look at the subjects' responses to various questions, and they find a striking range of error on certain sorts of questions. They conclude that they have found some belief-forming processes that are not sterling in their truth-conduciveness. How do they come to that conclusion? Presumably, they consult their own deliverances of rational intuition when they figure out the correct answers to the questions that their subjects have bungled. So it seems that the investigation of the truth-conduciveness of the pertinent belief-forming processes is not exclusively an empirical one.

The Benacerraf Problem receives much illuminating attention in various parts of Casullo's book. The problem is, roughly, as follows.[3] There is a strong intuition that there must be some sort of causal, or causal-like, connection between the knower and the subject matter of his knowledge. But if the apriorist holds that the subject matter of a priori knowledge is the realm of abstracta, then it is a mystery how one can gain such knowledge. This is because knowers do not stand in causal relations to abstracta. In discussing the Empirical Project, Casullo says that empirical investigation may well afford an explanation of how the processes that issue in beliefs with APJ produce *true* beliefs about the pertinent subject matters. Casullo then says that in understanding how this works, we will have "the key to providing a non-causal-perceptual explanation of how the . . . [processes] in question provide cognitive access to the subject matter of the beliefs they produce" (172). But if abstract entities constitute the subject matter of the a priori justified beliefs, then it is very hard to see how empirical investigation of our cognitive set-up can explain how our minds have access to this rarefied subject matter. I just do not see how there could be a cognitive-science-style answer to the Benacerraf Problem.

I will conclude with a brief consideration of one part of Casullo's rich discussion of what he calls the "relational questions": what are the relations between the a priori, the analytic, and the necessary? Casullo discusses

---

[3] See Benacerraf 1973.

Kripke's anti-Kantian claims about the necessary a posteriori and the contingent a priori.[4] One of Kripke's examples of the former involves the essentiality of origin. Given that Kripke's lectern is in fact originally made of wood, it is *necessary* that it is originally made of wood rather than, say, ice. But the necessary truth that the lectern is originally made of wood is not knowable a priori: it is only knowable posteriori, via empirical investigation of the guts of the lectern. Similarly, it is necessarily true that Hesperus = Phosphorus, but this identity is only knowable a posteriori, via astronomical investigation.

Casullo holds that Kripke's claims about reference-fixing and the contingent a priori stand in tension with his claims about the necessary a posteriori. Suppose that I stipulate that the term '1 meter' is to refer to the length of stick S at t. According to Kripke, I know "automatically, without further investigation" that S is 1 meter long at t; I know this a priori. But it is contingent that S is 1 meter long at t: S could have had a different length at t from the length that it actually has at t. So we have an example of the contingent a priori.

Casullo objects as follows. Suppose that I stipulate that 'wood' is to refer to the substance of which my lectern is made. Then the sentence 'The lectern is originally made of wood' expresses a necessary truth that is, by Kripke's own lights, knowable a priori. Casullo seems to be arguing that this runs counter to Kripke's claim that he has presented us with a case of the necessary a posteriori.

Casullo gives a second example. Suppose that I stipulate that 'Hesperus' is to refer to Phosphorus. Then the sentence 'Hesperus = Phosphorus' expresses a necessary truth that is, by Kripke's own lights, knowable a priori. Again, Casullo seems to be arguing that this runs counter to Kripke's claim to have found a case of the necessary a posteriori.

A natural reaction to Casullo's examples is to say that they are *irrelevant* to Kripke's, since in Kripke's, there is no stipulative reference-fixing that can serve to generate a priori knowledge regarding the lectern and regarding heavenly-body-identity. So Kripke's claim to have presented us with cases of the necessary a posteriori stands.

Though Casullo does not come out and say that this is what he is doing, he might respond in the following way to the charge of irrelevance. If Kripke accepts a Russellian, anti-Fregean view of the nature of the propositions that figure in his examples of the necessary a posteriori, then the Casullo examples engender a problem for Kripke. On a Russellian view, the sentence 'The lectern is originally made of wood' expresses the same proposition in both the situation that Kripke describes and the situation

---

[4] See Kripke 1980.

that Casullo describes, namely a *singular proposition* involving the lectern and the natural kind *wood*. Similar remarks apply to the two different Hesperus/Phosphorus examples: the same singular proposition involving a planet figures in both. Given these assumptions, Kripke cannot maintain that he has presented us a proposition about the lectern that is *only* knowable a posteriori; and he cannot maintain that he has presented us with a proposition about a planet that is *only* knowable a posteriori. The pertinent necessary propositions can be known in *both* an a priori *and* an a posteriori manner. This is not surprising, though, since mathematical propositions seem to have just that character.

In defense of Kripke, he has never subscribed to the Russellian approach to propositions. In "A Puzzle about Belief," he worries that the notion of proposition is in danger of breaking down under various pressures.[5] In *Naming and Necessity*, he speaks of a priori knowledge that certain *sentences are true* in discussing the contingent a priori. So Kripke could hold that given the normal, nonstipulative way in which I come to understand the pertinent sentences in the Kripkean examples of the necessary a posteriori, I cannot come to know a priori that the sentences are true. In order to know this a priori, I would need to come to understand the sentences in a different way, viz. by stipulating the reference of certain key terms.

It is in the nature of philosophers to criticize, criticize, criticize. Despite the foregoing worries about Casullo's book, I want to end by praising it. When BonJour's *In Defense of Pure Reason* was published, I thought that it was at that point the benchmark work on the a priori.[6] It seems to me that Casullo's *A Priori Justification* has supplanted it.

REFERENCES

Benacerraf, P. 1973. Mathematical Truth. *Journal of Philosophy* 70: 661–79.
BonJour, L. 1998. *In Defense of Pure Reason*. Cambridge: Cambridge University Press.
Casullo, A. 2003. *A Priori Justification*. Oxford: Oxford University Press.
Kripke, S. 1980. *Naming and Necessity*. Cambridge: Harvard University Press.
———. 1994. A Puzzle about Belief. In *Meaning and Use*, ed. A. Margalit, 239–83. Dordrecht: Reidel.

---

[5] See Kripke 1994.
[6] See BonJour 1998.

[5]

Experience as a Natural Kind: Reflections on Albert Casullo's *A Priori Justification*

ROBIN JESHION

It is a pleasure to have the opportunity to discuss Albert Casullo's book *A Priori Justification*. There are so many things to admire in it. It is remarkably clear and chockfull of argumentation. It is also extremely comprehensive and systematic in treating the contemporary literature on the a priori. What I admire most of all is Casullo's ability to examine all sides in the debate with an extremely fair and critical mind that is able to see the shortcomings in arguments even for views he favors. This book reaps rewards because he is offering up a bold wholesale criticism of pretty nearly all previous attempts to articulate and support moderate rationalism, and this criticism leads him to outline a novel, interesting, and probably promising way of going.

Casullo's central critical claim is that both proponents and opponents of moderate rationalism have offered uncompelling arguments for their positions. He sees the current debate as in a standoff. Proponents of the a priori typically appeal to a logical or rational faculty for recognizing logical or mathematical truths (and possibly others—modal, philosophical, ethical, as well) and often claim that they can recognize "from the inside" the operation of this faculty. The faculty, it is said, generates rational or logical intuitions that are identifiable at the phenomenological level and that ground beliefs independent of the justificatory services of sense perception. Opponents of the a priori typically maintain that these so-called logical and rational intuitions are entirely mysterious, and that there is no basis for the claims to a special nonexperiential faculty. Casullo sees fault on both sides. He carefully addresses the details but his main complaints are that neither proponents nor opponents of the a priori have advanced arguments that would be compelling to the other side. The basic strategy of advancing analytical arguments in support of or against moderate rationalism is both misguided and dialectically unproductive.

Casullo's main positive aim is to reorient how we go about establishing or undermining moderate rationalism. The best strategy, according to Casullo, is to advance theory-neutral empirical evidence that should be compelling to all participants in the debate, what Casullo calls "common ground." He thinks that such empirical evidence ought to be capable of generating a consensus about the standing of moderate rationalism. And he seems to be very doubtful that any nonempirical approaches could do the job. More specifically, the two main theses he argues for are (1) Empirical research is needed to clearly explicate the thesis of moderate rationalism. In particular, it is needed to articulate the concepts of experiential and nonexperiential sources of justification. (2) Empirical research is needed to discover whether moderate rationalism is true. So Casullo's project here, interestingly, is neither a defense of nor assault on rationalism, but rather a kind of metatheory about how we ought to go about investigating its truth.

Before I get going in what will be (alas—it is what we do) a largely clarificatory and critical discussion, I want to start off by noting how much I admire Casullo's intentions in drawing up this project. He is earnestly looking for a way to avoid what he rightly sees as a stalemate between opponents and proponents of moderate rationalism. Though, in the last thirty years or so there has been a resurgence of interest in the a priori, and there have been numerous conferences and volumes published on the a priori and the status of rational intuition, there have been remarkably few attempts to clearly and coolly assess the strengths and weaknesses of both sides of the debate and to try to find a means of attacking the problem that will, at least intially, be acceptable to all. In *A Priori Justification*, Casullo does exactly this. I can think of no other philosopher who has even approached the problem with as fair and clear a mind.

Casullo starts off by arguing that the concept of a priori justification is just the concept of "nonexperiential" justification. In particular, it does not involve certainty, indubitability, or infallibility. He claims that the key question in the contemporary debate is whether any of our beliefs are, in this sense, a priori justified. Moderate rationalism is the view that gives a positive answer to this question. In what follows, my comments will be largely confined to examining Casullo's arguments for and ideas in favor of the two main theses mentioned above. Though there are numerous interesting issues associated with whether we should understand a priori justification simply as "nonexperiential justification," here I shall simply grant this to Casullo.

In taking a priori justification to be nonexperiential justification, we need to understand the relevant notions of experience and to specify the sense in which nonexperiential justification is independent from experience. Casullo begins by distinguishing what he calls the broad and narrow notions of experience. The broad notion of experience "applies to any introspectively accessible state" of a thinker (Casullo, 149). So, if there are logical intuitions that are introspectively accessible, then they count as experiences in this broad sense. This notion of experience is broad precisely because it includes both introspectively accessible sense perceptual experiences and the experiences of logical intuitions that proponents of the a priori claim to be transparently identifiable. Plainly, this notion of experience does not cut a meaningful a priori /a posteriori distinction, so it is the narrow notion of experience—the one on which beliefs that are grounded on logical intuitions are not counted as experiences—that is relevant to the project of establishing or undermining moderate rationalism.

Casullo reviews and criticizes various ways of analyzing the narrow notion of experience. The first way is by enumerating all the varieties of experiences that a priori justified beliefs are not based upon. Standard candidates to be included are experiences had by the five senses. But there are problems with this approach, argues Casullo. First, it is not clear how to complete the list, especially since there is little agreement about whether introspection, memory, and testimony should count as experiences in this narrow sense. Second, even if the list is completed, it will have little explanatory value for it will not reveal why logical intuition does not itself count as an experience in this narrow sense. Third, once the list is completed, a hitherto unidentified source of justification (perhaps telepathy) would automatically count as nonexperiential. In effect, the enumerative approach automatically rules out the possibility of new experiential sources.

The main alternative to the enumerative approach is what might be called the conceptual approach, whereby one attempts to give a conceptual analysis of the narrow notion of experience. Casullo discusses conceptual analyses on which the following features of sense perceptual experience are singled out as relevant ones for capturing the nature of narrow experience: (1) phenomenological features; (2) the contents of the beliefs justified by sense experience; (3) the objects of sense experience; and (4) the relation between the thinker and the object of experience.

Casullo rejects all of these approaches. With respect to (1) he is doubtful both that there are any phenomenological features common to sense perceptual experiences and that they are also exemplified by all other experiences that would count as "narrow." He suggests, in particular, that it is wrong to characterize sense perceptual experience in terms of being appeared to in a particular way, for example having a sensuous appearance as of redness (for vision), as of thunder (for audition), and so on.

Casullo considers BonJour's version of (2) on which the relevant notion of experience "should be understood to include any sort of cognitive factor or element which, whatever its other characteristics may be, provides or constitutes information, input, concerning the specific character or the actual worlds as opposed to other possible worlds."[1] Casullo claims that on this proposal experiential justification reduces to justified belief in a contingent truth and nonexperiential justification reduces to justified belief in a necessary truth. He rejects the proposal because it automatically rules out necessary truths justified empirically and contingent truths justified a priori. Plus he holds that it lacks explanatory power insofar as it does not indicate the nature of the difference between justifications for believing necessary truths and justifications for believing contingent truths.

The version of (3) that Casullo discusses is, basically, Lewis's according to which sense experience involves a relation between a subject and a concrete object or event, whereas nonexperiential sources involve relations only to abstract objects (numbers, worlds, and so on). His criticisms here structurally parallel those advanced against BonJour. He sees problems in the fact that it automatically rules out sense perceptually justified beliefs about abstract objects and nonexperientially justified beliefs about concrete objects. And, again, he claims it lacks explanatory power because it fails to reveal the nature of the difference between justifications for belief about concrete objects and justifications for beliefs about abstract objects.

The last variety of conceptual analysis of the narrow notion of experience (4) pinpoints a relationship between subject and the object of experience, typically a causal relationship. Casullo's discussion here is complicated. Since it will not be significant in what follows, I will just signal here that he finds wanting each causally inspired analysis that he considers. In the end, Casullo maintains that there is a common reason why these four approaches have failed to turn up a viable analysis of experience. The failures are "a product of *a priori* reflection on introspectively accessible features of cognitive experience" (Casullo, 158).

I am doubtful that the problems associated with hitting upon a correct analysis of this narrow notion of experience are exclusively or primarily due to a priori reflection on introspectively accessible features of cognitive experience. While philosophers may make numerous mistakes in their attempts to put down the relevant features of experience, the failures do not themselves suggest or signal the need to look in an entirely different direction for an answer.[2] Instead, the failures may be correctable by further a priori reflection—engaging in considering counterexamples and explanatory worth of the explications (e.g., some of the critical work that Casullo

---

[1] BonJour, *The Structure of Empirical Knowledge*, 192.

[2] Casullo, of course, does not say that the failures do themselves suggest that we turn to empirical science to nail down the notion. He just sees this as the most fruitful option. I just wish here to suggest alternative reasons for problems with the conceptual analyses.

does himself). Indeed, I am inclined to think that the real reason for the problems with the analyses is because the concept of experience, in the sense of interest here, is a functional notion that is quite difficult to nail down analytically. I will develop this point further shortly.

As an alternative to giving an analytical account of experience, Casullo proposes that we instead look to empirical science to understand its nature. How can we do so? Casullo's key idea here is that we can draw on empirical evidence if we treat the term "experience" as a putative natural kind term. This proposal is, I think, one of the most interesting, original, and provocative ideas in the book. I'm going to take some time now to spell out the details.

Casullo's starting point is that we currently lack both an acceptable account and adequate understanding of the nature of experience. All that we have are a range of paradigmatic instances of types of experience, namely seeing, hearing, tasting, smelling, touching. These cognitive processes are identified by their having certain features at a kind of crude "macro" or "surface" level: they provide information about the actual world, they put us in causal relation to physical objects, and they possess a distinctive phenomenology. While these features are used to select the paradigm instances of experiences, they do not fix the extension of the term "experience." In fact, according to Casullo, no such analytical account or phenomenological identification fixes the extension of the term. And none could. For its extension is fixed, rather, by "the underlying nature of the paradigms" (Casullo, 158), by which Casullo means whatever it is that empirical science—here cognitive science, but perhaps neuroscience (were cognitive science ultimately to individuate kinds at a neurological level)—specifies as the underlying nature of those paradigms.

The idea is that "our present situation with respect to 'experience' is analogous to that of sixteenth century speakers of English with respect to 'water'"(Casullo, 159). In the sixteenth century, we were in position to identify the surface characteristics of water such as being a colorless, odorless liquid found in lakes and streams and its functional relational characteristics such as quenching thirst. But we were not then in position to identify its essential nature as H_2O. And since "water" was used as a natural kind term—as whatever it is that has the essential underlying structure of *that* stuff—we were not at that time in position to give the conditions for determining the extension of the term "water." Only after the identification of water as H_2O was made were we able to give the conditions for the extension of "water." According to Casullo, the "underlying chemical structure fixes the extension of 'water' in all possible worlds. In any possible world, something is water just in case it is H_2O" (Casullo, 158).

In evaluating this proposal, let me start off with a few points of clarification. In holding that "experience" be viewed as a "putative natural kind term," Casullo is not maintaining that *there is* a single underlying nature associated with the five senses. Since we are unaware of the underlying nature of experience, we are also unaware of whether there is in fact some common underlying nature that unifies the local paradigms of experience. It will be up to the empirical sciences of human cognition to determine whether there is a single underlying nature. Casullo uses "putative" to signal our present epistemic uncertainty about this matter.

It is important here to keep separate metaphysical and linguistic issues. "Putative" signals the epistemic possibility that there may be no single common underlying nature of experience—there might be many and there might be none. The term just functions to note that we don't at present know the existential facts—what the metaphysics is. But "putative" does not function as a way of qualifying Casullo's thesis in philosophy of language that "experience" is a natural kind term. Here it is worth noting again that according to Casullo our circumstances are analogous to those of sixteenth-century English speakers with respect to "water." Putnam's arguments about "water" aim to show that the term was at that time a putative natural kind term, even though it was discovered much later what exactly the nature of water is. Likewise, according to Putnam, "jade" was used as a natural kind term, even though, as it was later discovered, the paradigmatic applications of the term "jade" extended to two different things, what we now know as jade and jadeite. Although there were two different underlying natures discovered, "jade" was nevertheless a natural kind term. So, Casullo's claim that "experience" is a natural kind term should stand (if it does stand) independently of how the metaphysics turns out. To put a finer point on all of this, let us distinguish the following theses:

Metaphysics of Sense Experience: There is a single underlying nature associated with the five senses.

Natural Kind Term Thesis: "Experience" is a natural kind term the extension of which is determined by the underlying nature of the five senses.

These two theses, one in metaphysics, the other about language, are independent in the sense that neither thesis entails the other. This will be important in evaluating Casullo's claims, and I will return to it shortly.

Right now, I want to reflect on how Casullo construes the relevant reference-fixing paradigms of "experience." Casullo says the cognitive processes associated with the five senses are the reference-fixing paradigms of "experience." But this is insufficient for isolating the relevant paradigms, for there are various ways of specifying these cognitive processes. Drawing a simple distinction will illustrate this point. Like many, I think that I can have phenomenologically identical experiences, yet one is veridical and the other is merely a hallucination. I can visually perceive a brown cow in front of me and I can have a visual hallucination as of the very same scene—merely "before my eyes," as it were. Now, if this is the case, then, within the "narrow" notion that Casullo does specify, there remain two distinct notions of experience. One notion is linked exclusively to the phenomenological level and includes both the veridical and hallucination experiences. Let us call this the *phenomenological notion of experience*. The other is linked perhaps in part at the phenomenological level, but requires also causal connection to the objects of experience, and so it would rule out hallucinatory experiences. Note that it does not have to rule out all illusions (cases in which one misidentifies a perceived object, for example) and so need not be restricted to veridical perceptions. But hallucinations would not count. Let us call this the *causal notion of experience*. What we have here, then, are two notions of experience, one associated just with being appeared to in a certain way, and the other associated with further characteristics of information delivering perceptual experiences—being appeared to in a certain way because or in virtue of one's having causal contact with the objects that appear to one. (This is very crude but it will suffice for our purposes here.)

Here we have two ways of "picking out" the cognitive processes associated with the five senses. Both ways will do the trick. The phenomenological notion will pick up other stuff, such as hallucinations, as well, of course. What I wish to urge here is greater clarification: to properly characterize exactly what he is selecting for in taking "experience" to be a natural kind term, Casullo needs to settle on a fairly precise way of identifying or characterizing the reference-fixing paradigms. Now, given that Casullo always speaks about the five senses and never includes hallucinations as paradigms, it seems fairly clear that he is intending the causal notion of experience, and is intending to rule out from the get-go the phenomenological notion of experience.[3] That is, he is identifying a causal condition—being appeared to in a certain way in virtue of causal contact with the objects that appear to one—as necessary for being a reference-fixing paradigm. It is worth noting that though the causal condition may be necessary for counting as a paradigmatic instance of an experience, this does not rule out

---

[3] Casullo has confirmed this in correspondence. Notice that the fact that Casullo intends to treat "experience" as a natural kind term does not *itself* determine whether his notion is the phenomenological notion or the causal notion. For one might be interested in whether there is any (say) essential cognitive (neurological, perhaps) features to both visual hallucination and *bona fide* vision, auditory hallucination and audition, etc. Or one might be interested in whether there is any essential cognitive (neurological, perhaps) feature just to *bona fide* vision, audition, olfaction, etc.

the possibility that hallucinations will come to be found to have the same underlying nature as, say, visual or auditory experiences.

In attempting to specify the relevant thing that is supposed on this analysis to determine the extension of "experience," I have been quoting Casullo: he calls it the "underlying nature of experience." What does this come to? In particular, what is the appropriate level of scientific analysis for giving the underlying nature of experience? Casullo is not explicit on this in the book. But given that he maintains that "experience" is here a *natural* kind term, it must be some physical state or process—probably a brain state or process. My best initial guess was that he means at least that it is a variety of neurological state or process. In very helpful correspondence, Casullo says that because the issues here concern human cognition and the role of experience in acquiring knowledge, the appropriate level of scientific analysis should be that of cognitive psychology, in which case experience is to be treated as a psychological kind. This then raises the difficult issues about the relationship between psychological kinds and neurobiological kinds. This point will be important momentarily. In any event, if it does turn out that there is a certain underlying physical nature, call it nature N, identical to experience, then, according to Casullo, in all possible worlds, something is an experience just in case it is N.

So far so good. We have got a very interesting theory and interesting novel suggestion about how to construe "experience" and how we should view and then come to a deeper understanding of the nature of experience. I want to turn now to evaluating some of Casullo's central theses.

My first concern is about the natural kind term thesis. I am doubtful that "experience" is a natural kind term whose extension is determined by the underlying nature of the five senses. Natural kind terms are terms that are *in fact* used in a certain way in natural language. If "experience" is a natural kind term, then it should be used in natural language as such. Now, "experience"—as Casullo intends it here as a way to isolate the narrow notion—is (obviously) not in common usage in the way that "water" was in the sixteenth century. It is, rather, a technical expression used by philosophers with the aim to specify in some fashion what is common to experiences with the five senses. This fact does not itself show that "experience" is not used by philosophers as a natural kind term. Plenty of terms are technical, used within a specific community of speakers, yet are natural kind terms nevertheless (e.g., "gene" and "molecule"). But it suggests a salient difference and highlights the fact that whether something is a natural kind term will turn on facts about its usage in the relevant linguistic community.

Natural kind terms are terms used to speak about kinds in a way that bears certain important structural parallels to the way that demonstratives or proper names are used to speak about individuals (at least according to the new theory of reference that Casullo seems to be drawing on). A speaker uses the demonstrative or complex demonstrative (say "that" or "that cow") to refer directly to an individual in the sense that the demonstrative, complex or simple, is not synonymous with a description that uniquely identifies the individual. Typically, in the case of a demonstrative, the speaker perceptually (usually visually) focuses attention on the individual and uses the demonstrative as a device to draw others' attention to that individual. Even if the speaker has radically false beliefs about the individual, she still refers to the object she attends to, for she used the demonstrative with the intention to refer to *that* individual. Proper names differ from demonstratives in that speakers often use them to refer to individuals even in the absence of a current direct perceptual relation to such individuals. Nevertheless, according to the new theory of reference, they are like demonstratives in that speakers use them to refer to individuals without mediation via any uniquely identifying descriptions. Names are not synonymous with definite descriptions. And speakers who successfully use them need not have any uniquely identifying information about the intended referent.

Natural kind terms too are not synonymous with descriptions and are used competently by speakers who do not know how to uniquely identify the kind. What is usually regarded as fundamental for something being a natural kind term is that speakers use the term with certain linguistic intentions. The standard Putnam argument that "water" is a natural kind term whose extension is fixed by paradigms and not by a description presupposes the idea that sixteenth century speakers used "water" with the intention to refer to whatever is the same natural stuff as the clear liquid stuff that is in rivers, lakes, and comes out of faucets. Having the same "surface" properties—being clear, liquid, potable, and so on—is not sufficient for being water. In Putnam's famous thought experiment, XYZ has the same surface characteristics as H_2O. But, he argued, we would not and, in the sixteenth century, did not use "water" to apply to both H_2O and XYZ. Those convinced by the argument find that they have the intuition that we use and our sixteenth-century fellows used "water" with the intention to apply it exclusively to one and the same natural stuff (at the essential, micro-level) as is in our lakes and rivers, etc.

Let us apply the Putnam style argument to "experience." Suppose that nonhuman rational beings on twin earth take in information about their local environment in a certain fashion that is very much like the way that we take in information about out local environment. They are appeared to in a certain way. They have a distinctive phenomenology in that there is something it is like for them to take in such information via this channel to the local environment. Also, the objects that appear to them cause those appearances. In short, they have all the marks of the "surface characteristics" of human sensory experiences. But they are not human and so have no common biological history as us. The processes that secure information about their local environments are realized by different biological stuff. We have eyes, they have shmeyes. We have brains, they have schlains. Call what they have twin-experience. Now, if "experience" is in fact a natural kind term whose extension is determined by the underlying nature of the paradigms, then in all possible worlds, something is an experience only if it is identical to N, some physical, probably neurological, state of a human being. So then we would have to say that we would not apply this term to cover their twin-experience. But would we really refrain? As philosophers interested in isolating sense experience from rational insight, is our current use of "experience" limited only to creatures whose conscious, causally-mediated, information-gathering systems are biologically like our own? My sense here is no—I think that there is a marked asymmetry between our past and current use of "water" and our use of "experience."

The argument could be altered slightly. Instead of simply having different realizing systems for visual experience, we can have beings with a very different means of taking in information about the external environment. Imagine nonhuman rational beings that, in addition to using other sense modalities, also echolocate. I think we'd count such beings' echolocatings as instances of sensory experience, even though they are realized in something vastly different (at the physical level) than neurons. They have a distinct phenomenology and bring in information about the environment by means of causal interaction with that environment.[4]

It is important to remember here that in evaluating the natural kind term thesis, the relevant issues are not the metaphysical ones about what neurological processes scientists might discover in fact unify cognitive processes associated with the five senses. The issue is rather the linguistic one concerning whether we use "experience" to apply exclusively to such processes. It seems to me fairly clear that our current professional use of "experience" allows for application to states and processes that realize perception in different physical media. I would suggest that this shows that "experience" is not a natural kind term, but rather a functional kind term.

---

[4] Could Casullo get around this argument if he grants that our current use of "experience" allows us to extend it to differently realized-perception but denies that his natural kind term thesis is incompatible with such use? No. One might be tempted to take this line if one failed to distinguish using a term as a natural kind term and using a term with the bare intention to allow that it is whatever it turns out to be. If "experience" is a natural kind term and is used in the way that sixteenth-century speakers used "water," then there are constraints on how it has been used. It will be used with the intention to isolate a *natural kind* like a neurological or biological process—something with a particular distinct physical make-up, and not, for example, a functional kind like whatever underlying processes realize causally mediated information giving states that have a distinctive phenomenology.

I think that the arguments above about our use of "experience" not being limited to our own neurological states and processes contain the strongest case against the natural kind term thesis. But a challenge from the other direction is interesting and, though it is probably flawed, is worthy of discussion. Consider scenarios in which an individual is in state N, yet has nothing register at the phenomenological level. No matter how carefully she attends to what she experiences (or reconsiders after the fact), she finds nothing "registering" in her perceptual field that correlates with information that she secures.[5] I have in mind here cases of blindsight, the phenomena in which, usually following certain types of brain lesions, patients report that they cannot see ordinary medium-sized objects right in the middle of what would be their attended-to visual field yet, if pressed to locate the objects (by reaching for them) they are able to do so with significant accuracy. Here we have instances in which a subject takes in information and forms beliefs about objects in virtue of a causal contact with the objects, but has no associated phenomenology and no conscious awareness of seeing those objects. But, by hypothesis, it is epistemically possible that the subject is in N. Would we apply "experience" to a patient with respect to an object that she claims not to see but can respond differentially to? I do not have any clear idea here but it is not apparent to me that we would regard her as having a sensory experience.[6] Despite the indefiniteness of cases like this, I think that they are probably not good tests for the natural

---

[5] I mean to exclude here cases in which our attention is on one thing and we secure only flickers of information from something outside that locus of attention, perhaps peripherally. In the APA session, Casullo offered an interesting case in which someone is driving in a car, yet focused on a construction site. Suddenly, the driver slams on the breaks because he believes that a ball is approaching the car and does not want to hit a child that might try to retrieve it. This is not the type of case I have in mind as an instance of nothing registering phenomenologically. For, in my view, though the driver's attention is on the construction site, he sees the ball with peripheral vision, which *is* registered at the phenomenological level, even though it is not the main locus of attention. Issues here about the relationship between attention and perception are complex, but I am looking here for a more definite case of securing information without any relevant associated phenomenology.

[6] Cases of blindsight are such strange but perhaps also fruitful sources of investigation precisely because they seem to suggest that mechanisms of information receipt and mechanisms for conscious information receipt can come apart. Investigators currently aim to discover whether such phenomena occur only in brain lesion patients or whether it is a feature of intact brain functioning as well. It might well be that it is constitutive of our use of "experience" that it requires securing information through conscious channels. Nevertheless, I have no doubt that philosophers interested in isolating sources of a priori justification from all other sources of justified beliefs would count the subpersonal deliverances to the blindsighted person as empirical. But I doubt that they would do this primarily because instances of blindsight have the same underlying nature as normal visual experience. They would count it as empirical because of the role that the environmental information plays in supporting the patient's locatings of objects.

kind term thesis because the parallel argument for "water" might not be good either. Consider: is ice water? It is, to be sure, H_2O, but it is far from clear, probably false, that it is also water. This suggests that the discovery that water's underlying nature is H_2O reveals only that if something is water, then it is H_2O, not that it is water if and only if it is H_2O.[7]

In any case, the key point against the natural kind term thesis is that having the same underlying nature as the cognitive processes associated with the five senses is not necessary to count as in the extension of "experience." Now, Casullo does say a great deal that suggests that he is fully behind the natural kind term thesis. He claims that others' attempts at coming up with the right analysis of experience failed basically because they did not realize that the natural kind term thesis holds. Those that took the enumerative approach fail because, he says, they "propose to fix the extension of "experience" prior to identifying the underlying nature of the local paradigms" (Casullo, 160). Those that took the conceptual approach fail because "they treat the surface characteristics that are used to identify the local paradigms of experience as necessary and sufficient conditions for being an experience" (Casullo, 160). And he says that his own alternative "both explains the failure of the previous attempts to analyze the concept and offer the prospect of arriving at that goal by alternative means" (Casullo, 160).

But if the natural kind term thesis is false, then there are two worries associated with Casullo's project. First, it seems that Casullo has not explained previous failures to understand the nature of experience. Those who favored the enumerative approach will not have been mistaken in attempting to fix the extension of the term prior to discovering the underlying nature of human sense experience.[8] Those who favored the conceptual approaches will not have been mistaken for attempting to articulate the necessary and sufficient features of experience—indeed, this is the right approach if "experience" is a functional kind term. Second, if the natural kind term thesis is false, then it would seem that Casullo's positive approach does not succeed in providing necessary and sufficient conditions for something being an experience. For even if one good route to discovering facts about sense experience is by investigating the underlying nature

---

[7] Many theoretical statements (like "water is H_2O") that look like identity statements with the logical form A=B are better understood as having the logical form $\forall x(Ax \equiv Bx)$. If the example with "water" does not convince, perhaps this statement will: "lightning is electricity." By endorsing the identity, Casullo would have to maintain that something is lightening if and only it is electricity. But there is electricity that is not lightning. Cf., Soames 2005 (22-24).

[8] While I do not agree with Casullo in *this* criticism of the enumerative approach, I think he is exactly right in his criticism that providing an exhaustive list is not explanatory and that it automatically rules out additional possible varieties of experience.

of cognitive processes associated with the five sense, the extension of "experience" is still not determined by those processes.

One funny thing in all of this, though, is that while Casullo often says that his key suggestion is that "experience" is a putative natural kind term whose reference is fixed by the underlying nature of the paradigms, he does not really try to make a case for this descriptive thesis about how "experience" is used. For example, he does not offer Putnam-style arguments, like the one I advanced previously, that turns on linguistic intuitions about how we have been using the term "experience." This leads me to wonder whether there is another thesis that Casullo is advancing that he has not distinguished from the descriptivist natural kind term thesis and which is a kind of *revisionist* thesis about how we ought to use the term "experience." That is, he might be suggesting that we ought to stop using "experience" to apply to the cognitive processes by which we secure information about the world via causal relations to objects in the world accessed through distinctive conscious phenomenological states. What we should do instead is take the five senses as paradigms and think of experience as whatever it is that physicalistically (not functionally) unifies them. As it happens, sometimes Casullo speaks this way. He writes: "My suggestion is that "experience" *be viewed* as a putative natural kind term"; "I argue that attempts to articulate the experiential/non-experiential distinction by means of conceptual analysis fail and that a more fruitful approach is *to treat* 'experience' as a putative natural kind term . . ." (Casullo, 159, 181, my emphasis). So we have a very different thesis than the natural kind term thesis under consideration.[9]

What should we think about this revisionist thesis? It is hard to say, I think, because it is somewhat difficult to say what it amounts to. What does it mean to say that we should treat a term as natural kind term? Perhaps what Casullo is suggesting is simply that we revise and reorient how we think of experience: we should think of it as just those underlying (probably neurological, but in any event, psycho-biological) processes that unify the five modes of perception in humans. And if we do this, then empirical science must be called upon to identify those underlying processes that realize vision, audition, and the rest. To connect this up with the linguistic issue, Casullo would presumably have to say (if he agreed that the descriptive natural kind term thesis is false) something to the effect

---

[9] To drive home the importance of the difference between this and the natural kind term thesis, it is worth reflecting on the comparison with "water." The whole purpose of the Putnam twin-earth thought experiments was to bring out intuitions that XYZ was not in the extension of "water"—not even prior to the discovery of its underlying chemical structure. And this showed that "water" was even then being used as a natural kind term. Putnam was not arguing for the revisionist thesis that we *ought to view* the extension of "water" as being fixed by the underlying nature of paradigmatic instances of water.

that "experience," as philosophers have previously been using and understanding it, has not captured the relevant notion or concept of experience that ought to be at the center of our discussions about nonexperiential justification. The revisionist thesis above should then more formally be about a new term "experience*" that has not previously been employed in our epistemic debates but which captures how we should understand the concept of experience.

> *Revisionist Thesis about "Experience":* Experience should be viewed as a natural kind and a new term, "experience*," expresses this concept as a natural kind term whose extension is determined by the underlying nature of the five senses.

This revisionist thesis would have the advantage of not being subject to any Putnam style of arguments because it is not a claim about how a term in our language is used. Its success will, however, ultimately depend upon whether theorists are willing to count the underlying nature of the five senses as giving the necessary and sufficient conditions for being an experience. Those who find it more natural to think of experience as a functional kind (and I count myself among those) will, probably, resist.

But what, for Casullo, really hinges upon either the natural kind thesis or the revisionist thesis? As far as I can see, there is little of deep significance in his overall project that must turn on it. His overarching aim is to answer the question of whether there are nonexperiential sources for justifying beliefs. The main thrust of his book is that we should and must bring in empirical investigation to answer this question. Let us bracket (for now) whether we must do so. It is completely consistent with this main aim that we allow that "experience" is a functional kind term. For we can still draw on empirical research in cognitive science to discern the underlying processes that realize the five sense modalities in humans, and to use these in attempting to isolate physical features of empirically justified beliefs in humans. We can also use empirical research in cognitive science to discern underlying processes associated with the cognitive states identified at the phenomenological level as justifying beliefs a priori.

Casullo outlines two projects to be carried out in attempting to answer whether there are any a priori justified beliefs, what he calls the *Articulation Project* and the *Empirical Project*. The Articulation Project is the project of describing the cognitive states that confer a priori justification, specifying the scope of the beliefs they justify, and the conditions under which they do so. The Empirical Project is the project within cognitive science to isolate underlying cognitive processes for the cognitive states identified phenomenologically (in the Articulation Project), to show that such processes play a role in producing the relevant beliefs, and to show that the processes are truth conducive. What I have been saying is that these two central projects can still stand, even if the concept of experience applies to a wider range of states than those that have the same underlying nature as the cognitive processes associated with the five senses.

Perhaps Casullo will think this will not work because (he thinks) he needs necessary and sufficient conditions for being an experience. This is not clear to me. Suppose the Empirical Project showed that there is a single type of distinctive underlying cognitive processes associated with the cognitive states identified at the phenomenological level, that they are relevantly different from the underlying processes associated with the five senses, and that these processes are truth conducive. In such circumstances, I would think that we would have nondefinitive but solid empirical grounds for thinking that moderate rationalism obtains. True, there would be other modes of belief formation (via memory, introspection, testimony) that would be outstanding and difficult to classify, perhaps. But this alone would be a very weak basis for regarding the positive results of the Empirical Project as suspect or compromised.

I have been spending most of this discussion examining Casullo's arguments and ideas surrounding his first thesis that empirical research is needed to clearly explicate the thesis of moderate rationalism, especially to articulate the concepts of experiential and nonexperiential sources of justification. I want now to turn to his second main thesis that empirical research is needed to underwrite moderate rationalism.

Casullo spends some time addressing central challenges to his project to underwrite moderate rationalism with empirical evidence, and here I think he is spot on the mark (Casullo, 173–75). In particular, there are two "in principle" (or, one might say, structural) challenges to moderate rationalism that have previously been regarded as major obstacles to any project like Casullo's. The first is that introducing empirical considerations to identify what experience is or to isolate cognitive processes and show they are truth conducive will "trickle down" and make the beliefs under investigation themselves empirically grounded. Casullo gives compelling reasons for thinking this objection involves a levels confusion by assuming that one's a priori justified belief will necessarily become empirical if empirical evidence is marshaled to demonstrate that the relevant cognitive processes (say involved in mathematical reasoning) are truth-conducive. The second challenge maintains that employing empirical evidence to underwrite moderate rationalism makes a justification circular because it involves the use of logical and mathematical principles. The idea is that because supporters of moderate rationalism will regard such principles as justified a priori, they are somehow illegitimately assuming that there are nonexperiential sources of justification. I agree with Casullo in thinking that this objection is just confused: the defender of moderate rationalism does not need to assume anything about the source of our logical and mathematical beliefs in order to draw upon them in supplying the relevant empirical evidence for underwriting moderate rationalism.

Supposing there are no solid *in principle* "structural" objections to an empirically based case for moderate rationalism, what can we say about the project's prospects for success? The first point to make reiterates what I said at the outset. The appeal to empirical evidence to decide the truth of moderate rationalism is, as Casullo emphasizes, common ground between both main parties in the current debate. Certainly Casullo has an excellent dialectical strategy for making headway on the debate. We have everything to gain by looking to empirical evidence as a way to make a case on behalf of (or against) moderate rationalism. Maybe it will pan out. There is, to be sure, plenty of work that has already been carried out within cognitive psychology that pertains to these issues. I have in mind here especially the fascinating work by Gallistel and Gelman, Spelke and Carey, and others about the origins/development/nature of basic arithmetical knowledge.[10] There is every reason, I think, to interpret this research as providing prima facie evidence that such knowledge is in some sense nonexperientially *based*. However one interprets these findings on the acquisition and mastery of basic arithmetical knowledge, to count as part of Casullo's Empirical Project, they would have to be greatly supplemented so as to show that the processes that such beliefs stem from are truth-conducive.

This brings me to some more general concerns about the process reliabilist terms that Casullo favors. In proposing to advance a case for moderate rationalism by looking for reliable underlying cognitive processes, possibly at the neurological level, Casullo seems to me to have left out one of the key reasons for our interest in a priori justification in the first place: in understanding the nature of human understanding. While I do not doubt that some notion of truth conductivity is central to an account of epistemic justification, I wonder, however, whether reliability is *the* correct notion for cashing out that truth conductivity, especially within a theory about a priori justification. Perhaps there are other ways to establish that some of our beliefs must be grounded nonexperientially, solely on the basis of our understanding of the contained concepts. For example, I am sympathetic with certain transcendental arguments that aim to show that believing what we take to be obvious—i.e., propositions we accept based exclusively on our conceptual understanding of contained concepts—is necessary for coming to possess logical, mathematical, and probably philosophical knowledge. This idea does not incorporate the process reliabilism that runs wholesale through Casullo's work, but it does emphasize the spe-

---

[10] The literature is vast. Here is a small sample. R. Gelman and C. R. Gallistel's pioneering work in their 1978. Cf., Gelman and Gallistel's more recent work, including, their 2005 and their 2004. Cf., also, for example, Carey 2001and Dehaene, et al. 1999.

cial role of the understanding within cognition, a role not had by perception. I doubt that we can shed maximal light on such understanding, and can see how it differs from perception if we treat it primarily in terms of the reliability of underlying cognitive processes.

One last remark. Casullo's Articulation and Empirical projects aim to isolate the cognitive processes associated at the phenomenological level with a priori justified beliefs and then to call upon empirical research to discover the underlying nature of these cognitive processes, and to demonstrate their role in producing the relevant beliefs and their truth conduciveness. According to this approach, whether moderate rationalism is true will depend upon the underlying nature of these cognitive processes, and, in particular, whether they in fact differ from the underlying nature of the cognitive processes associated with perceptual experiences. I wonder whether such an approach can capture the difference between using your fingers to support your belief that you have five fingers and using your fingers as a heuristic device to support your belief that two plus three is five. Both beliefs draw upon perception. On traditional versions of rationalism, the latter belief can still be grounded a priori because the subject *used* the perceptual information in a distinctive way, solely as a means of triggering her rational insight. This marks off a sense of justificatory independence of experience that Casullo's account seems to be hard pressed to accommodate—for his notion of experience independence seems rather to be one on which a belief does not involve the underlying processes associated with the five senses. Neither one of these last two critical points confronts Casullo on his own terms. They merely signal that there may be alternative (admittedly more traditional) ways of attempting to establish moderate rationalism.

REFERENCES

Carey, S. 2001. Evolutionary and Ontogenetic Foundations of Arithmetic. *Mind and Language* 16: 37–55.
Casullo, A. 2003. *A Priori Justification*. Oxford: Oxford University Press, 2003.
Dehaene, S., E. Spelke, P. Pinel, R. Stanescu, and S. Tsivkin. 1999. Sources of Mathematical Thinking: Behavioral and Brain-imaging Evidence. *Science* 284: 970–74.
Gelman, R., and C. R. Gallistel. 1978. *The Child's Understanding of Number*. Cambridge: Harvard University Press.
———. 2004. Language and the Origin of Numerical Concepts. *Science* 306: 441–43.
———. 2005. Mathematical Cognition. In *Cambridge Handbook of Thinking and Reasoning*, ed. Holyoak and Morrison. Cambridge: Cambridge University Press, 559–88.
Soames, S. 2005. *Reference and Description*. Princeton: Princeton University Press.

[6]

Reply to my Critics: Anthony Brueckner and Robin Jeshion

ALBERT CASULLO

In *A Priori Justification*, I offer a systematic treatment of the primary epistemological issues associated with the a priori that is sensitive to recent developments in the field of epistemology. I argue for three primary conclusions. First, the concept of a priori justification is minimal: it is simply the concept of nonexperiential justification. Second, the basic question that must be addressed to resolve the controversy over the existence of a priori knowledge is whether there are nonexperiential sources of justified beliefs. Third, and most importantly, articulating the concept of nonexperiential justification and establishing that there are nonexperiential sources of justified belief requires empirical investigation. Anthony Brueckner and Robin Jeshion offer insightful assessments of my project. In this essay, I attempt to address their questions and respond to their criticisms.

1. The Concept of A Priori Knowledge

A Priori Justification is organized around four questions originally posed by Kant:

1. What is a priori knowledge?
2. Is there a priori knowledge?
3. What is the relationship between the a priori and the necessary?
4. Is there synthetic a priori knowledge?

I approach the first question by examining conditions on a priori justification proposed by various theorists. I argue that only two survive critical scrutiny, leaving us with two competing analyses of a priori justification:

(AP1) S's belief that p is justified a priori if and only if S's belief that p is nonexperientially justified.

(AP2) S's belief that p is justified a priori if and only if S's belief that p is nonexperientially justified and cannot be defeated by experience.

I maintain that (AP1) offers the superior analysis.

Brueckner raises two issues with this aspect of my project. First, he (2011, 85–86) suggests that proposals like (AP1) and (AP2) are not best viewed as examples of conceptual analysis, since he doubts that such a concept is a part of either "our shared conceptual repertoire" or "the shared conceptual repertoire of philosophers." Brueckner favors an alternative picture. Apriorists think that there are cases of knowledge, mathematics and logic being the paradigms, that are in important ways different from our knowledge of physical objects. The respect in which these cases are special is that they are "in some sense 'independent of experience'," and this special form of justification is called *a priori*. Apriorists then examine these cases, try to figure out what is special about them, and come up with different conclusions about the "nature of the special justification that seems to them to be present." So what is the upshot? Consider the following proposal due to (the early) BonJour (1985, 192): "a proposition is justified *a priori* when and only when the believer is able . . . to intuitively "see" or apprehend that its truth is an invariant feature of all possible worlds." I take this to be an analysis of the concept of a priori justification and argue that it is too strong since mathematicians who lack the concept of necessity can have a priori justification for their mathematical results. Brueckner takes my example to show that BonJour is simply mistaken about the nature of the justification involved in the paradigm cases.

I agree with Brueckner that the concept of a priori justification is not part of our ordinary repertoire of concepts. I believe, however, that it is part of the shared conceptual repertoire of at least some philosophers. Since this concept is technical, I offer two criteria for evaluating purported analyses of it: sensitivity to historical precedent, and compatibility with more general assumptions about justification and knowledge. I think that Brueckner's picture highlights the core of the shared concept: justification that is in some sense independent of experience. Any account of the concept that did not include this element would violate my first criterion since it would effectively divorce the concept from the set of issues posed by Kant and subsequent attempts to answer them. What remains to be done, however, is to articulate the relevant sense of 'independence', and this is where most of the contemporary debate centers.

There are two more observations worth making about Brueckner's reading of the situation. First, it conflicts with what apriorists say that they are doing. Prior to introducing his proposal, BonJour (1985, 191) tells us that his aim is "to clarify both the concept of *a priori* justification itself and some closely related concepts and distinctions." Plantinga (1993, 107), in the context of defending a similar proposal, maintains that "the question here is whether the term '*a priori* knowledge' expresses the concept of knowledge independent (in the right way) of experience, or whether it expresses a stronger concept: the concept of knowledge independent of experience accompanied by the conviction that what is known is necessary." Philosophers sometimes err in their characterizations of what they are doing, but Brueckner's picture entails a particularly pervasive and systematic error on the part of apriorists.

Second, radical empiricists also offer proposals articulating the special character of a priori justification. It is not clear how these proposals fit into Brueckner's picture. Since radical empiricists reject the contention that there is anything different going on in the special cases, they are not making claims about the nature of that special justification. One might suggest that they are simply reporting what apriorists claim to be different about the special cases. But that cannot be right because they often dispute the characterizations offered by apriorists. Instead, they also claim to be offering an analysis of the concept of a priori justification. For example, Philip Kitcher (1983, 24) maintains that "X knows a priori that p just in case X has a true belief that p and that belief was produced by a process which is an *a priori warrant* for it," proposes conditions that distinguish a priori warrants from other warrants, and presents his results as follows: "Summarizing the conditions that have been uncovered, I propose the following analysis of a priori knowledge."

The second issue raised by Brueckner concerns the dispute between proponents of (AP1) and proponents of (AP2). I view it as a dispute over the analysis of the concept of a priori justification. Brueckner (2011, 86) recasts the dispute as follows: "in the special cases, in which one's justification seems to be nonexperiential, is one's belief nevertheless defeasible by experience?" and contends that "this question cannot be answered by analyzing some shared concept." It is a "substantive" philosophical question. I agree. It is a difficult and complex matter to determine whether some nonexperientially justified belief is defeated by experience. I spend a great deal of time trying to sort out the relevant issues, and draw some general conclusions about the conditions under which justification is defeated. Nevertheless, three points need to be stressed in this context. First, we must distinguish two questions: (1) Is indefeasibility by experience a necessary condition for a priori justification? (2) Are nonexperientially justified beliefs defeasible by experience? Second, from the fact that the second question cannot be answered by analyzing some shared concept, it does not follow that the first question cannot be answered by analyzing some shared concept. Third, if the answer to the first question is negative—i.e., if (AP1) is the correct analysis of a priori justification— then the difficult issues surrounding the second question need not be settled in order to determine whether some beliefs are justified a priori.

Brueckner concludes this part of his discussion with the observation that one aspect of my treatment of (AP1) and (AP2) is peculiar. I maintain that proponents of the two positions can agree that intuition yields nonexperiential justification, but still disagree over whether it yields a priori justification. Brueckner (2011, 86) maintains that the proponent of (AP2) "should hold instead that rational intuition yields nonexperiential justification only if that justification is indefeasible." On the contrary, I contend that the proponent of (AP2) cannot offer that response. Moreover, my framework, which views (AP2) as an analysis of the concept of a priori justification, allows us to see why this is so.

A theory of a priori justification is part of a broader theory of justification, which includes a general concept of justification as well as a concept of a priori justification. The function of the latter is to articulate the differences between a priori and a posteriori justified beliefs, while the function of the former is to articulate the essential features of all justified beliefs. If a theorist maintains that S's belief that p is justified a priori only if it is indefeasible by experience, this claim may be a consequence of either the theorist's general concept of justification or the theorist's concept of a priori justification. If being indefeasible by experience is a necessary condition of a belief's being justified, then it is also necessary condition of a belief's being justified a priori. But this requirement is not a consequence of the requirements of a priori justification as such. Hence, when I examine conditions on a priori justification, I assume that they are conditions imposed by the narrower concept of a priori justification and not conditions imposed by the general concept of justification.

Let us now consider the position of Philip Kitcher (1983), the most prominent proponent of (AP2). He endorses a reliabilist account of warrant, but introduces the indefeasibility condition to distinguish between a priori and a posteriori warrant. The indefeasibility condition on a priori warrant is not a consequence of his general conditions on warrant. Suppose that intuition is a nonexperiential belief forming process and that it is sufficiently reliable to meet Kitcher's general conditions on warrant. It follows that intuition is a nonexperiential source of warrant. Kitcher cannot deny that it yields nonexperiential warrant or, alternatively, maintain that it yields nonexperiential warrant only if that warrant is indefeasible, since it satisfies his general condition on warrant.

2. The Concept of Experience

One of the virtues of (AP1) is that it is not open to the charge of radical empiricists that the concept of a priori justification is incoherent. Radical empiricists cannot coherently maintain that the concept of nonexperiential justification is incoherent since their leading claim, which is that every justified belief is ultimately justified by experience, involves the concept of experiential justification. Nevertheless, there is a lingering concern. If the distinction between experiential and nonexperiential justification cannot be articulated, then the framework of concepts employed by both apriorists and radical empiricists remains suspect. Hence, we need to provide a characterization of the distinction or, at least, some reason to think that one is forthcoming.

I begin by distinguishing two senses of 'experience'. Apriorists often claim that "intuition is a familiar kind of experience," or that "intuition is a phenomenologically unique type of experience." This sense of 'experience', which I call the *broad* sense, refers to any occurrent conscious state of the cognizer. But, clearly, it is not the sense relevant to the distinction between a priori and a posteriori justification. If the contention that intuitions are a source of nonexperiential justification is coherent, then there is another sense of 'experience' on which they are not experiences. Our target is this sense of 'experience', which I call the *narrow* sense.

I examine and reject two approaches to analyzing this concept: enumerating the relevant types of experience, and providing a general characterization of them. In light of these failures, is there any reason to be sanguine that a characterization of the distinction is forthcoming? My proposal is that we view the narrow sense of 'experience' as a putative natural kind term, like 'water', whose reference is fixed by local paradigms. The local paradigms are identified by characteristic surface features, but these features do not fix the extension of 'experience'. Its extension is fixed by the underlying nature of the paradigms, which is discovered by empirical investigation. This approach offers both an explanation of why the enumerative and general approaches fail and a new direction for finding an answer. Brueckner (2011, 88), however, maintains that there is a crucial disanalogy between the two cases. In the case of 'water', there is an associated semantic rule in terms of surface characteristics, such being a clear, thirst-quenching liquid that delivers the paradigms for empirical investigation. But what are the surface characteristics for 'experience'? It appears that I have eliminated all the likely candidates in arguing against the various proposals for offering a general characterization of the narrow sense of 'experience'.

I believe that the apparent tension between my negative conclusion and positive proposal can be reconciled. My proposal (2003, 159) is that we treat the cognitive processes associated with the five senses, which are identified in terms of surface characteristics such as "providing information about the actual world, involving a causal relation to physical objects, and perhaps having a distinctive phenomenology," as the local paradigms of the narrow sense of 'experience'. The general characterizations that I reject, however, treat the surface characteristics of the processes associated with the five senses as logically necessary or sufficient conditions for being an experience in the narrow sense. The fact that a feature F fails to be logically necessary or sufficient for something to be X is compatible with F's being a surface characteristic of the local paradigms that fix the reference of 'X'. Although being liquid is neither logically necessary nor sufficient for being water, it is a surface characteristic that is useful for identifying local paradigms of water.

Let me try to make the issues and my proposal a bit more concrete. The cognitive processes associated with the five senses are our paradigms of experiential sources of justification. Some theorists maintain that other sources of justification should be classified as experiential by virtue of their similarity to the paradigms. Such claims, however, remain controversial. The idea behind my approach is that we investigate the underlying features of the cognitive processes associated with the five senses as well as those associated with the controversial cases, such as memory, introspection and testimony. The goal is to see whether there are underlying features that are essential to the processes associated with the five senses and, if so, whether those features are shared by any of the controversial cases. If they are, that would provide a basis for grouping them together as experiential in the narrow sense. The fact that the surface characteristics of the processes associated with the five senses do not provide logically necessary or sufficient conditions for something's being an experience in the narrow sense does not entail either that those processes do not have a common underlying nature or, if they do, that no other cognitive processes share those essential underlying properties. Only empirical investigation can determine whether this is the case.

3. The Existence of A Priori Knowledge

Our concern to this point has been with the concept of a priori justification. We now turn to the question of whether there exists a priori knowledge. I maintain that neither apriorists nor radical empiricists offer convincing arguments for their respective positions. Moreover, their arguments are typically negative. Each side attempts to show, typically by a priori argument, that the rival position is deficient in some respect. The strategy is both ineffective and misguided. It is ineffective because it results in an impasse in which each side attempts to blunt the criticisms of the other, while maintaining that the other side has failed to blunt its criticisms. It is misguided because no argument to the effect that one position does *not* offer an adequate account of some domain of knowledge can establish that the other *does* offer an adequate account of such knowledge. Therefore, I contend that advancing the debate over the existence of a priori knowledge beyond this impasse requires offering evidence in support of one position that is compelling to both sides.

Since the central dispute is over the existence of nonexperiential sources of justification, advancing the case for the a priori requires offering supporting evidence for the existence of such sources. In order for the case to be compelling, it must be based on common ground. Since both parties agree that we have mathematical, logical, and scientific knowledge, despite their disagreement over the source of such knowledge, these areas of agreement can be exploited in arguing for the existence of a priori knowledge. Hence, I conclude that apriorists should offer empirical support for their position rather than limiting themselves to offering negative arguments against radical empiricism. Two considerations support this strategy. First, a case for a priori knowledge that is based on considerations endorsed by radical empiricists is one that they must acknowledge by their own lights. Second, by relying solely on a priori arguments, proponents of the a priori place themselves in a needlessly handicapped position.

In order to implement the general proposal, I sketch out two related projects. The first is aptly described by Brueckner (2011, 88) "as a kind of philosophical, nonempirical regimenting and ground-clearing project that will pave the way for an empirical defense of the a priori." I (2003, 164) refer to this project as the Articulation Project and characterize it as follows:

> (AP) Provide (a) a generally accepted description, at least at the phenomenological level, of the cognitive states that noninferentially justify beliefs a priori; (b) the type of beliefs they justify; and (c) the conditions under which they justify the beliefs in question.

The second, the Empirical Project, seeks the empirical supporting evidence, and I (2003, 169) characterize it as follows:

> (EP) Provide (a) evidence that the cognitive states identified at the phenomenological level are associated with processes of a single type or relevantly similar types; (b) evidence that the associated processes play a role in producing or sustaining the beliefs they are alleged to justify; (c) evidence that the associated processes are truth-conducive; and (d) an explanation of how the associated processes produce the beliefs they are alleged to justify.

Brueckner raises three issues regarding (EP). The first is whether it can get off the ground given what I say regarding (a) of (AP). In response to the charge that a priori justification is "mysterious" or "obscure," apriorists offer phenomenological descriptions of the relevant cognitive states. My survey of the descriptions offered by sophisticated, reflective apriorists, who have carefully considered the question, reveals enormous variation. Consequently, I argue that proponents of the a priori are faced with a dilemma. Either we have direct introspective access to the cognitive states that justify a priori or we do not. If we do, apriorists should be able to agree on the correct description of those states. If we do not, some alternative rationale must be offered to support the claim that there are such states. So where does this leave us with respect to (EP)?

First, I agree with Brueckner that unless the situation is resolved in some way, (EP) cannot get off the ground. We need to be able to identify the cognitive states that are alleged to justify a priori before we can investigate whether there is a common process responsible for those states, and whether that process is truth conducive. Second, the problem must be resolved for *any* plausible theory of a priori justification to get off the ground. If one cannot offer a generally accepted description of the cognitive states that are alleged to justify a priori, one is not in a position to offer any interesting material epistemic principles that articulate conditions sufficient for (prima facie) a priori justification. Third, apriorists have two broad options for resolving the problem. The first is to agree that the states that justify a priori are familiar and directly accessible, and to address the apparently divergent descriptions of those states. There are several strategies here. They might further introspect, discuss the adequacy of various descriptions of the states, and converge on a generally accepted description. Alternatively, they might argue that there are many different sources of a priori justification, which are aptly described by the divergent characterizations. Finally, they might argue that the descriptions are not divergent, and that the problem of heterogeneity is merely apparent. The other option is to deny that the states in question are familiar cognitive states that are easily accessible by introspection. Instead, they might maintain that it is by philosophical argument that we establish the existence and character of such states. This strategy would be analogous to using versions of the Argument from Illusion to establish that the cognitive states that non-inferentially justify beliefs about the external world are ways-of-being-appeared to.

Brueckner's two remaining issues pertain to the details of the (EP), assuming that it gets off the ground. Suppose that we are able to identify processes of a particular type that are associated with the phenomenological states that are alleged to justify a priori. I contend that empirical investigation is relevant to determining whether such processes are truth-conducive. For example, critics of the a priori frequently question the evidential value of intuition by citing specific examples, such as the case of Euclidean geometry, where intuition is alleged to have led us astray.

Suppose we grant that, in these specific cases, intuition did indeed lead us astray. Clearly, this result alone does not establish that intuition is an unreliable belief forming process. On the other hand, the familiar response of apriorists to the effect that the alleged failures of intuition pale in comparison to its evident successes in the case of the elementary truths of arithmetic and logic also clearly fails to show that intuition is, after all, a reliable belief forming process. Two additional pieces of information are necessary. First, we need to know whether the same type, or relevantly similar types, of processes are involved in the case of geometrical, arithmetical, and logical beliefs. Second, for each relevant type of process, we need a more complete picture of its track record of reliability. In the absence of such information, apriorists and radical empiricists can only offer anecdotal, but incomplete, evidence in support of their claims.

My contention is that empirical investigation can help on both fronts. First, it can help to determine whether there is a single type of belief forming process or several relevantly different types of belief forming processes associated with the cognitive states identified at the phenomenological level. Second, it can provide a more complete picture of the range of beliefs produced by each of the processes, whether these processes produce all and only the beliefs typically cited by apriorists, whether there is widespread variation across subjects with respect to the beliefs produced by the processes, and the extent to which the processes produce conflicting beliefs in the same cognizer over time.

In this context, Brueckner (2011, 90) claims that investigators, such as Kahneman and Tversky, rely on their own intuitions to determine which answers on their questionnaires are the correct ones and, hence, that the investigations they conduct are not *exclusively* empirical. Two points here. I did not intend to suggest that the investigations are exclusively empirical. My claim is that the investigations have an empirical component. Second, Brueckner's point underscores the dialectical effectiveness of the strategy of exploiting common ground that I propose. If the investigations in question, including the construction and scoring of the questionnaires that they utilize, meet the standards of the scientific community, then they meet the standards of knowledge espoused by the radical empiricist. Therefore, the radical empiricist is not in a position to dismiss their results as question-begging or suspect.

Finally, I maintain that empirical investigation of the cognitive processes associated with the states that are alleged to justify a priori might provide a better understanding of how the processes in question produce true beliefs about their subject matters, and also suggest that such understanding might provide the key to answering Benacerraf's problem. Brueckner (2011, 90) does not see how there could be a "cognitive-science-style answer" to this problem. First, I acknowledge that I have no answer to offer, but here is how I was thinking about the issue. The core of Benacerraf's problem is an explanatory challenge. How do we explain cognitive access to the subject matter of our justified beliefs? How do we explain the reliability of our belief-forming processes? Our answers to these questions in the empirical realm depends on causal considerations. Moreover, the causal model appears to be the only currently available explanatory model. So the difficulty that we face in answering Benecerraf's problem is that, once we are barred from employing the causal model, we have nowhere else to turn. My suggestion is that as we come to better understand the workings of our cognitive processes and, in particular, those associated the subject matters that fall victim to the Benacerraf problem, alternative models of reliable belief formation might emerge. Of course, I want to stress, there are no guarantees here. But it is also important to recognize that our philosophical conception of what constitutes a good explanation of some type of phenomenon is informed by, and evolves with, the standards of a good explanation of that type of phenomenon within the relevant scientific domain.

4. A Priori Knowledge and Necessary Truth

Contemporary interest in questions about the relationship between a priori knowledge and necessary truth is largely due to the work of Saul Kripke (1971, 1980), who rejects two claims traditionally associated with Kant:

(K1) All knowledge of necessary propositions is a priori.

(K2) All propositions known a priori are necessary.

According to Kripke, "Hesperus is Phosphorus" and "If the lectern is not made of ice, then necessarily it is not made of ice," provide examples of necessary a posteriori knowledge; and "S is one meter long at t" provides an example of contingent a priori knowledge.

There are, however, two readings of (K1):

(KT) All knowledge of the *truth value* of necessary propositions is a priori.

(KG) All knowledge of the *general modal status* of necessary propositions is a priori.[1]

I (2003, 187–94) argue that Kripke's examples of the necessary a posteriori contravene (KT) but not (KG). Moreover, as Kripke points out, there are less exotic counterexamples to (KT) since people often have a posteriori knowledge of some mathematical propositions.

Kripke regards his more exotic examples of the necessary a posteriori as significant because they, unlike the mathematical examples, contravene both (KT) and the weaker

(KT*) If p is a necessary proposition and S knows that p, then S *can* know a priori that p,

since their truth values are knowable *only* a posteriori. Here I maintain that there is a tension between Kripke's claim that the truth values of the exotic examples are knowable only a posteriori and his claim that reference-fixing stipulation generates a priori knowledge since it appears that one can have a priori knowledge that Hesperus is Phosphorus and that the lectern is made of wood via suitable reference-fixing stipulations. For example, if S stipulates that 'wood' is to be the substance out of which lectern L is made then, if reference-fixing stipulation generates a priori knowledge, S knows a priori that L is made of wood. Similarly, if S stipulates that 'Hesperus' is to be the planet identical to Phosphorus, then S knows a priori that Hesperus is Phosphorus.

Brueckner (2011, 91) questions my contention on the grounds that my examples are irrelevant to Kripke's examples since in his examples, "there is no stipulative reference-fixing that can serve to generate a priori knowledge regarding the lectern and regarding heavenly-body-identity." But he also goes on to argue, in my defense, that if Kripke accepts a Russellian view of the propositions that figure in his examples, then my examples do create a problem. Since, on the Russellian view, the sentence "The lectern is made of wood" and the sentence "Hesperus is Phosphorus" express the same proposition in both the situation that Kripke describes and the situation that I describe, the propositions expressed by those sentences are knowable both a priori and a posteriori.

Brueckner (2011, 92), however, offers a response to this line of defense, which is based on the observation that Kripke does not subscribe to the Russellian approach to propositions and, moreover, talks about a priori knowledge that certain *sentences* are true in his discussion of the contingent a priori:

---

[1] S knows the *truth value* of p just in case S knows that p is true or S knows that p is false (assuming truth is always bivalent); S knows the *general modal status* of p just in case S knows that p is a necessary proposition (i.e., either necessarily true or necessarily false) or S knows that p is a contingent proposition (i.e., either contingently true or contingently false).

Kripke could hold that given the normal, nonstipulative way in which I come to understand the pertinent sentences in the Kripkean examples of the necessary a posteriori, I cannot come to know a priori that the sentences are true. In order to know this a priori, I would need to come to understand the sentence in a different way, viz. by stipulating the reference of certain key terms.

Here I agree with Brueckner that, in his discussion of the contingent a priori, Kripke speaks in terms of knowing that sentences are true. But I do not see how the response that Brueckner offers on behalf of Kripke relieves the tension in his position. Let us grant that in the normal, nonstipulative way in which I come to understand the relevant sentences in Kripke's examples, I cannot come to know a priori that the sentences are true. To know them a priori, I would need to come to understand the sentences in a different way. But here it seems that if we have available to us the two different ways of coming to understand each of the sentences, and each way of understanding each of the sentences opens up a different way of coming to know that each of the sentences is true, then we have the possibility of knowing each of those sentences is true both a priori and a posteriori. Most of us do not understand the term 'one meter' by reference fixing stipulation and, as a consequence, in the normal nonstipulative way in which we come to understand the sentence 'S is one meter long', we cannot come to know a priori that it is true. But, in that special situation, in which we come to understand the sentence by stipulating the reference of 'one meter', we can know a priori that the sentence in question is true. So, it appears that if we consider the three Kripke sentences that are in play here—the lectern sentence, the heavenly-body sentence, and the meter-stick sentence—each can be known either a priori or a posteriori depending on how one comes to understand the sentence. It follows, then, that it is not the case that the first two are knowable only a posteriori.

5. Experience as a Natural Kind

Robin Jeshion's reflections focus on my proposal to view the narrow sense of 'experience' as a putative natural kind term. Her comments fall into four broad categories. The first consists of three points of clarification. The second offers two arguments against my proposal and suggests an alternative account of the semantics of 'experience'. The third explores the possibility that my proposal is revisionist rather than descriptive. The fourth addresses the relationship between my proposal to view 'experience' as a natural kind term and my contention that empirical investigation is relevant to determining whether there are non-experiential sources of justified belief.

5.1. Three Points of Clarification

Jeshion (2011, 98) maintains that in order to understand my proposal to view 'experience' as a putative natural kind term, it is important to distinguish two theses:

> *Metaphysical Thesis* (MT): There is a single underlying nature associated with the five senses.

> *Semantic Thesis* (ST): 'Experience' is a natural kind term the extension of which is determined by the underlying nature of the five senses.[2]

According to Jeshion (2011, 98), the two theses are independent in the sense that neither entails the other, and that the term 'putative' in my proposal qualifies only the metaphysical thesis—i.e., it "signals the epistemic possibility that there may be no single common underlying nature of experience." She concludes that (ST), if true, is true independently of how the metaphysics turns out.

Jeshion (2011, 98) bases her contention on the following observations:

> according to Putnam, 'jade' was used as a natural kind term, even though, as it was later discovered, the paradigmatic applications of the term 'jade' extended to two different things, what we now know as jade and jadeite. Although there were two different underlying natures discovered, 'jade' was nevertheless a natural kind term. So, Casullo's claim that 'experience' is a natural kind term should stand (if it does stand) independently of how the metaphysics turns out.

Jeshion's argument can be recast as follows:

(J1) (ST) does not entail (MT).
(J2) Therefore, (ST), if true, is true independently of how the metaphysics turns out.

I agree with Jeshion that Putnam's jade example shows that (J1) is true. (J1), however, does not entail (J2). Moreover, the point of the jade example is not to support the claim that 'jade' is a natural kind term independently of how the metaphysics turns out. To the contrary, the example, when examined in the broader context of Putnam's discussion of the semantics of 'water', actually supports the denial of (J2).

---

[2] Jeshion calls the first thesis "metaphysics of sense experience," and the second "natural kind term thesis."

In order to establish (J2), Jeshion must show that (ST) does not entail *any* substantive metaphysical thesis. Her argument establishes only that (ST) does not entail *one* particular metaphysical thesis—i.e., (MT). But from the fact that (ST) does not entail (MT), it does not follow that it does not entail *any* substantive metaphysical thesis. (MT) is a very strong metaphysical thesis. There is, however, a weaker metaphysical thesis,

> *Weak Metaphysical Thesis* (WMT): There is a common underlying nature associated with the five senses,

which is entailed by (ST) and, moreover, this contention is supported by the broader context of Putnam's discussion of jade.

Three paragraphs prior to his discussion of jade, Putnam (1975, 241) offers the following observations about 'water': "It could have turned out that the bits of liquid we call 'water' had *no* important common physical characteristics *except* the superficial ones. In that case the necessary and sufficient condition for being 'water' would have been possession of sufficiently many of the superficial characteristics." Here Putnam maintains that in order for the semantic thesis—that the extension of 'water' is fixed by the underlying nature of its associated paradigms—to be true, the metaphysical thesis—that the paradigms have *some* common physical characteristics other than the superficial ones—must be true. Putnam (1975, 241), however, also maintains that, in order for the paradigms to have *some* common physical characteristics, they need not have a *single* underlying nature: "If H_2O and XYZ had both been plentiful on earth, then we would have had a case similar to the jadeite/nephrite case: it would have been correct to say that there were *two kinds of 'water'*. And instead of saying the 'the stuff on Twin Earth turned out not to really be water', we would have to say 'it turned out to be the *XYZ kind of water*'." In the envisaged scenario, the semantic thesis remains true with respect to 'water' despite the fact that the local paradigms of water have two different hidden structures. But, as he (1975, 241) goes on to make clear, he is not maintaining that the semantic thesis that 'water' is a natural kind term is true no matter how the metaphysics turns out: "if there is a hidden structure, then generally it determines what it is to be a member of the natural kind, not only in the actual world, but in all possible worlds. . . . But the local water, or whatever, may have two or more hidden structures—or so many that 'hidden structure' becomes irrelevant, and superficial characteristics become the decisive ones." If it should turn out that the local paradigms have *too many* hidden structures, then those structures do not determine the extension of 'water'.

Two points are clear from Putnam's discussion. First, in order for the hidden structure of the paradigms of 'water' to determine its extension, they need not have a *single* underlying structure. Second, if the paradigms of 'water' have *too many* hidden structures, then the extension of the term is not fixed by the underlying nature of its paradigms. Admittedly, Putnam's second point is vague in that he does not articulate what counts as *too many* underlying structures. I have expressed the vague idea that for the extension of a term to be fixed by the underlying nature of its paradigms, the paradigms must not have too many different underlying natures but need not have a single underlying nature by saying that the paradigms must have some common underlying nature. Thus, (ST) entails (WMT), and this contention is supported by Putnam's remarks about jade.

Returning now to Jeshion's first point of clarification, two observations are in order. First, the semantic thesis that 'experience' is a natural kind term is *not* independent of how the metaphysics turns out. If the paradigms associated with 'experience' fail to have some common underlying nature, then its extension is not determined by the underlying nature of the paradigms. Second, my use of the term 'putative' is intended to qualify both (WMT) and (ST). On my view, if the paradigms of experience do not have some common underlying nature, then 'experience' is not a natural kind term—i.e., its extension is not determined by the underlying nature of the paradigms.

Jeshion's (2011, 98–99) second point of clarification pertains to the details of my proposal to treat 'experience' as a natural kind term. She contends that there are two different ways of identifying the reference fixing paradigms and that each yields a different notion of experience. The first, which identifies the paradigms solely by reference to phenomenological characteristics, yields the *phenomenological* notion of experience. The second, which identifies the paradigms in terms of both phenomenological characteristics and causal connection with the objects of experience, yields the *causal* notion. Here she observes that since I identify the paradigms as the cognitive processes associated with the five senses, it is the causal notion that interests me.

Jeshion's observation is correct. I focus on the causal notion of experience because my ultimate goal is to identify the essential features of the types of experience that are incompatible with a priori justification. The hope is that identifying the features essential to sense experience will provide a principled way of adjudicating the more controversial cases of experience. It is unlikely that the most important epistemological differences between the experiences that are compatible with a priori justification, such as rational insight, and those that are not, such as perception, are phenomenological. The persistent use of visual metaphors to describe the cognitive states alleged to justify a priori suggests that, at the phenomenological level, there may be more similarity between perceptually seeing red squares and rationally seeing that red squares are possible than between seeing red wines and tasting red wines.

Jeshion's (2011, 100) third point of clarification raises the question: "What is the appropriate level of scientific analysis for giving the underlying nature of experience?" In *A Priori Justification*, I (2003, 159) maintain that "the critical question for our purposes is whether the scientific study of human cognition will uncover some significant underlying properties that unify the local paradigms of experience and play some role in formulating laws and theories about how humans acquire knowledge." I took the reference to "the scientific study of human cognition" to indicate that the appropriate level of scientific analysis is that of cognitive psychology. Jeshion (2011, 100) maintains that I was not sufficiently clear on this point: "But given that he maintains that 'experience' is here a *natural* kind term, it must be some physical state or process—probably a brain state or process. My best initial guess was that he means at least that it is a variety of neurological state or process." She (2011, 100) acknowledges, however, that the issue was clarified in correspondence in which I indicated that "the appropriate level of scientific analysis should be that of cognitive psychology, in which case experience is to be treated as a psychological kind." Nevertheless, in her (2011, 100) canonical formulation of my position, which is the formulation that provides the starting point for her critical remarks, she maintains: "if it does turn out that there is a certain underlying physical nature, call it nature N, identical to experience, then, according to Casullo, in all possible worlds, something is an experience just in case it is N."

Jeshion's third point of clarification is puzzling in two respects. She begins by presenting a line of argument that led to her best initial guess of my view:

(J3) All natural kinds are physical kinds—i.e., their underlying nature is some common physical structure or make-up.

(J4) Therefore, if experience is a natural kind, then it is a neurological kind.

This line of argument is puzzling. Jeshion offers no support for (J3). Moreover, whether all natural kinds are physical is a question to be settled by a posteriori, scientific considerations. Our best indication of which natural kinds exist is provided by our best scientific theories. The natural kinds are those referred to by the fundamental laws of our best scientific theories. Jeshion is not entitled to assume a priori that those kinds are physical. What is even more puzzling, however, is that she acknowledges that the issue of the appropriate level of scientific analysis for giving the underlying nature of experience was clarified in correspondence and that my position is not (J4) but

(C1) If experience is a natural kind, then it is a psychological kind.

Despite acknowledging this point, she immediately goes on to offer the following canonical formulation of my position:

(J5) If there is some underlying physical nature of experience, then experience is identical to that physical nature in all possible worlds,

which restates her initial guess that, on my view, experience is a physical (neurological) kind. Since my position is that experience is a psychological kind, Jeshion's canonical formulation of my position is incorrect. I will ague in the next section that Jeshion's leading argument against my proposal rests essentially on that incorrect formulation.

5.2. Two Opposing Arguments

Jeshion's leading argument against the view that 'experience' is a natural kind term employs a variation on Putnam's classic twin earth argument to highlight an alleged asymmetry between 'water' and 'experience'. Jeshion invites us to envisage a twin earth inhabited by rational beings who secure information about objects in their environment via causal relations to those objects accessed through distinct conscious phenomenological states. The cognitive processes of these rational beings possess all the surface characteristics of the paradigms which, according to my view, are associated with the term 'experience'. These rational beings, however, are not human: their biological history is different from ours; their cognitive processes are realized by different biological stuff. The problem, according to Jeshion (2011, 102), is that

> if 'experience' is in fact a natural kind term whose extension is determined by the underlying nature of the paradigms, then in all possible worlds, something is an experience only if it is identical to N, some physical, probably neurological, state of a human being. So then we'd have to say that we would not apply this term to cover their twin-experience. But would we really refrain? As philosophers interested in isolating sense experience from rational insight, is our current use of 'experience' limited only to creatures whose conscious, causally-mediated, information-gathering systems are biologically like our own? My sense here is no.

So the alleged asymmetry comes to this. If we were to discover on twin earth a substance that has the same surface characteristics as our water but with a different chemical structure, we would not say that it is water. If we were to discover on twin earth beings with cognitive processes that have the same surface characteristics as human experience but realized by different biological stuff, we would say that they have experiences.

Jeshion's argument can be reconstructed as follows:

(J6) If 'experience' is a natural kind term, then the state N that science discovers to be identical with experience in the actual world is a physical (neurological) state.

(J7) If 'experience' is a natural kind term and scientists discover that experience is identical to N in the actual world, then experience is identical to N in all possible worlds.

(J8) There is a possible world in which cognizers have experiences but are not in the same physical (neurological) state as their human counterparts; their psychological states are realized by different biological stuff.

(J9) Therefore, 'experience' is not a natural kind term.

(J6) clearly reiterates (J4) which, as I maintained in the previous section, misrepresents my position. Moreover, if (J6) is replaced by an accurate statement of my position,

(C2) If 'experience' is a natural kind term, then the state N that science discovers to be identical with experience in the actual world is a psychological state,

then the argument fails since (a) the fact that the twin earth cognizers and their human counterparts are in different neurological states does not entail that they are in different psychological states, and (b) she offers no independent argument in support of the claim that the twin earth cognizers and their human counterparts are in different psychological states. Therefore, Jeshion's argument against my position depends essentially on an incorrect formulation of it: one that assumes that the appropriate level of scientific analysis for giving the underlying nature of experience is that of neurology as opposed to psychology.

Jeshion seems to be aware of this point since she (2011, 102, n. 4) raises the question of whether I can maintain both (a) "that our current use of 'experience' allows us to extend it to differently realized-perception" and (b) that such use is compatible with the thesis that 'experience' is a natural kind term. Her answer is negative. If 'experience' is a natural kind term then, according to Jeshion (2011, 102, n. 4), "it will be used with the intention to isolate a *natural kind* like a neurological or biological process—something with a particular distinct physical make-up, and not, for example, a functional kind like whatever underlying processes realize causally mediated information giving states that have a distinctive phenomenology."

There are two problems with this contention: one metaphysical and the other semantic. There are no a priori metaphysical constraints on the nature of natural kinds. Our best scientific theories provide the best indication of which natural kinds exist and the nature of those kinds. If our best psychological theories involve functionally characterized psychological processes, then that is strong evidence that there are functional as well as physical and neurological natural kinds.

The semantic issue is more complex. To get our bearings, let us return to Jeshion's useful comparison between the semantics of proper names and the semantics of natural kind terms. Names are not synonymous with definite descriptions. A speaker can use a name to refer to an object in the absence of possessing information that uniquely picks out that object. Moreover, even in those situations in which a speaker introduces a name using a definite description, the name is not synonymous with the description. The semantic function of the description is not to give the meaning of the name but to fix its reference. Similar points can be made with respect to natural kind terms. They are not synonymous with definite descriptions. A speaker can use a term to refer to a natural kind in the absence of possessing information that uniquely picks out that kind. Moreover, when a speaker introduces a natural kind term using a definite description, the description does not give the meaning of the term but fixes its reference.

Suppose that we have a term that is introduced by some functional characterization—i.e., in terms of its typical causes and effects. Jeshion's functional characterization of 'experience' provides an example. The fact that a term is introduced by some functional characterization is semantically neutral. It does not show that the term is a functional kind term in Jeshion's sense—that is, one that is analytically equivalent to the functional characterization—and it does not show that the term is not a natural kind term—that is, one whose extension is fixed by the underlying nature of the functionally characterized paradigms. The correct semantic account will turn on whether the functional characterization fixes the reference of the term or provides its meaning. A functional characterization of a term can play either role. Once we recognize that natural kinds are not restricted to physical kinds and that a functional characterization can fix the reference of a term, we can see that there is no incompatibility in maintaining both (1) that 'experience' is a natural kind term, and (2) that it can apply to differently realized cognitive states. Whether this account is correct will turn on the semantic role of the functional characterization. In the next section, I will argue that Jeshion's functional characterization of 'experience' does not provide its meaning.

Jeshion advances a second argument against my position, which she ultimately does not endorse.[3] One of the consequences of my proposal to treat 'experience' as a natural kind term is that the surface characteristics used to identify the paradigms need not be necessary conditions for being a member of the associated natural kind. Since I have maintained that a distinctive conscious phenomenology is a surface characteristic of the paradigms used to fix the reference of experience, I have left open the epistemic possibility that one might be in state N, where N is the state that empirical science discovers to be identical with experience, and yet one lacks any associated conscious phenomenology.

Jeshion, however, invites us to consider the case of a blindsighted cognizer, who forms accurate beliefs about the location of objects in her immediate environment but lacks any associated conscious phenomenology. Suppose that she is in state N when she forms such a belief about the presence of some object. According to my account, she experiences the object in question. Jeshion (2011, 103), however, is not so sure: "I do not have any clear idea here but it is not apparent to me that we would regard her as having a sensory experience."[4]

My response to this case is less tentative since I think that there are many ordinary and quite familiar cases where we readily agree that someone experiences an object despite the absence of any relevant phenomenology. Suppose I am driving down the street focused on the construction taking place at the next intersection, which has disrupted the flow of traffic. Suddenly I slam on the brakes. A ball rolls in front of my car and a young child pulls herself to a stop within inches of my car. Presumably, my slamming on the brakes was not a random act on my part. It was brought about, in part, by my belief that a ball was approaching my car, along with some associated background beliefs about balls and the proximity of children. The belief that the ball was approaching my car was, presumably, a visual belief. The information that led me to step on the brakes was processed by the visual channels of my cognitive system. Here it seems perfectly mundane and ordinary to say that I saw the ball approaching the car

---

[3] Jeshion ultimately rejects this argument on the grounds that so-called theoretical "identity" statements are better understood as conditionals rather than biconditionals. By pursuing this objection in more detail, I am not dismissing her insightful suggestion for defusing it. I am pursuing it in order to respond to a (hypothetical) critic of my position who insists that theoretical identities are biconditionals.

[4] In the next section, I will argue that Jeshion's tentativeness about this case is at odds with other things that she says about the concept of experience.

despite the lack of appropriate phenomenology. Whatever visual phenomenology I had was associated with the construction site ahead of me. Jeshion (2011, 103, n. 5) questions this case on the grounds that the driver "sees the ball with peripheral vision, which *is* registered at the phenomenological level." I agree that the driver sees the ball but, as the case is described, the driver has no conscious, occurrent visual experiences that can plausibly be construed as of the ball approaching the car. If he is registering something at the phenomenological level, it is not something of which he is consciously aware.

5.3. An Alternative Proposal

Jeshion offers a lucid summary of my criticisms of extant proposals for analyzing the narrow sense of experience. Although she does not dispute my claim that these proposals all fail, she disagrees with my diagnosis of why they fail. My contention is that the source of their failure is methodological: they all attempt to provide an analysis of the relevant concept by a priori reflection on introspectively accessible features of cognitive experience. Jeshion (2011, 96–97) maintains that "the failures may be correctable by further a priori reflection," and that "the real reason for the problems with the analyses is because the concept of experience, in the sense of interest here, is a functional notion that is quite difficult to nail down analytically."

Jeshion is not explicit about the details of her alternative proposal. The clearest indication occurs in a passage where she (2011, 105) introduces the idea that my proposal might be construed as a revisionist thesis, a thesis about how we ought to use the term 'experience', as opposed to a descriptive thesis, a thesis about our actual use of 'experience': "he might be suggesting that we ought to stop using 'experience' to apply to the cognitive processes by which we secure information about the world via causal relations to objects in the world accessed through distinctive conscious phenomenological states." This passage suggests that Jeshion believes that our actual use of 'experience' can be articulated roughly as follows:

(J) X is an experiential process if and only if X is a cognitive process by which we secure information about the world via causal relations to objects in the world accessed through distinctive conscious phenomenological states.

Moreover, according to Jeshion, the semantic role of (J) is to provide the meaning of the term 'experience'. Hence, (J) is analytically true and knowable a priori.

There are two reasons for rejecting (J). First, (J) places the burden of distinguishing between experiential and nonexperiential processes entirely on the character of the relation between the cognizer and the object of experience. If 'causal' is deleted from the right side of the biconditional, then it satisfied by cognitive processes, such as rational insight, that apriorists posit as the source of nonexperiential justification. Rational insight is alleged to be a cognitive process by which we secure information about the world via some relations to objects in the world accessed through distinctive conscious phenomenological states.

Apriorists defend proposals such as (J) by pointing out that experiential processes provide information about the nature of contingent objects: they provide knowledge of contingent truths. Nonexperiential processes provide information about the nature of necessary or abstract objects: they provide knowledge of necessary truths. Since abstract objects cannot stand in causal relations, the nonexperiential processes are those that secure information about the world via noncausal relations.

As Jeshion (2011, 96) notes, I (2003, 152–58) consider and reject accounts of the distinction between experiential and nonexperiential processes that are similar to (J). Here is the problem. Apriorists typically claim (as they should) that some necessary truths are known on the basis of experience. So the apriorist who endorses (J) is committed to the following three claims:

(1a) We secure information about the nature of necessary objects via experience.

(2a) Securing information about an object via experience requires standing in a causal relation to that object.

(3a) Necessary objects do not stand in causal relations.

Clearly, the position is untenable. The source of the problem is (J), which entails that an experiential process secures information about an object by standing in a causal relation to that object.

The second reason for rejecting (J) emerges in the context of Jeshion's discussion of the phenomenon of blindsight. In a note she (2011, 103, n. 6) states, "I have no doubt that philosophers interested in isolating sources of a priori justification from all other sources of justified beliefs would count the subpersonal deliverances to the blindsighted person as empirical." Hence, the apriorist who endorses (J) is committed to the following claims:

(1b) A process is experiential only if it involves a distinctive conscious phenomenological state.

(2b) The process of blindsight does not involve such a state.

(3b) Beliefs justified by the process of blindsight are justified by experience.

Once again, the position is untenable. The source of the problem is (J), which entails that the presence of a distinctive conscious phenomenological state is a necessary feature of experience.

5.4. Two Remaining Issues

There are two remaining questions that Jeshion raises regarding my proposal to treat 'experience' as a natural kind term. First, she asks whether the proposal is descriptive or revisionist. Since I have rejected the argument that is alleged to show that it is not descriptive, I am free to maintain that it is descriptive. Nevertheless, I do not think that much hangs on this. My goal is to articulate the concept of a priori justification as it is employed by proponents of the a priori. Among the things that apriorists say is

(N) Some necessary truths are justified by experience.

Such apriorists are faced with a dilemma. Either what they say is coherent or it is not. If it is coherent then 'experience' is not a term whose meaning is captured by (J), and they need to provide an alternative account of its semantics. If it is not coherent, then apriorists need to revise their use of 'experience'. If they opt for the first horn, I maintain that my proposal captures the semantics of their current use. If they opt for the second horn, I recommend that they replace their current use with one that treats 'experience' as a natural kind term. My inclination is to be charitable—i.e., to regard (N) in the mouth of the apriorist as coherent, and to view my proposal as descriptive of their actual use. But, once again, not much hangs on this. The primary question is whether there is a coherent concept of a priori justification. Whether the articulation of the concept of experience that is necessary to provide a coherent articulation of the concept of a priori justification is descriptive or revisionist is of secondary interest.

Finally, Jeshion raises an interesting question about the relationship between the two leading claims of my account: (1) 'experience' is a natural kind term whose extension is fixed by the underlying nature of its associated paradigms, and (2) empirical investigation is relevant to answering the question of whether there are a priori justified beliefs. She maintains these claims are independent of one another in the sense that even if my claim that 'experience' is a natural kind term is wrong it does not follow that we cannot employ empirical investigation to support the claim that are a priori justified beliefs. In particular, she argues that if 'experience' is a functional kind term, then we can still employ empirical research to discover the underlying nature of the states that realize experience in humans and utilize this information to articulate the distinctive features of experiential processes. Moreover, we can also employ empirical research to determine whether there is some unique process underlying the cognitive states, identified at the phenomenological level, that apriorists claim justify beliefs nonexperientially. If there is such a process and it is different in relevant ways from those associated with the five senses, we can employ empirical investigation to determine whether that process is generally reliable.

Jeshion is correct in maintaining that my two claims are independent. One can consistently reject my claim that 'experience' is a natural kind term, as Jeshion does, but still agree that the program of empirical investigation that I propose, which consists of the Articulation Project and the Empirical Project, provides a fruitful way of addressing the question of whether a priori knowledge exists. Moreover, I also agree with Jeshion that we do not need a fully articulated concept of the a priori in order to embark on the two projects.

Jeshion (2011, 106), however, also contends that, "there is little of deep significance in his overall project" that turns on the claim that 'experience' is a natural kind term since its "overarching aim is to answer the question of whether there are nonexperiential sources for justifying beliefs." Here it is important to remember that my aim in *A Priori Justification* is to address four questions (see section 1), the first of which is: What is a priori knowledge? This question is important for two reasons. We cannot address the second question, Is there a priori knowledge?, in the absence of a sufficiently clear articulation of the concept of a priori knowledge. The articulation that I defend in terms of nonexperiential justification is adequate for this purpose. But the first question is also important for intrinsic theoretical reasons. One goal of a philosophical theory is to provide fully articulated analyses of its basic concepts. But I have not provided such an analysis of the concept of a priori knowledge since I have not offered an analysis of the relevant concept of experience. Moreover, I have argued that all extant proposals for analyzing that concept fail. My proposal offers an alternative strategy for articulating the relevant concept of experience. So Jeshion is correct in maintaining that the significance of my proposal to view 'experience' as a natural kind term does not lie in the fact that my program for employing empirical investigation to determine whether there exists a priori knowledge depends on it. Its significance lies in the fact that one central goal of my overall project is to articulate the concept of a priori knowledge and my proposal offers a strategy for overcoming the final hurdle to providing a full articulation of that concept.[5]

REFERENCES

BonJour, L. 1985. *The Structure of Empirical Knowledge*. Cambridge: Harvard University Press.
Brueckner, A. 2011. Albert Casullo's *A Priori Justification*. In *What Place for the A Priori?*, ed. M. Shaffer and M. Veber [the present volume], ch. 4. Chicago: Open Court.
Casullo, A. 2003. *A Priori Justification*. New York: Oxford University Press.
Jeshion, R. 2011. Experience as Natural Kind: Reflections on Albert Casullo's *A Priori Justification*. In *What Place for the A Priori?*, ed. M. Shaffer and M. Veber [the present volume], ch. 5. Chicago: Open Court.
Kitcher, P. 1983. *The Nature of Mathematical Knowledge*. New York: Oxford University Press.
Kripke, S. 1971. Identity and Necessity. In *Identity and Individuation*, ed. M. K. Munitz, 135–64. New York: New York University Press.
———. 1980. *Naming and Necessity*. Cambridge: Harvard University Press.
Plantinga, A. 1993. *Warrant and Proper Function*. New York: Oxford University Press.
Putnam, H. 1975. The Meaning of 'Meaning'. In *Mind, Language and Reality: Philosophical Papers*, vol. 2, 131–93. Cambridge: Cambridge University Press.

---

[5] This essay is a revised version of my contribution to the symposium "Author Meets Critics: Albert Casullo, *A Priori Justification*," American Philosophical Association Pacific Division Meetings, March 23–27, 2005. Anthony Brueckner and Robin Jeshion were my co-symposiasts. I would like to extend my appreciation to the 2005 Pacific Division Program Committee, and especially Tim Black, for organizing this session. My thanks to my colleagues at the University of Nebraska-Lincoln and, in particular, to John Gibbons for helpful discussions of earlier versions of this paper.

[7]

Epistemological Empiricism

HAROLD I. BROWN

I will argue that no a priori truths play a substantive role in physical science.[1] I refer to this view as *epistemological empiricism* to emphasize that it does not include the semantic and antirealist views often associated with empiricism. Still, my thesis is not sufficiently specific; I must say more about my use of "a priori" and "substantive," beginning with the former.

The term "a priori" is commonly used in several different ways; I make no claim to having captured its "correct" meaning. I aim only to make my thesis clear—although it is important that the meaning I specify have a recognizable role in the history of philosophy. Note first that I am using "a priori" as a predicate of propositions. Arguably, there is a more basic use of "a priori" as an epistemic predicate—one that properly characterizes a way of knowing. Its application to propositions is then derivative: a priori truths are those we know in a particular way. I accept with this claim, but I will focus on these derivative products because this will allow us to avoid a variety of disputes. One of these is the precise characterization of this way of knowing, which is controversial, although various accounts converge on the nature of the outcome: True propositions that we are justified in believing, and whose justification is not subject to challenge by any empirical evidence.[2]

---

[1] I note a possible exception: deductive logic. I consider the epistemic status of logic to be an open question, and will not discuss it here. One approach to including logic under my thesis would take off from the recognition that the validity of an argument form can be challenged by finding an instance with true premises and a false conclusion. A well-known example is provided by the indeterminacy relations of quantum theory, which seem to provide an empirically established counter-example to distribution of conjunction over disjunction. If we claim to know that no empirical counter-instances are possible in specific cases, we are under the obligation of explaining how we know this.

[2] This is not the same as claiming that such beliefs are infallible. Peacocke, for example, holds that a priori justifications are fallible (e.g., 1992, ch. 7; 2000) but can be corrected only by a priori methods.

Consider another reason for focusing on these products. However we characterize the a priori mode of knowing, its core feature is its account of justification: An a priori way of knowing provides a mode of justification that does not depend on any empirical claims. Among the various disputes about justification, the dispute between naturalistic and nonnaturalistic accounts has particularly general scope. Naturalists typically give an account of justification in terms of the cognitive processes that generate a belief. Antinaturalists, following Frege, reject this appeal to processes, viewing justifications as objective propositional structures consisting of some set of premises and some appropriate logical relation between these premises and the conclusion to be justified. But the premises must themselves be justified, and this justification too must be immune to empirical challenge. I will not review the history of attempts to break the lurking regress.[3] The two approaches converge on justified beliefs so that by focusing directly on these beliefs we can look at their possible roles in science without entering into disputes about their source. Indeed, if my claim that there are no substantive a priori truths in science is correct, we need not provide an account of the way such truths are justified.

Next, I characterized these truths as immune to empirical *challenge*, rather than as immune to empirical refutation, because of the contemporary recognition that scientific propositions face empirical tests as members of sets—although not as the whole corporate body of science. Consider, then, a situation in which we deduce an empirically testable result from a set of premises, and the evidence contradicts that result; something in our corpus must be revised. I want to contrast two ways of looking at this situation. One view sharply distinguishes the premises we used to deduce the contradicted result from the empirical evidence. We then focus on the premises and require that the revision occur here. An a priori truth would be a proposition in this set that is in principle not a possible candidate for reconsideration. This separation of the propositions yielding the prediction from the result of an empirical test allows for the possibility that some empirical results are indubitable. Such results are immune from reconsideration but are not a priori. There are, however, overwhelming grounds for denying that indubitable empirical results occur in scientific testing. Two familiar points will underline the reasons for this. First, it is not observations understood as psychological events or physical states of instruments that enter into the evaluation of scientific propositions, it is reports of those observations. But these reports must be expressed in the conceptual framework of a theory in order to be relevant to its evaluation. Theory change

---

[3] Neither approach has any problems with the use of concepts derived from experience in an a priori justification. It is only the propositions in which these concepts occur that are the subject of concern.

can change these reports while the outcome of a test remains stable. Second, empirical reports that are relevant to the evaluation of scientific theories must have units attached. We may agree, for example, that if I see 5 on a digital readout it is highly unlikely that I am mistaken. But this result is not relevant to any theory until we specify whether it is five kilograms, or five feet per second, or five neutrinos in the last month. At this point the theory of the instrument enters, along with the usual reasons for acknowledging dubitability. These considerations will serve to introduce the second view noted above (which I will adopt henceforth): Once the observation reports have been formulated we have a set of propositions that includes both the original premises and these reports. When a prediction fails this set is inconsistent; one or more propositions in the set must be rejected. Any a priori truths in this set are not subject to rejection for some appropriately deep reason. My thesis, then, is that there are none of these. I will begin exploring candidates shortly.

I want to note how the Duhem-Quine thesis is to be understood in this context. According to this thesis, any specific claim in a set can be protected by making revisions elsewhere in that set. However, Greenwood (1990) pointed out that this is not so simple when we are dealing with a set of tightly integrated propositions—which is what we find in a well-constructed scientific theory. Any change we make in the set in order to accommodate a particular anomaly is liable to generate new consequences that will introduce new empirical anomalies. When multiple attempts to protect a proposition fail in this way, we accumulate empirical evidence against that proposition. As long as we acknowledge the possibility of solving our problem by replacing that proposition—however unpleasant this may be—that proposition is not an a priori truth. Quine suggests that in extreme cases we can overcome "recalcitrant experience by pleading hallucination" (1961, 43), but this is not to be taken seriously in contemporary science. Scientific theories are not tested against momentary psychological events—they are tested against stable, intersubjective evidence. Often this evidence is embodied in photographs or computer printouts (see Brown 1995; 2005 for discussion). Rejecting evidence by an appeal to hallucination requires claiming a persistent, widespread hallucination—a claim that requires empirical evaluation. There are familiar cases of persistent widespread illusions, such as the Müller-Lyer illusion. But exactly because of their persistence and intersubjectivity we are not fooled by them; rather, we have learned how to overcome them—for example, by measuring the picture that generates the illusion.

I am dealing here with a tough-minded conception of a priori truths, but—as Popper might say—this enhances the content of the claim that such truths occur in science. If we can identify such, we will have something well worth having (I will contrast a weaker notion of the a priori below). The strength of this notion of an a priori truth depends on our extending the notion of an empirical challenge beyond that of a direct confrontation between a single proposition and a single empirical result. But this is not an arbitrary extension. It is justified because it captures the way that empirical testing is actually carried out in science.

By a "substantive truth" I mean one that states a constraint on either nature or the practice of science. The claim that every alteration has a cause is one candidate for a substantive truth. This claim purports to tell us something about what is going on in nature and also generates a task for research. Scientists who accept this claim are not only constrained to seek causes, but to accept the blame when causes are not found. Moreover, by focusing attention on the search for causes, the causal principle guides research. Various conservation principles are also substantive in this sense. A failure of, say, the energy balance in an interaction indicates that something is going on in nature that researchers have missed, and provides a goal for further research on this interaction. By way of contrast, definitions that are introduced as abbreviations for more complex constructions are not substantive. Abbreviations may facilitate our thought, but they do not constrain either nature or the practice of science. Such definitions may be a priori in that we can maintain the meanings of our terms in the face of all experience, but they are not substantive truths. A different kind of example is illustrated by the cogito. We may grant that "I exist" is indefeasibly true at each moment at which I am conscious, but this is not a truth that plays any role in science.[4]

I now want to begin looking at the familiar candidates for a priori truths in science, beginning with analytic propositions. Explicit definitions provide a clear example of analytic propositions; their truth is not in question, and they cannot be contradicted by any empirical result. Such definitions are substantive to the extent that they introduce a new concept into a scientific framework—as opposed to just giving an abbreviation for some previously adopted expression. The decision to include a concept in a theory is typically not arbitrary. We introduce concepts because we believe that they have instances in the relevant domain or that they can play a role in predictions and explanations.[5] Concepts are eliminated from the active scientific repertoire when evidence indicates that they do not play these roles. Van Fraassen (1975, 242) captures this point in a remark on Kant's thesis that there is an apodictic basis to our science of matter:

---

[4] It is debatable whether the cogito is established by an a priori procedure, but we need not pursue this issue here.

[5] In classical empiricist semantics all definitions are abbreviations of the sort noted in the previous paragraph. But even here the decision that a particular term is worth including in our repertoire can be a substantive decision.

"what we *refer* to as matter may not be an instance of our concept of matter. The pure part of the theory of matter cannot become wrong: in principle it can be propounded in the form of a definition. But although it is apodictic, it can certainly become irrelevant." This is what famously occurred with the Aristotelian concept of natural place, phlogiston, and caloric, and less famously with telegony. "The concept of telegony, which was almost universally believed in by nineteenth-century breeders and fanciers and widely accepted within the zoological community, attributed to the 'previous sire'—usually understood as the father of a female's first child—the power of influencing her subsequent offspring" (Ritvo 1997, 107–8; cf. Banton 1998, 42–43). Telegony was held to describe an actual phenomenon, and belief in telegony formed the basis for some advice found in the literature of animal husbandry. For example, owners of a purebred bitch that had become pregnant by an undesirable male were advised to eliminate her from the breeding stock. Similarly, cattle breeders were advised never to start a herd with a purchased cow since they had no control over her previous mates. Belief in telegony provided an addition to the prevailing reasons for insisting on female virginity in human marriages; Darwin is included among the scientists who believed in telegony (Ritvo 1997, 109–10). So the concept played a serious role in nineteenth-century theoretical and practical thought, but has vanished from our repertoire even though the definition has not been refuted. In this case the concept became irrelevant as it became clear that it has no instances.

This point about individual analytic propositions also applies to entire conceptual systems: Whether a system is instantiated in nature is always an empirical question. No matter how tightly structured and coherent a conceptual system may be, it does not constrain nature. Aristotelian mechanics is a clear example. The concepts of natural and violent motion, as specified within this system, are contraries; thus it is a conceptual truth that an object cannot engage in both forms of motion at the same time. Working within this framework, there is no reason to check whether an actual projectile instantiates both forms of motion simultaneously; it is known a priori that it cannot. But when Aristotelian physics was refuted, its identification of a projectile's vertical motion as natural and its horizontal motion as violent was rejected. In other words, accumulating evidence showed that the Aristotelian framework is not instantiated in this world, and its concepts became irrelevant to the practice of physics. We reject Aristotelian physics as a description of the actual world even though we have not shown that the conceptual truths built into the theory are false. The conceptual truths of a framework are a priori only relative to that framework; since acceptance of the framework is under empirical control, so is the role of these truths in science. The upshot, then, is that we must admit two modes of empirical rejection of a proposition: showing that it is false and showing that it is irrelevant.

This result has direct bearing on another sense of "a priori" that has a precedent in Kant and has recently been emphasized by Friedman: "The Kantian notion of the a priori included two distinguishable meanings: In the first, 'a priori' means necessarily and unrevisibly true, but in the second it means only constitutive. . . ." Friedman then specifies two characteristics of propositions that are constitutive in the sense he intends: "first, they are not themselves subject to straightforward empirical confirmation or disconfirmation by measuring parameters and instantiating laws, and second, they first make possible the confirmation and disconfirmation of empirical laws properly so-called . . ." (1999, 61). Friedman is especially concerned with the role of these constitutive propositions in the work of the logical positivists. He argues, for example, that geometry plays this role in Reichenbach's early work. To be sure, the development of physics from Newton to Einstein involved a change in the accepted geometry, and Friedman acknowledges that this change was motivated by empirical considerations: "In special relativity, however, we change—under pressure of new empirical findings—precisely the background space-time structure" (61). Moreover, by the time we get to general relativity, Euclidean geometry—which was constitutive for Newtonian mechanics—has lost this constitutive role and become empirically false (69). Still, Friedman holds, new propositions play a constitutive role in the new physics, and we find a generally satisfactory account of this constitutive a priori in Carnap's distinction between L-rules and P-rules (70). The upshot is a relativized notion of the a priori: These propositions are constitutive of a particular framework, although they cease to be part of science when that framework is rejected. For the positivists these constitutive propositions are analytic, which is why I am considering them at the present point in our discussion.

Clearly, these propositions are not candidates for a priori truths in science, as I am using the term, exactly because they are subject to empirical challenge. Friedman emphasizes that they are not subject to *straightforward* empirical evaluation, where this presumably means that they cannot be individually evaluated on the basis of evidence and logic alone. But none of the central propositions of a science are subject to this kind of evaluation. Note also that I am not challenging the view that the internal structure of a theory is hierarchical (Friedman 2002, 189–90) and that some propositions may play a special role in making empirical tests of a theory possible. I am only claiming that these propositions are subject to empirical challenge—a point that Friedman seems to concede. If these constitutive propositions are analytic they cannot be falsified by experience, but they are subject to rejection as irrelevant—and empirical evidence plays a key role in this assessment. My concern here is with propositions that cannot be evaluated as either false or irrelevant on the basis of empirical evidence. This is close to Kant's other sense of a priori, although unlike Kant I do not require that such a priori truths are necessary truths. Note especially that for Kant the causal principle and Euclidean geometry cannot be put aside as part of the process of improving the empirical success of science.

The admittedly overworked analogy between a theory and a game may help clarify the notion of a constitutive a priori, and my reasons for not pursuing it. Baseball is defined by a set of rules that are constitutive of the game. According to Gould (1997), these rules have not been changed for a century—although there have been substantial changes in the game. For example, while the number of bases and the rules for scoring a run have remained constant, the height of the mound and size of the strike zone have been altered by those who run professional baseball. Moreover, Gould claims, these changes have been made in response to an empirically evaluable goal: keeping the outcome of the central battle between pitcher and batter—as measured by the average batting average—essentially constant. Still, in spite of the constitutive role of the rules, I may choose not to play or follow baseball. And I may make this choice on such empirical grounds as that I find the game boring. The a priori truths that Kant and others have claimed for science are made of stronger stuff—or would be if they existed.

The distinction between the internal structure of a theory and its empirically evaluable application to some external subject matter applies directly to the role of mathematics in science. The axioms and theorems of a mathematical structure such as linear algebra or group theory form an internally a priori system, but whether this system applies to the physical world cannot be determined a priori. This is familiar from discussions of geometry, but a different example, one as fundamental as geometry in the development of physics but not often discussed, may help drive home the point: the velocity-addition formula required by special relativity (SR). Recall a typical situation. In reference frame F1 a rocket ship is moving at velocity u along the x-axis in the positive x direction. Call the frame of reference of the ship F2. The ship emits a projectile in the positive x' direction—where the x'-axis is stationary in F2 and coincides with the x-axis of F1. In F2 the velocity of the projectile is v. What is the velocity of the projectile relative to F1? While it may seem obvious that it is $u + v$, and while this may be built into both classical and folk physics, SR requires a different rule for adding these velocities: $(u + v)/(1 + uv/c^2)$. This result is entailed by the postulates of SR and is thus a priori with respect to this framework. But the reasons for adopting this framework—and rejecting its predecessors—are empirical.

Now consider a variation on this case. We have two rules for adding fractions that we use in different situations. R1 is the familiar rule that requires expressing the fractions in terms of a least common denominator and then adding the numerators. R2 requires that we add the numerators and add the denominators. We use R2 when we calculate batting averages, but let me take a different example since not everyone is familiar with this concept from baseball. Suppose that for each class in session in a university at a given time we know the fraction of students that are women. If we want to use this data to determine the total fraction of women in class at that time we must use R2. This has significant ramifications, which can be brought out by considering a simplified example. Suppose that only two classes are meeting, and that one class has four students of whom two are women, while the other has two students of whom one is a woman. The fractions we begin with are 2/4 and 1/2; the total we are interested in is 3/6. Note especially that when R2 applies we cannot reduce fractions or replace fractions with decimals. In such cases 2/4 is not equivalent to either 1/2 or .5. Indeed, suppose we are giving monetary awards in accordance with the following rule: Each person who is in class when the data are taken receives $100, and each woman receives an additional $50. Use of reduced fractions or decimals at any stage of the calculation will prevent us from determining how much money to appropriate. There is nothing mysterious about this situation once we recognize that there are multiple mathematical structures, and the application of a particular structure to some external domain requires independent exploration of that domain. The mathematics does not itself guarantee its application. Moreover, we now know that a mathematical structure may be in use in some domain for a long time before new evidence leads to its reconsideration.[6]

There is another respect in which the application of mathematics to a particular domain is under empirical control: whether a body of mathematics can be interpreted at all in that domain. The application of arithmetic to money will illustrate the point. Dollars add, but dollars do not multiply: there is no such thing as six dollars^2. The usual rule of multiplication is irrelevant here because we lack a relevant interpretation of multiplication for this case. By way of contrast, we multiply lengths because we have found a relevant and useful interpretation of length^2.

Some will hold that by introducing mathematics I have moved from considering analytic propositions to synthetic a priori propositions. For present purposes I need not take a stand on this issue, but I do want to directly confront the claim that there are synthetic a priori propositions in

---

[6] A second step towards an argument for the empirical status of logic begins from the recognition that modern mathematical logic is an interpreted formalism. A formalism alone does not constitute a logic; it becomes a logic only when interpreted in terms of some subject matter—say a body of discourse. But then it is an empirical question whether a particular interpreted formalism adequately captures the logical features of that discourse.

science. It is characteristic of these propositions that we recognize cases that could pose empirical challenges to them but, for appropriately deep reasons, never accept such challenges. It is not just that we always choose to modify our framework in ways that protect these propositions, but that we are rationally constrained to proceed in this way. The key issue is the nature of this rational constraint. Kant's transcendental deduction is the grandmother of attempts to establish such constraints. The aim of the deduction is to establish that we have a right to use concepts in order to organize experience. Kant emphasizes that he is using "deduction" in a special sense taken from jurisprudence where deductions establish rights, as opposed to facts. But even given this special usage he is still offering an argument which must have premises and a logical form that is either deductive or nondeductive.[7] The conclusion of this argument is that pure a priori concepts—which are subjective conditions of thought—are objectively valid conditions for the possibility of experience. Clearly this is not an analytic proposition, and Kant emphasizes that it cannot be established empirically. The only option, then, is that this conclusion is synthetic a priori. I want to consider both options for the form of the argument and investigate the nature of its premises.

If the argument is deductive it is clear that these premises must be synthetic a priori propositions. But now we are in danger of begging the question since the transcendental deduction is supposed to be one step in the proof that we know some synthetic a priori propositions. We cannot assume such knowledge in order to prove that it exists. Moreover, if we ignore this objection a familiar regress threatens since we need justified premises. The only way of breaking this regress that the philosophical tradition offers is some form of intellectual intuition. Such a solution would avoid the charge of begging the question since it amounts to admitting one class of synthetic a priori propositions in order to establish a different class. But Kant denies that such intuition is available to human beings and I know of no reasons for disagreeing. Note, however, that we have been pushed to a consideration of human cognitive capabilities: our aim is not just to establish propositions that are in fact synthetic a priori, but to establish them as propositions that we are justified in continuing to accept in the face of all apparent empirical challenges. This requires the ability to *recognize* their synthetic a priori status—which requires an account of how we are able to do this. Such an account would presumably be based on empirical evidence and points in the direction of a nondeductive argument

---

[7] Kant believed that he had discovered a new branch of logic—transcendental logic—which also deals with form: the form of experience. The first *Critique*'s table of contents underlines how much of this book Kant presented as a book on logic. I do include transcendental logic in my use of "logic."

for Kant's key conclusion. But this proposal immediately raises another question: does it even make sense to claim that we might decide on non-a-priori grounds that some proposition is an a priori truth? I want to explore this option.

It will help to return briefly to analytic propositions. In the section in which Kant introduces the analytic/synthetic distinction he writes: "For it would be absurd to found an analytic judgment on experience. Since, in framing the judgment, I must not go outside my concept, there is no need to appeal to the testimony of experience in its support" (A7, B11, 1963, 49; Kant is using "judgment" as a synonym for "proposition"). But while it may be a fact that the predicate of a proposition does not go beyond the subject, this does not guarantee that we can always recognize this fact and appeal to it in justifying our belief in that proposition. Disputes among analytic philosophers about whether specific propositions are analytic illustrate the difficulties we encounter. In such cases we may have empirical grounds for believing that a proposition is analytic (such as the behavior of members of a community when we question its truth) and thus seek an appropriate analysis. To further underline this point consider an alien anthropologist who arrives on earth with limited knowledge of English. After interviewing a few English speakers our anthropologist might discover that all aunts are female on purely empirical grounds. Later, after learning more English, the anthropologist finds that the empirical procedure was unnecessary. "All aunts are female" is analytic and its truth *can* be discovered by reflection alone. A human observer of our anthropologist's early work could describe her as having discovered an a priori truth empirically.[8] Moreover, after several such experiences the anthropologist might begin entertaining the hypothesis that certain deeply held propositions are analytic even though she cannot display the analysis.

A similar situation is provided by the recent advent of computer-assisted proofs of mathematical theorems. Proofs establish relations between propositions. Statements of these relations provide a paradigm case of a priori truths independently of whether the premises and conclusion of a proof are analytic or synthetic. But computer-assisted proofs depend for their acceptability on our understanding of the physical behavior of our computer, and are empirical to the extent that our knowledge of

---

[8] Chisholm (1977, 46–47) notes this possibility when a logical theorem is accepted on the basis of expert testimony. It is also built into Kitcher's account of the a priori. Kitcher defines a priori truths as "those propositions which could be known a priori" (2000, 66), while also emphasizing (later on the same page) that we must not collapse the distinction between "a priori knowledge and empirical knowledge of propositions that could have been known a priori."

this behavior is empirical: "The operation of computers depends on properties of copper and silicon, on electrodynamics and quantum mechanics. Confidence in computers comes from confidence in physical facts and theories. These are not a priori. We learn the laws of physics and the electrical properties of silicon and copper from experience" (Hersh 1997, 53). Hersh also notes that "the physical processes that make computers work aren't fully understood" (54). For example, our understanding of computers is no better than our understanding of transistors, which is no better than our understanding of quantum theory. In addition, our acceptance of a computer program as doing what we have designed it to do is empirical. To be sure, the first step in accepting a program is the programmer's grasp of its logical structure. But it is virtually certain that on first running any moderately complex program we will turn up unnoticed errors in its logic; indeed this is a good reminder of the limits of human insight into such structures. Debugging then proceeds by running test cases for which we know what the outcomes should be, and correcting those errors that we find. The conclusion arrived at through this process—that a program is free at least of important bugs—is often false; this is familiar to anyone who uses professionally written programs.[9] Moreover, the reliability of a traditional proofs depends on the behavior of brains. Currently these are no better understood than computers although we do have strong evidence that "human beings are *less* reliable at long computations than a Cray or a Sun" (Hersh 1997, 54). This should be familiar to anyone who has learned to trust a pocket calculator over her own arithmetic.

With this clarification in place, we can turn to our current concern: Can we have empirical grounds for believing that a scientific proposition must never be rejected even though this is a logically admissible option in response to experience? The burden of evidence indicates that we have not yet discovered any such propositions. Nevertheless, there is an important point to Kant's introduction of synthetic a priori propositions and to the notion of a constitutive a priori emphasized by Friedman. This point, deriving from Hume, is that logic and evidence alone are not sufficient to guide our response to the empirical world. Hume developed this theme in his analysis of confirmation; I want to highlight two stages of Hume's discussion. First, given A alone, we have no grounds for deciding what other items are associated with A:

> Let an object be presented to a man of ever so strong natural reason and abilities; if that object be entirely new to him, he will not be able, by the most

---

[9] Tymoczko notes a case in which two mathematicians "proved the negation of a certain computer based result and only afterwards learned that the original program was in error" (1998, 243).

accurate examination of its sensible qualities, to discover any of its causes or effects. Adam, though his rational faculties be supposed, at the very first, entirely perfect, could not have inferred from the fluidity and transparency of water that it would suffocate him, or from the light and warmth of fire, that it would consume him. No object ever discovers, by the qualities which appear to the senses, either the causes which produced it, or the effects which will arise from it; nor can our reason, unassisted by experience, ever draw any inference concerning real existence and matter of fact. (1975, 27)

Second, even when we have observed a constant association between two items, logic still leaves us without sufficient grounds for concluding that they will be associated in cases we have not examined.

Kant's attempt to solve this problem by means of synthetic a priori propositions embodies his recognition that only synthetic propositions can fill the gaps. Note how these propositions play a double role. They are descriptive propositions in that they state universal features of the (phenomenal) world. But they are also normative in that they guide research. For example, the causal principle enjoins us to study the physical world by seeking causes and never accepting the failure to find a cause as evidence against the principle. Still, in Kant hands this normative guidance is minimal since it tells us little about how to recognize a causal relation when we see one. Kant's key idea is that a cause is operating when we encounter succession in accordance with a rule—although such succession indicates only that a causal relation is present; it does not imply that the cause is found in the observed succession. Moreover, Kant points out (in a footnote to the second analogy) that succession in accordance with a rule is not sufficient to guarantee that a cause is in play: "It should be carefully noted that I speak not of the alteration of certain relations in general, but of alteration of state. Thus, when a body moves uniformly, it does not in any way alter its state (of motion); that occurs only when its motion increases or diminishes" (A207, B252, 1963, 230). Kant's footnote is a recognition that according to Newtonian physics no cause is needed to sustain uniform motion.

A bit of historical reflection on this footnote will introduce another theme. In the language of the seventeenth and eighteenth centuries *states* are properties of physical objects that do not change spontaneously. Descartes's first law of nature asserts that simple objects do not change their state without an external cause. This tautology gains substance because Descartes maintains that uniform motion (motion in a straight line at constant speed) is a state. Such motion is not a state in Aristotelian physics, so Descartes's claim expresses a different tautology than the same words would express if uttered by an Aristotelian. In stating his laws of nature Descartes writes:

> The first of these laws is that each thing, provided that it is simple and undivided, always remains in the same state as far as is in its power, and never changes except by external causes. Thus if some part of matter is square, we are easily convinced that it will always remain square unless some external intervention changes its shape. Similarly, if it is at rest, we do not believe that it will ever begin to move unless driven to do so by some external cause. Nor, if it is moving, is their any significant reason to think that it will ever cease to move of its own accord and without some other thing which impedes it. (1991, 59)

In the ensuing discussion Descartes makes it clear that this persistence applies only to uniform motion; he explicitly excludes circular motion on the earth and in the heavens.

This extension of the concept of a state to include uniform motion is taken over by Newton—although with further conceptual innovations. In particular, Descartes holds that while uniform motion and rest are both states, they are different kinds of states that are governed by different laws; these are embodied in his rules of impact (1991, 64–69). For Newton, uniform motion and rest are states of the same kind, governed by the same laws. In addition, for Descartes change of direction and change of speed are different kinds of change; Descartes does not have the vector concept of velocity. As Garber notes, "Descartes recognized the importance of both magnitude and direction, without knowing exactly how to combine them" (1992, 246). Newton knew how to combine them. (See Brown 2007, ch. 9 for a detailed analysis).

The role of conceptual innovation in the development of science is another blow to the thesis that some set of a priori truths provides a permanent part of science. It suggests that we may not yet have developed the concepts we will need for future formulations, and that central concepts of current formulations may vanish. I submit that recognizing the possibility of conceptual innovation is the key contribution of Goodman's new riddle of induction, but that his conservative response—stick with entrenched predicates—is the wrong response. This is clear if we turn away from Goodman's artificial example and look at the history of science. Reflection on this history underlines a further factor that contributes to the need for conceptual innovation and extends the reasons for doubting that we are in a position to permanently fix any feature of science: this is the growing scope and precision of our evidential base. The most important contributor to this development is the introduction of instruments that allow us to detect and study items that we cannot examine with our native senses—either because they are too small or too distant, or because none of our senses respond to them. We have been making use of such instruments at least since the discovery of the magnetic compass—which allows us to see the direction of the earth's magnetic field even though none of our senses responds to magnetism. This line of development took a major leap with Galileo's use of the telescope early in the seventeenth century, and the rapid adoption of telescopes as the central tool for astronomy. It took another major step when Herschel (1800) discovered infrared radiation by examining temperature variations in the spectrum of sunlight that continue beyond the red end of the spectrum, and Ritter (shortly afterwards) discovered ultraviolet radiation by studying the way sliver chloride darkens when exposed to light at the blue end of the spectrum and beyond. (For discussions see Brown 2005; Guiot 1985; Hacking 1983, 176–78; Wetzels 1990.)

Our ability to study items we cannot sense, and the need to introduce new concepts to accommodate new evidence, accelerated with the discovery of radioactivity in 1896. Consider just one example: introduction of the concept of an isotope (Brown 2007 provides many further examples.) In nineteenth-century chemistry the thesis that every element is characterized by a specific atomic weight functioned as if it were a synthetic a priori proposition: it described a key feature of the physical world and it played a normative role in chemical research. While elements could be identified through chemical reactions and spectroscopic analysis, it was considered especially important to determine their characteristic weights. Failures to find such weights were interpreted as failures of chemical analysis, not as evidence against the fundamental role of weight. Yet such failures occurred throughout the century, and in 1886 Crookes put forward the "audacious" speculation that the weight standardly associated with an element was that of the majority of its atoms, and that some might have slightly different weights (Bruzzaniti and Robotti 1989, 309); this was not immediately embraced. The evidence that led scientists to accept multiple weights for an element—and thus reject weight as the defining feature of an element—came from the completely unexpected discovery of radioactivity. Once this phenomenon was recognized, and the difference between alpha and beta radiation established, it became clear that transformations occur in which an element emits an alpha particle and two beta particles (in any order). Beta emission could be treated as involving no change of weight, so the transformations in question leave an element's slot in the periodic table unchanged while its weight drops by four units (see Fajans [1913] 1970, 207–19; Soddy [1913] 1970, 219–28).[10] This makes it strikingly clear that a single element can have two different atomic weights, a discovery that was encapsulate in the new concept of an *isotope*. Other radioactive transformations could result in two different elements

---

[10] It was generally believed at this time that the nucleus contains protons and electrons, but that electrons make no significant contribution to an element's weight, although it was recognized that electrons have mass. The neutron would not be discovered for two decades.

with the same atomic weight (known as *isobars*). Both the nature of the physical world and the aims of chemistry had to be rethought. Soddy captures the impact of the latter change:

> There is something, surely, akin to if not transcending tragedy in the fate that has overtaken the life work of that distinguished galaxy of nineteenth-century chemists, rightly revered by their contemporaries as representing the crown and perfection of accurate scientific measurement. Their hard-won results, for the moment at least, appears as of as little interest and significance as the determination of the average weight of a collection of bottles, some of them full and some of them more or less empty. (1932, 50)

The use of instruments burgeoned throughout the twentieth century vastly extending the scope and precision of the empirical evidence at the basis of science. In astronomy, for example, we now gather data throughout the electromagnetic spectrum, from radio waves to gamma radiation. Since 1987, when a supernova was first registered by neutrino detectors that were deployed for other purposes, scientists have been designing and deploying neutrino telescopes. We have learned more about the constituents of the universe since we began extending our probes beyond the optical portion of the electromagnetic spectrum than we learned in the entire previous history of astronomy. The development of detectors used to study sub-atomic particles—whether coming from space or produced in laboratories—is another major part of the story (see Galison 1997 for this history). We have learned more about the material world since the discovery of radioactivity than we learned in the previous millennia of studying the easily available properties of physical objects.[11] Examples can easily be multiplied and we have no reasons for believing that this process of extending our probes, encountering surprises, and introducing new concepts will end any time soon.

Still, coherent scientific research requires something that plays the normative role of synthetic a priori propositions. This becomes fully clear with the twentieth-century recognition that scientific propositions face empirical evaluation only as members of sets; that in cases of a negative outcome, logic does not tell us which member(s) of a set should be rejected; and that rejected propositions may be superseded by propositions that involve new concepts. If synthetic a priori propositions existed, they would ameliorate this problem by reducing the permissible options. Since the 1950s there has a been a persistent search for a substitute for the synthetic a priori—that is, for propositions that can play

---

[11] A physicist friend emphasizes that contemporary particle research would not be possible without modern computational power.

the descriptive and normative roles of the synthetic a priori without being either permanent or known a priori.[12] Following the terminology introduced in Laudan et al. (1986) I will refer to these as *guiding assumptions* (henceforth GAs). Quine attempted to deal with this issue in his thesis that while all propositions are subject to reconsideration in response to evidence, some are more central to our thinking and we are reluctant to reject them. Such rejections do occur, although only under extreme circumstances. But Quine ignored conceptual innovation. For my purposes it will be more illuminating to consider attempts that integrate the need for GAs with such innovation. I will give brief sketches of three such attempts—due to Sellars, Putnam, and Kuhn—in order to underline the pervasive sense that such propositions are needed.[13]

Beginning with Sellars, I will note just two of his central themes. (See especially Sellars 1953, 1963, 1965, 1973; Brown 1986, 2007, chs. 4–5.) *First*, concepts occur only as members of systems of interrelated concepts. At least part of every concept's content is determined by implications which hold between that concept and other concepts in the system.[14] While holistic, this view should be read as a local holism; it does not require that all concepts link together into a single massive conceptual scheme. Rather, each of us deploys many different conceptual systems that have a variety of relations to each other. I have concepts that I use for thinking about baseball, and some of these concepts have close ties to concepts I use for thinking about other games, but they have little connection with concepts I use for thinking about carpentry, transcendental arguments, or plate tectonics. I also have two conceptual schemes for thinking about space and time—one from everyday experience and one from SR. There are complex relations among the concepts in the two schemes, and there are good reasons for describing both as systems of space and time concepts. Still, they are distinct conceptual schemes and I can shift from one to the other without confusing them.

Second, each of the implications that are constitutive of a concept is associated with a firmly accepted universal generalization—which may be either analytic or synthetic. The idea is that firmly accepting the generalization "All A are B" is equivalent to acquiring a license to infer "x is B" from "x is A"—a license that is valid independently of whether the infer-

---

[12] Kant's attempt to establish a priori knowledge of synthetic propositions leads to his conclusion that these propositions can describe only a phenomenal world; this style of antirealist argument is eliminated when we drop the attempt at an a priori justification.

[13] Other variations on this theme include Toulmin's ideals of natural order, Lakatos hard core, and Laudan's research traditions.

[14] Sellars distinguishes three kinds of conceptual systems—formal, descriptive, and normative—on the basis of whether and how relation to an extra-systemic subject matter plays a role in constituting conceptual content.

ence is based on an analytic or a synthetic proposition.[15] That is, we build all of our firmly accepted generalizations concerning A into our concept of an A. In the course of our cognitive history (both as individuals and as a species) we engage in frequent conceptual change as new evidence and new reflections lead us to change our firm beliefs. But as long as we are working within a particular conceptual system, the synthetic generalizations that we firmly accept function as if they were synthetic a priori propositions that guide research while also providing part of the content of our concepts. Sellars describes these propositions as true *ex vi terminorum* but not analytic. They provide GAs as long as they are in force, but are subject to change as our cognitive situation changes.

This theme is also central to Putnam's (1962) paper on the analytic/synthetic distinction. Approaching the question in terms of Quine's attack, Putnam argues that there is a genuine distinction between analytic and synthetic propositions, although it does not have the importance attributed to it by analytic philosophers. More importantly, the empiricist version of the distinction—which admits only analytic a priori and synthetic a posteriori propositions—fails because it is not exhaustive. To understand the nature of scientific knowledge, Putnam argues, we need to recognize a *third class of propositions* that does not fit the standard empiricist dichotomy. Members of this class are not known a priori; they are adopted on empirical grounds although they are protected from refutation for substantial periods of time. Still, they can be overthrown as part of the process of accommodating empirical evidence. Putnam also holds that these propositions have a special tie to the central concepts of a scientific discipline, and that their overthrow involves changes in the discipline's conceptual framework.

Provision of GAs is also a central function of Kuhn's paradigms (1962; for discussion of this theme see Brown 1975; Hoyningen-Huene 1993). These propositions (along with skills embodied in individual scientists) constitute "normal science" which Kuhn describes as "research firmly based upon one or more past scientific achievements, achievements that some particular scientific community acknowledges for a time as supplying the foundation for its further practice" (1962, 10).[16] Once again these propositions are closely connected to the conceptual structure of a field.

---

[15] The analytic/synthetic distinction becomes important when we consider the justification of a generalization. Sellars also considers probabilistic generalizations but I will not pursue this issue.

[16] I am focusing here on just one aspect of these prior achievements. For Kuhn these achievements provide models that can be adapted to solving new problems, and that are used for training new generations of researchers. The propositions I am concerned with are, Kuhn holds, derivative from these models.

Recall that for Kuhn fundamental scientific concepts are constituted independently of experience. According to the prevailing view in 1962, the concepts of a scientific theory divide into observation concepts—that get their content directly from experience—and theoretical concepts. The content of theoretical concepts is partly constituted by implicit definitions provided by the theory's axioms, but these concepts lack cognitive content unless they are associated with observation concepts—although the association can be quite indirect. Kuhn, however, held that fundamental concepts are completely defined by relations to other concepts and—rather than deriving meaning from their association with observation—provide meaning to our experience. The propositions linking these concepts serve as GAs (although to my knowledge Kuhn never put the point this way).

All these developments underline the recognized need for something in addition to empirical evidence and logic in order to make sense of how science works without admitting any propositions into science that are not subject to challenge as our expanding probes of nature turn up new phenomena. GAs serve this purpose. As long as a GA is in force it takes on a methodological role so that without appropriate historical perspective we can easily mistake it for an a priori truth. The key question then becomes how GAs are justified. It is clear that this requires an account of justification that goes beyond just evidence and formal relations. I will not pursue this question here.

The upshot of this discussion is a picture of science that recognizes that research—which is what living science is all about—requires fixed points that focus inquiry by reducing the number of options that are left after we take logic and empirical evidence into account, and by indicating fruitful lines for research. While some might think it desirable that we establish such fixed points once and for all, reflection on both the history of science and our own cognitive capabilities show pretty clearly that we are not in a position to do this—we just do not know enough about the universe. As was suggested above, we have every reason for expecting that science will continue to develop new ways of probing nature, that these probes will yield phenomena that challenge established GAs, and that the adoption of new GAs will go hand-in-hand with the adoption of new concepts. [17]

---

[17] I want to thank Dr. Herman Stark for comments on an earlier version and for help with an article written in German.

REFERENCES

Banton, M. 1998. *Racial Theories*. 2nd ed. Cambridge: Cambridge University Press.
Brown, H. 1975. Paradigmatic Propositions. *American Philosophical Quarterly* 12: 85–90.
———. 1986. Sellars, Concepts and Conceptual Change. *Synthese* 68: 275–307.
———. 1995. Empirical Testing. *Inquiry* 38: 353–99.
———. 2005. On the Epistemology of Theory-Dependent Evidence. In *Cognitive Penetrability of Perception*, ed. A. Raftopoulos, 73–95. Hauppaugae, NY: Nova Science Publishers.
———. 2007. *Conceptual Systems*. London: Routledge.
Bruzzaniti, G., and N. Robotti. 1989. The Affirmation of the Concept of Isotopy and the Birth of Mass Spectrography. *Archives Internationales D'Histoire des Sciences* 39: 309–34.
Chisholm, R. 1966. *Theory of Knowledge*. 2nd ed. Englewood Cliffs, NJ: Prentice-Hall.
Descartes, R. 1991. *Principles of Philosophy*. Trans. V. Miller and R. Miller. Dordrecht: Kluwer.
Fajans, K. [1913] 1970. The Placing of the Radioelements in the Periodic System. In *Radiochemistry and the Discovery of Isotopes*, ed. A. Romer, 205–19 New York: Dover.
Friedman, M. 1999. Geometry, Convention, and the Relativized A Priori: Reichenbach, Schlick, and Carnap. In *Reconsidering Logical Positivism*, 59–70. Cambridge: Cambridge University Press.
———. 2002. Kant, Kuhn, and the Rationality of Science. *Philosophy of Science* 69: 171–90.
Galison, P. 1997. *Image and Logic*. Chicago: University of Chicago Press.
Garber, D. 1992. *Descartes' Metaphysical Physics*. Chicago: University of Chicago Press.
Gould, S. 1997. Why the Death of .400 Hitting Records Improvement of Play. In *Full House*, 111–28. New York: Three Rivers Press.
Greenwood, J. 1990. Two Dogmas of Neo-Empiricism: The "Theory-Informity" of Observation and the Quine-Duhem Thesis. *Philosophy of Science* 57: 553–74.
Guiot, J. 1985. *Zur Entdeckung Der Ultravioletten Strahlen Durch Johann Wilhelm Ritter*. Archives Internationale d'Historie des Sciences 35: 346–56.
Hacking, I. 1983. *Representing and Intervening*. Cambridge: Cambridge niversity Press.
Herschel, W. 1800. Experiments on the Refrangibility of the Invisible Rays of the Sun. *Philosophical Transactions of the Royal Society of London*: 284–92.
Hersh, R. 1997. *What Is Mathematics, Really?* New York: Oxford University Press.
Hoyningen-Huene, P. 1993. *Reconstructing Scientific Revolutions*. Trans. A. Levine. Chicago: Chicago University Press.
Hume, D. 1975. *Enquiries Concerning Human Understanding and Concerning the Principles of Morals*. 3rd ed. Ed. L. A. Selby-Bigge; revised by P. H. Nidditch: Oxford: Clarendon Press.
Kant, I. 1963. *Critique of Pure Reason*. Trans. N. Smith. London: Macmillan.

Kitcher, P. 2000. A Priori Knowledge Revisited. In *New Essays on the A Priori*, P. Boghossian and C. Peacocke, 65–91. Oxford: Clarendon Press.

Kuhn, T. 1962. *The Structure of Scientific Revolutions.* Chicago: University of Chicago Press.

Laudan, L., et al. 1986. Scientific Change: Philosophical Models and Historical Research. *Synthese* 69: 141–223.

Peacocke, C. 1992. *A Study of Concepts.* Cambridge, MA: MIT Press.

———. 2000. Explaining the A Priori: The Programme of Moderate Rationalism. In *New Essays on the A Priori*, ed. P. Boghossian and C. Peacocke, 229–85. Oxford: Clarendon Press.

Putnam, H. 1962. The Analytic and the Synthetic. In *Minnesota Studies in the Philosophy of Science* III, ed. H. Feigl and G. Maxwell, 358–97. Minneapolis: University of Minnesota Press.

Quine, W. 1961. Two Dogmas of Empiricism. In *From a Logical Point of View*, 20–46. New York: Harper Torchbooks.

Ritvo, H. 1997. *The Platypus and the Mermaid and other Figments of the Classifying Imagination.* Cambridge, MA: Harvard University Press.

Sellars, W. 1953. Inference and Meaning. *Mind* 62: 313–38.

———. 1963. Is There a Synthetic *A Priori*? In *Science, Perception and Reality*, 298–320. New York: Humanities Press.

———. 1965. Scientific Realism or Irenic Instrumentalism. In *Boston Studies in the Philosophy of Science* 2, ed. R. Cohen and M. Wartofsky, 171–204. Dordrecht: Reidel.

———. 1973. Conceptual Change. In *Conceptual Change*, ed. G. Pearce and M. Maynard, 77–93. Dordrecht: Reidel.

Soddy, F. [1913] 1970. The Radio-Elements and the Periodic Law. In *Radiochemistry and the Discovery of Isotopes*, ed. A. Romer, 219–28. New York: Dover.

———. 1932. *The Interpretation of the Atom.* London: John Murray.

Tymoczko, T. 1998. Computers and Mathematical Practice: A Case Study. In *New Directions in the Philosophy of Mathematics*, ed. T. Tymoczko, 242–45. Princeton: Princeton University Press.

van Fraassen, B. 1975. Theories and Counterfactuals. In *Action, Knowledge, and Reality*, ed. H. Casta?eda, 237–63. Indianapolis: Bobbs-Merrill.

Wetzels, W. 1990. Johann Wihlelm Ritter: Romantic Physics in Germany. In *Romanticism and the Sciences*, ed. A. Cunningham and N. Jardine, 199–212. Cambridge: Cambridge University Press.

[8]

A Dilemma for Naturalized Epistemology?

SHANE OAKLEY

We are like sailors who must rebuild their ship on the open sea, never able to dismantle it in dry-dock and to reconstruct it there out of the best materials.

—OTTO NEURATH, "Protocol Sentences"

1. Introduction

Neurath's statement in the epigraph has come to be something of a mantra for epistemologists of a naturalistic stripe, particularly as it is a metaphor that is meant to capture the actual epistemic state of humans. It is an expression of the limits of human knowledge, of the very prospects of epistemology. On the face of it, Neurath is denying the very possibility of a foundationalist epistemology by claiming that there are no grounds outside of our current system of beliefs that are capable of validating those beliefs that we possess. However, such a claim hardly entails a naturalized epistemology. More is needed to show that this is the case, and indeed more can be said in support of this view. For in the open sea of beliefs, there are those beliefs that include our current scientific beliefs and beliefs about the methods employed in science. Perhaps more importantly, as Neurath and Quine accept, science constitutes our paradigmatic example of epistemic success. Science, in the application of its methods, appears to have made significant epistemic progress, if any real epistemic progress has been made by any discipline. Given that there is no privileged epistemic framework outside of our current set of beliefs, no Archimedean point from which to make judgment, it seems that the only hope to develop an adequate epistemology is by taking the current methods of science to both constitute our epistemic norms and to be the source of future norms.[1] The underlying theme of naturalism is, of

---

[1] I am not here claiming that this is the view of any particular naturalized epistemologists,

course, that the empiricist methods of science are those that *should* be utilized in the project of epistemology and concomitantly that there are no extrascientific reasons that one can appeal to in order to validate their use.[2] In other words, there are no grounds outside of science, a priori or otherwise, that can serve to determine the epistemic viability of the methods of science. To put it yet another way, there is no first philosophy according to the naturalists.

The merits of the naturalized view of epistemology have been challenged on many fronts and for many different reasons. Here, I will be concerned with certain arguments against naturalized epistemology articulated by Harvey Siegel (1980, 1984) and Robert Almeder (1998). These arguments go right to the heart of the matter by questioning the feasibility of the entire program itself. They conclude that either naturalism is false because it is self-defeating or that naturalism is vacuous because it is circular. In order to respond to these critical arguments, I will here investigate in detail this apparently damning dilemma for naturalism.[3] Of course the conclusions of both horns of this dilemma do not bode well for naturalized epistemology, and so it is certainly a worthwhile project to see if the naturalist has resources sufficient to avoid it. My approach to this problem will be to argue that the dilemma presented by Siegel and Almeder does not pose a special problem for naturalism, because the presuppositions that are required for the argument to go through are just the presuppositions behind the adequacy of *any* epistemological theory, naturalistic or otherwise. To show this I develop an analogous argument against a priori justification that has the same general structure as the argument leveled against naturalism. Given such an argument we can see that it is dialectically ille-

---

nor am I claiming that it is the accepted view. In Quine's seminal 1969 essay, he seems to take the view that the job of epistemology is explanatory, i.e. that epistemology is in the business of explaining how we can come to have this torrential output of theoretical scientific beliefs given such a meager input of retinal irritations. My concern in this essay will not be with any particular version of naturalism in epistemology *per se*, but rather with the possibility of justifying extreme naturalism, i.e. with what Kornblith (1994) has dubbed the "replacement thesis." I do present a sketch of a particular version of naturalism that is appealing to me in particular, but nothing said in this essay will necessarily rest on this.

[2] We may include here the requisite mathematical and logical theories that facilitate those methods and their success. One might, however, immediately claim that the question has already been begged by the naturalist, as logic and mathematics are a priori disciplines. Hence, insofar as one of the tenets of naturalism is the denial of the a priori, the naturalists must explain these disciplines naturalistically, otherwise there is no epistemic justification for mathematical truths. I will remain silent on this issue, although I think that it is legitimately in the purview of a naturalized epistemology to make use of mathematics and logic.

[3] From this point on when I use the term "naturalism" I will have in mind only naturalism in epistemology as opposed to naturalism in other areas of philosophy.

gitimate to utilize such an argument to eliminate one theoretical standpoint in favor of another.

The reason that the problem presented by Siegel and Almeder is so interesting and in need of attention by naturalized epistemologists rests on a general failure on the part of many naturalists to appreciate the need to legitimize their position. In this respect, the dilemma that will be discussed here is akin to a skeptical challenge against a thesis. In the face of general epistemological skepticism it seems that most naturalists have simply waved their hands when confronted with the issue of justifying naturalism, and this seems to be intellectually unsatisfactory.[4] So it is especially important to see what sort of response a naturalist might give to the challenge.

2. What is Naturalism?[5]

One interesting observation that can be made with respect to the philosophical literature on Naturalism is that this position is often either inadequately defined or simply not defined at all.[6] Also, some authors have offered such trivial accounts of naturalism that the justification of our beliefs includes rational insight or a priori judgment.[7] Other authors seem to understand naturalism in a much more austere way taking it to be the thesis that what only counts as evidence is evidence of the sort character-

---

[4] I am not sure that this is really a fair statement as it appears that many naturalists do not necessarily neglect skeptical challenges to their view in so much as they concede something to the skeptic. In fact, I think that a concession of some sort to the skeptic puts the naturalists in a much better dialectical position than those who criticize the view, but that is an issue for another paper.

[5] I should note here that I will be speaking of naturalism as a thesis about the nature of evidence and justification quite broadly. The thesis will be discussed in terms of those concepts being derived from that which is sanctioned by science, where science is very broadly understood to be the practice that we actually engage in when formulating our beliefs. Some understand the thesis to be the thesis that epistemology should be subsumed under or at least heavily integrated with the psychological study of our actual belief forming processes. With respect to this latter claim I take it to be subsumed under the naturalistic thesis as I have so construed it. Nothing should be lost with respect to the argument by taking the thesis of psychologism as such. For a good discussion of the latter conception of naturalism see Kornblith 1994.

[6] Some do not feel the need to define the thesis as such as they take it to be a stance, akin to van Fraassen's (2002) empirical stance, or research program rather than a thesis that can be asserted as a proposition. Thanks to Risto Hilpinen (personal communication) for discussion of this idea with me.

[7] Though she might not claim this, I take the view reached by Haack (1993) to defend a thesis of this sort.

[8] Perhaps the classic statement of such an austere view is Quine's 1969. Of course, one might claim that the latter's view is simply a descriptive thesis and that my statement of it

istic of the empirical methods of the sciences.[8] Between the two extremes there seem to be a variety of theses that form a continuum.[9] In order to facilitate discussion of the variants of naturalism in the context of the argument against naturalism, it will prove fruitful to first give a schematic definition of naturalism that is broad enough to incorporate all of the naturalistic theses, from the most trivial to the most extreme. In so doing we will be able to construct the alleged dilemma against "naturalism" in a more precise and comprehensive form.

Upon examination of both the extreme and trivial versions of naturalism we find that the key idea they share is that principles of evidence and epistemic justification should be seen to be the principles that are employed in or are discoverable by the methods of science. Hence, what one takes science to consist in will determine the form of the naturalized epistemology that one adopts. In order to capture the theses that constitute the total set of "naturalized" epistemologies let us first consider a set of propositions E having as members those propositions e that serve as evidence and hence justify one's beliefs. Assuming that it is possible for our beliefs to be justified and that the evidence for our beliefs is propositional evidence[10] we can presently understand the set E as a nonempty set with an undefined extension. The elements of E will be determined in accordance with the correct epistemological theory and will be those propositions that are implied by that theory to be evidential. Understanding E in this way we are now in a better position to understand why the trivial and extreme versions of naturalism are in fact trivial and extreme. According to the trivial version of naturalism the scope of E (were the trivial thesis true) would be quite large, as the set would consist of empirical propositions as

---

incorporates a normative element. In any case, I would still claim that Quine's 1969 view of the elimination of traditional epistemology for psychology still involves a normative element; viz. only empirical evidence can determine the best description of the development of science from such a meager input in the world.

[9] E.g. reliabilism as developed by Goldman (see his 1967 and 1979), just to take a couple of examples. One might also consider the view of Laudan (1996) as an in-between view as well. For other ways to carve the joints of what is to count as naturalism see the introduction to Kornblith 1994 as well as Kitcher 1992 and Rosenberg 1996.

[10] We could develop the notion of that which justifies a belief nonpropositionally if we pleased, which is what I would be inclined to do in the end. However, utilizing the idea of a proposition and the concept of propositional justification will allow for a much less cumbersome presentation. I should note that my use of the notion of propositional justification is a bit idiosyncratic as what I mean for a proposition to justify a belief is for that proposition to express that something was observed, or something was intuited, or whatever the theory of justification says evidence for beliefs should be. Evidence in and of itself need not be propositional. If I believe p I will site as my justification for that belief some proposition q that expresses what is the evidence for the belief in question. The proposition serves as my reason for the belief as that evidence is provided to a third party.

well as a priori propositions.[11] On the other hand, the extreme version of naturalism, were it true, would determine a set E with a very narrow scope and it would consist mainly of empirical propositions, although it would not necessarily include all empirical propositions. The triviality of the former view and the narrowness of the latter view will be even more apparent once we have developed the schematic version of naturalism.

Again, broadly speaking, naturalism in epistemology is the claim that the present principles of evidence and justification employed in the sciences, including those that will be discovered in accordance with presently employed principles, exhausts the set of epistemic principles. There are simply no more to be had. Given those principles of evidence and justification we can determine the set of evidential propositions that follow from them, i.e. the set of propositions that provide probative support for our beliefs. Let the set S consist of those propositions e that are deemed to be justificatory in terms of both the presently employed and discoverable principles of evidence and justification employed in the sciences. So it should be very clear that how broadly or narrowly one understands science will determine the elements of S. Assuming that a tenet of naturalism is that the principles of evidence and justification are those that are presently employed in science and the evidential propositions that follow from them determine the set S, we can see that the naturalists claim that the naturalistic thesis N entails the following general statement:

(1) $(\forall e)(e \in S \rightarrow e \in E^*)$.

Here E^* is thought to be co-extensive with E. Note that (1) is a trivial entailment from any N. Furthermore, the naturalist is committed to the claim that all and only those propositions that are evidence for beliefs follow from the present and future principles of evidence and justification employed in the sciences. Hence, N entails:

(2) $(\forall e)(e \in E^* \rightarrow e \in S)$.

In this expression E^* is to be regarded as co-extensive with E. Thus, from (1) and (2) we get the bi-conditional definition schema for N:

(3) $(\forall e)(e \in E^* \leftrightarrow e \in S)$

---

[11] Again here, I will understand an empirical proposition as one that expresses that something was observed or otherwise obtained empirically and by an a priori proposition I will understand a proposition expressing an a priori reason or that one had a rational insight, etc. I do not think that this affects the argument presented here.

Here we can see that (3), as a definition scheme, is rather trivial. However, the triviality of (3) is a virtue rather than a vice because it allows for a continuum of naturalistic theses to be defined dependent on how liberally or austerely each version of naturalism determines the extension of S. Although the definitions of the various theses might be rather thin, each thesis would nevertheless be uniquely identifiable. Given that the theses that are instances of (3) are provided by specifying identity conditions we can begin to construct a more refined set of definitions of "naturalism," thus allowing for more precise articulations of particular naturalized epistemologies.[12] Of course, here (3) will remain in schematic form, as I have no intentions to defend any particular version of naturalism.

One thing to note about (3) is that using the general scheme one can schematically define a general continuum of epistemic theories. Again, this point makes (3) smack of triviality, but, as I will try to show below, this is a virtue not a vice of (3) itself. Essentially this will allow us to underwrite the claim that the dilemma presented against naturalism is not a particular problem for naturalism, because it is a problem for any epistemological theory. In the next section I will give a nonformal exposition of the alleged dilemma for naturalism. Using (3), I will then prove that one of the premises of the dilemma is true and show that one of the premises is not obviously true. In doing this I will formalize the tacit presuppositions that the proponents of the dilemma must accept in order to defend the premises of the argument. In any case, the response to the dilemma presented here is not meant to be a final refutation of the claim that this dilemma poses serious problems for naturalism, but it will at least undermine the initial prima facie force that the argument has.

3. An Informal Statement of the Dilemma

The dilemma to which I have been referring arises for the naturalistic thesis in the event that someone challenges the thesis of naturalism. Hence, suppose that Jones confronts Quine and asks Quine why he, Jones, should accept a naturalized epistemology as the correct theory of knowledge and rationality. Should Quine respond that he is justified in accepting his naturalized epistemology on the basis of the Quine/Duhem thesis and his rejection of the analytic synthetic distinction, then it seems that Quine has presupposed that which he intends to deny by adopting an austere naturalized epistemology in the first place, viz. the utilization of reasons that are not sanctioned by or discoverable through the methods

---

[12] Again, this is assuming that a naturalized epistemology is a thesis that can be stated and is either true or false rather than a stance.

of the empirical sciences. For we are free to ask, as Siegel (1984) so poignantly does, "is it the case that the Quine/Duhem thesis is justified by an appeal to empirical data or by reference to a scientific theory?"[13] Moreover, is the rejection of the analytic/synthetic distinction based on empirical data or scientific theory? The answer to both of these questions seems to be no. Both the Quine/Duhem thesis and the rejection of the analytic/synthetic distinction appear to be philosophical theses that were reached through philosophical argument and not through principles of justification sanctioned by or discoverable through the methods of empirical science.[14] Hence, the Quine/Duhem thesis and the rejection of the analytic/synthetic distinction cannot be used in support of Quinean "extreme" naturalism on pain of self-defeat. More generally, any independent reason that goes beyond those propositions that are declared to be evidence in terms of the naturalistic thesis will not serve to justify the thesis without also falsifying it. The only other response to Jones's request for a reason to accept Quinean naturalism that is then open for Quine is to offer some empirical, or otherwise scientifically sanctioned, proposition from within the theory itself. On the face of it, however, such a move seems to be viciously circular. It would, so the critic claims, be an illegitimate dialectical move on Quine's behalf to offer up such a proposition in defense of his own theory.[15],[16]

In a more schematic form then, the dilemma that is leveled by Siegel and Almeder is established as follows:

---

[13] See Siegel 1984 (667) for this criticism.

[14] One might argue quite convincingly that Quine did reject the analytic/synthetic distinction at least in part on empirical grounds, as one reading of his argument is that Quine was concerned that there were no behavioral criteria that led to a meaningful cleavage between the analytic and the synthetic. The distinction, that is, has no empirical content and is hence a dogma. For a good discussion of this interpretation of Quine's (1951) attack on the analytic/synthetic distinction see Creath 2004. Putnam's 1976 revisiting of Quine's "Two Dogma's" also suggest that there may well be empirical reasons based on an historical induction to reject the distinction, which Putnam takes to really be a rejection of the *a priori/a posteriori* distinction as opposed to a rejection of the analytic/synthetic distinction.

[15] One might understand Bealer's (1992) so-called "starting-points" argument as an argument in defense of this very sort of criticism, at least as it applies to Quine's variant of coherentism. However, for a good critique of that argument see Shaffer and Warnick 2004.

[16] For this sort of criticism see Siegel 1980 also, where he criticizes Quine's view in a similar, although not necessarily identical, way. The argument is that empirical psychology itself may be able to explain why a particular theory was chosen, but it fails to explain why that choice was good or bad. It fails to account for the epistemic status of the choice of theory, which is the task of epistemology. Generalizing that result, if we used empirical psychology to explain how naturalism is reached, we have provided no reason for accepting the thesis on that basis unless we beg the question and presuppose that that thesis is in some way epistemically privileged to begin with, which is exactly what the conclusion was supposed to establish.

If there is an independent justification of naturalism, then it cannot be justification in the terms of the naturalistic thesis, i.e. naturalism is false.

If there is no independent justification for naturalism, then any defense of the thesis is viciously circular.

<u>Either there is an independent justification for naturalism or there is not.</u>

Therefore, either naturalism is false or any defense of naturalism is viciously circular.

The arguments that support premises 1 and 2 are obviously central to determining whether or not the argument is sound. Assuming that one of those arguments fails, we then would have no reason to suspect that the dilemma presents a serious problem for naturalism. I will reconstruct a formal argument for premise 1 that shows the premise to be necessarily true given the definitional scheme of naturalism offered above. The focus of the attack on the purported dilemma will then be on premise 2. A formal examination of the tacit presuppositions that one must hold in order to maintain that the consequent of premise 2 follows from the antecedent will be made, and, given a variant of the definitional scheme offered above, it will be shown that it is in fact possible for there to be a justification of naturalism in terms of the naturalistic thesis itself. Hence, the reasoning of the original dilemma cannot be sustained in the form in which it has been presented. However, what ultimately justifies the naturalistic thesis will not be a concern in the present work. Rather, the aims here are simply to show that naturalists ought not to give up the search for acceptable justifications of their versions of naturalism and that the dilemma stated above is not a special problem for naturalism.

4. A Formal Defense of the Self-Defeating Claim against Naturalism

The basic argument for premise one of the dilemma is elegantly stated by Siegel (1984, 675) to be a deep problem for naturalized epistemology. This is because, in attempting to justify their own thesis, naturalists, "must assume the legitimacy of, and strive to achieve, the very sort of justification [they] seek to show cannot be had."[17] Hence, we seemingly must con-

---

[17] In fairness to Siegel, his 1984 discussion is limited to Quine's naturalized epistemology and Roth's (1983) defense thereof. Hence, the charitable reading of that paper should have it such that his conclusion does not extend to all naturalized epistemologist, but rather

clude that naturalism is in some way self-defeating, i.e. any justification that can be sited for the naturalistic thesis will need to be justified and that such a justification can only come by way of extrascientific reasons. In terms of the definitional scheme provided above we can thus provide a straightforward *reductio ad absurdum* against the possibility that there is such an extrascientific reason, i.e. an independent reason, in support of any naturalistic thesis N. Recall that the set S is the set of propositions that are the evidential propositions capable of justifying the things that we believe that are entailed by a given N. Again, the elements of S will be determined according to the way a particular thesis N specifies what science is like. Hence, for the set Ψ of every set S_i of evidential propositions there will be a one-to-one mapping of the elements from the set Φ of all naturalistic theses N_j to the elements of the set Ψ. Given this one-to-one mapping from Φ to Ψ we can prove by reductio that premise one is true for arbitrary N, S, and E* in terms of the definition scheme (3) above, and is thus true with respect to any naturalistic thesis.

In order to show this we must suppose that there is some proposition e that serves to justify some naturalistic thesis N, that e is an element of the set E* of evidential propositions, and that e is not an element of S. Under such a supposition we then have an independent proposition that is said to serve as a justification of some arbitrary naturalistic thesis N. Formally this would be represented as follows:

(4) $(\exists e)(eJN \ \& \ e \in E^* \ \& \ e \notin S)$.

Here 'xJy' is the two-place relation of justification and N is some arbitrary naturalistic thesis. Recall the definition scheme given above:

(3) $(\forall e)(e \in E^* \leftrightarrow e \in S)$.

Here the domain of quantification is the set of all propositions. From (3) and the supposition of (4) one can easily deduce a straightforward contradiction.[18] Hence, it follows that:

(5) $\{(3) \ \&(4)\} \Rightarrow \bot$.

---

to that (perhaps) large number whom, like Quine and Roth, see the Quine-Duhem thesis and the alleged collapse of the analytic-synthetic distinction to entail Quinean naturalized epistemology. Siegel has, perhaps, shown that such versions of naturalized epistemology are in some important sense self-defeating, but I think it is an overstatement of the conclusion to extend it to "all naturalized epistemologies." However, Almeder (1998) has extended the conclusion as such and added his own bells and whistles to the argument, so I find it necessary to write Siegel's quote here in its very bald form.

[18] For the sake of specificity I have given the proof as Appendix 1.

In other words, there is no model in which both (3) and (4) can be jointly true. Given also that (3) and (4) are mutually exclusive we can conclude that premise 1 of the purported dilemma for naturalism is necessarily true. There can be no independent justification of any thesis N such that the thesis comes out to be true. To put it another way, if there is an independent justification for some thesis N then that thesis is necessarily false.

That premise one of the argument above comes out true in accordance with our definitional scheme (3) seems to provide some support for considering (3) to be a comprehensive definition of the set of versions of naturalism with respect to the dialectical situation we have been considering. The proponents of antinaturalism appear to accept that a general criterion that any epistemological theory must meet is that it cannot be justified by propositions or reasons that are not sanctioned as probative by the theory itself. As any epistemological theory that can be defined in terms of (3) meets this requirement, using (3) to combat the argument does not involve one in begging the question against the proponents of the dilemma. Moreover, as mentioned before, (3) must be formally correct in some way because in order to be non-self-defeating any epistemological theory must also conform to a formal scheme such as (3). This should come as no surprise because (3) is neither substantive nor controversial. Working within the constraints accepted by the proponents of the dilemma we must conclude then that not only is there no naturalistic thesis N such that N has an independent justification, but also that there is no epistemological theory of justification C such that C is true and such that there is an independent reason in favor of C. By extension then we see that premise 1 in the dilemma is true for any epistemological theory and so it cannot be a premise that is specifically a problem for naturalism.

From these reflections on (3) and its relation to premise 1 of the dilemma we can see that insofar as we accept as a criterion of adequacy for an epistemological theory that it not have a justification that is not sanctioned by the theory itself we can begin to appreciate the fact that premise 2 of the Siegel/Almeder dilemma is doing all of the real work. In particular, given the generality of premise 1, viz. that it is true for any epistemological theory, it is apparent that the Siegel/Almeder dilemma poses no special problem for naturalism unless premise 2 is true given the naturalistic thesis. Interestingly there is no straightforward way to prove premise 2. In fact, once the underlying presuppositions that motivate the introduction of premise 2 into the argument against naturalism are uncovered we have a straightforward proof of the possibility of a self-justifying naturalistic thesis.

5. The Possibility of a Self-Justifying Naturalized Epistemology

Suppose that we accept as a negative criterion of adequacy for any epistemological theory of justification C that C cannot have as its metajustification a proposition or set of propositions that are not entailed to be evidential by the theory itself. We have then committed ourselves at that point to a further positive criterion of adequacy if we accept the claim that it is possible for some theory to have a metajustification at all. The positive criterion of adequacy that follows from our acceptance of the negative criterion states that an epistemological theory is justified just in case it is self-justifying. Hence, for any epistemological theory C and any evidential proposition e, e justifies C just in case e is an element of the set of propositions that are entailed to be evidential propositions by C. For clarity's sake, let us put this criterion of adequacy in symbolic form. This will make it easy to see if we can make use of it in justifying premise 2 of the argument:

(CA) $(\forall X)(\forall e)\,(eJX \leftrightarrow e \in E^*)$.

Here the extension of E is determined by an instance of C. Now, (CA) appears to be a condition of adequacy both on any actual and any possible C, at least insofar as we accept *tout court* the negative criterion of adequacy discussed above. Hence, it must be taken to be necessary if it is applicable and should be understood as follows:

(CA') $\Box(\forall X)(\forall e)\,(eJX \leftrightarrow e \in E^*)$

Taking (CA') to be the condition of adequacy imposed on epistemological theories, insofar as those theories are justified, we can now clearly see the underlying presuppositions behind the Siegel/Almeder Dilemma against naturalism. Moreover, if the conclusion of that argument is to follow, then what must be shown is that naturalism fails to meet (CA').

So, does naturalism fail to meet (CA')? Is it true that it is not possible for versions of naturalism to include internal mechanisms that allow that epistemological theory to justify itself? As I will show here this is not the case. It is in fact possible for a naturalistic thesis to justify itself. In fact, the proof goes through for arbitrary N, and so even if the extreme replacement version of naturalism is not, more must be said about why that is the case over and above the claim that replacement naturalism is circular. Despite these provisos, merely showing the bare possibility that naturalism is self-justifying is sufficient to cast doubt on the truth of the second premise of the Siegel/Almeder argument. However, before giving the proof of this claim it is first necessary that we uncover a tacit presupposition of the debate to which the proponents of the Siegel/Almeder dilemma are committed. The presupposition is quite simple, viz. if Siegel, Almeder, et al. want to avoid being epistemological skeptics, then they must believe that it is at least possible for there to be some epistemological theory C and some proposition e, such that e justifies C and $e \in E^*$, where E^* is determined by that particular instance of C.[19] Moreover, the range of possible justified epistemological theories must be restricted to those theories that are possible to develop and verify in some way within the constraints of human cognitive limitations. Otherwise, there would be no reason to engage in this debate to begin with because we should simply be conceding that skepticism is true, i.e. *humans* can never be sure that we are ever justified in any of our beliefs.[20] Hence, formally, proponents of the Siegel/Almeder dilemma are committed to the following thesis:

(PE) $\Diamond(\exists C)(\exists e)(eJX \ \& \ e \in E^*)$.

I take it that anyone who does not believe that skepticism about the justification of epistemic theories is true is committed to (PE) and that including the claim (PE) as a premise in an argument is unobjectionable.

Restricting the notion of possibility and necessity to worlds or situations in which humans are cognitively identical, or at least sufficiently similar, with respect to all essential properties of actual humans, we introduce a generalized version of (3) that serves as a definitional scheme for any epistemological theory. Here we are exploiting the broad generality of (3) that was noted above. When we speak of justification, evidence, and belief the general idea is that if a belief is justified it is justified by the subjects pos-

---

[19] It should be noted here that it is possible in terms of (PE) that a theory could be non-viciously circularly justified without being justified *simpliciter*, as in the case where $e \in E^*$ and $e \notin E$. Self-justification is thus a property of a theory rather than a final epistemic arbiter of the *actual* justification of the theory. Epistemologists pushing the Siegel/Almeder type dilemma should take heed to this in order to avoid begging important questions to skeptics.

[20] In formulating a proof for the possibility of a self-justifying naturalism I utilize the apparatus of possible worlds semantics for the sake of ease. The restriction of possibility and necessity with respect to epistemic theories should be understood to be a restriction on the possible worlds that are accessible from the actual world. Only those worlds where beings with relevantly similar cognitive structures to humans should be considered accessible, as other sorts of beings may have radically divergent epistemological features depending on the nature of their cognitive abilities. Some may say that this begs the question against the traditionalists. However, I think this to be a reasonable constraint insofar as the traditionalists is hoping to come up with some sort of necessary criteria of justification that is self-supporting. It begs the question to the skeptic to think that we, humans, would have the epistemological theory that is the best in all possible worlds given that we are cognitively constrained in many ways.

sessing some evidence that supports the believed proposition. One role of a theory of justification then is to codify the types of propositions that are capable of serving as evidence for beliefs. In accord with the role that a theory of justification must play we can then say that any theory of justification, be it naturalistic or rationalistic, determines a unique set of evidential propositions constituted by a subset of the set of all propositions.[21] Moreover, it seems reasonable to suppose that the set of evidential propositions that follows from an epistemic theory are, for the proponents of that theory, the exhaustive set of evidential propositions E. Hence, the following principle appears to be an extension of (3) as it applies to all epistemic theories of justification:

(3') $\Box(\forall Y)(\forall e)(e \in E^* \leftrightarrow e \in Y)$.

In this expression Y is a variable ranging over any set of evidential propositions corresponding to any possible epistemic theory. (3') should, however, be read carefully, especially under the supposition that there is some epistemological theory that is the correct epistemological theory. (3') explicates a commitment to the way in which we would go about providing a definition of an epistemological theory as determining the extension of E, whatever E may actually be. In any case, for any epistemological theory C there is a set U of evidential propositions such that those propositions are claimed to be co-extensive with E. Presumably, this latter claim holds in any of our restricted possible worlds, and hence (3') is an acceptable definitional scheme. Necessarily, the quantified statement in (3') provides a definitional-scheme for any epistemological theory in any possible world.

To get a better handle on the content of (3') consider some set of evidential propositions Q that follow from the epistemic theory T. Proponents of T must then claim that the set Q of evidential propositions is co-extensive with the set E, where E is the actual set of evidential propositions. We can then say that Q determines a set E* such that $(\forall e)(e \in E \rightarrow e \in E^*)$, which may well actually be false. However, the proponents of a theory, insofar as they believe their theory to be correct, are committed to the truth of the co-extensiveness of E* and E. Hence, (3') should not be read as stating that it is necessarily the case that every epistemological theory determines the elements of E because such a claim would be absurd. Assuming that there is one correct epistemological theory, there will then be some Y and some E* such that Y, E*, and E are co-extensive. This is consistent with (3'). So (3') does not appear to be objectionable.

---

[21] The expression "all propositions" here should be understood tenselessly, i.e. as the set of past, present, and future propositions.

At this point, one might wonder what the purpose of all this "logic chopping" is. The reason for formalizing the scheme introduced earlier and for elucidating the underlying presuppositions of the proponents of the Siegel/Almeder dilemma is, as stated earlier, to formally demonstrate that it is possible for some naturalistic thesis N to be self-justifying. For from (CA'), (PE), and (3') it follows that it is possible that there is some propositions e that justifies N where e is an element of S. Symbolically:

(6) $\{(CA'), (PE), (3')\} \Rightarrow \Diamond(\exists e)(e J N \ \& \ e \in S).$[22]

Given (CA'), (PE), and (3') it is possible that naturalism is self-justifying. In fact, accepting (CA'), (PE), and (3') commits one to the possibility that any epistemological theory X could be self-justifying.[23] As a result, we cannot maintain that premise 2 of the Siegel/Almeder dilemma is obviously true. For, as this proof demonstrates, if it is possible for any theory to be self-justifying, then it is possible for even extreme naturalism to be self-justifying. However, if this were to be denied then the proponents of the Siegel/Almeder dilemma are simply skeptics about the justification of epistemic theories.[24] Of course, if one does in fact wish to maintain that circular justification can never really be justification, another strategy (which I am sympathetic to) for attacking the proponents of the Siegel/Almeder dilemma would be to argue that the positive criterion of adequacy discussed above is overly demanding. To demand that a theory of justification must be capable of justifying itself in terms of its own criteria is tantamount to asking for a proof where no proof can be had. So it would be absurd to do this. What we should seek are explanations of why it is reasonable to accept a theory of justification that are internal to the theory itself.[25] Following up on this suggestion would involve accepting the first premise of the dilemma and it would constitute a weakening of the criterion of adequacy that motivates the second premise. However, the project of defending this suggestion will not be pursued here. To conclude I propose a

---

[22] I have offered the proof of this as Appendix 2.

[23] I should note however that this result does not hold for relativism as there is no unique E* that is determined by the thesis. Relativism then does not fit the general schemata (3') and is non-self-justifiable. Thanks to Jeremy Morris for bringing the problem of relativism to my attention in a discussion of this paper.

[24] Interestingly there are several intriguing pieces in the literature that may well serve the naturalists well in the attempt at self-justification. For an interesting Bayesian account of non–vicious circular justification see Shogenji 2000. Hal Brown has also contributed some interesting work to the literature on circular justification and theory-laden justification in Brown 1993 and Brown 1994. For an older piece on the justification of induction inductively see Black 1958. For a reply to Black see Achinstein 1962.

[25] Thanks to Keith Lehrer for discussion of this point. This seems to be part of Lehrer's (1990) project. Also see Lehrer 1999.

dilemma for a priori theories of justification that is analogous to that of Siegel and Almeder. Doing so will complete the project of showing that naturalism is not especially vulnerable to the Siegel/Almeder dilemma.

6. A Dilemma for A Priori Justification

Constructing this dilemma is quite simple. In schematic form it can be stated as follows:

4. If there is an independent justification for rationalism, then rationalism is self-defeating, and hence false.

5. If there is no independent justification for rationalism, then any defense of the thesis will be viciously circular.

6. <u>Either there is an independent justification for rationalism or there is not.</u> Therefore, either rationalism is false or is circular.[26]

Formulating principle (R) as a schematic definition for any rationalistic thesis we get:

(R) $(\forall e)(e \in E^* \leftrightarrow e \in R)$

where R is the set of evidential propositions that follow from any particular rationalistic thesis and E^* is thought to meet the condition $(\forall e)(e \in E \rightarrow e \in E^*)$, where again this may well be false. Assuming R and that $(\exists e)(e J R \;\&\; e \in E^* \;\&\; e \notin R)$ is true, we can prove by *reductio ad absurdum* that premise 4 of this argument is true. Again, by reasoning similar to that used above, we can also show that it is possible that there is a self-justifying rationalistic thesis for arbitrary R, and hence for every R. Therefore, the dialectical situation from the standpoint of this sort of metaepistemological dilemma is the same for both naturalism and rationalism, as well as for any

---

[26] Casullo (2000) constructs a similar, if not identical argument, against the rationalists. He then proceeds to argue that what would be premise 4 of the above argument is false as the rationalists, insofar as they accept two sorts of justification, viz. rational and empirical, can feasibly offer a metajustification for rationalism in terms of empirical evidence. I concede that certain rationalists may well have such a move open to them, but the target that I have in mind here is the theorists that either takes a priori justification to have more weight than empirical justification claiming that an empirical justification of rationalism somehow undermines a priori justification, e.g. BonJour 1998, or the rationalists that claims that a priori justification has the upper hand in matters of metajustification. With respect to the latter two sorts of theorists, the argument seems to be sound as premise one seems not to be deniable.

other epistemic theory for that matter. We cannot, therefore, legitimately use an argument of this form to favor one epistemic theory over another.

Reflecting on these results, I cannot claim to know how one might go about justifying naturalism in terms of itself. Moreover, I cannot claim to know how one could go about justifying rationalism or a priorism in terms of itself. One might claim that those propositions that are a priori justified are so justified because they are self-evident. But the proposition that self-evident propositions are a priori justified is not itself self-evident.[27] Hence, it appears that the rationalist and the more empirically inclined naturalists are in the same dialectical position with respect to the dilemma. Therefore the Siegel/Almeder dilemma is not a special problem for naturalists. Moreover, as I have shown, the dilemma is really ill formed as it stands, because the truth of the second premise of that dilemma is questionable. Also, one may simply deny the appropriateness of such a strong positive criterion of adequacy like that discussed above. However, if one were to reject that criterion, then it seems to be the case that the proponents of naturalism in fact have a dialectical advantage over antinaturalists. This is because science seems, through empirical inquiry and explanatory methods, to be able to explain why naturalism should be accepted. The success of science itself seems to offer the starting point for such an explanation. This response is not, of course, decisive, but rationalism, at least in this respect, seems incapable of explaining why it is acceptable without begging the question. That is a topic for another essay. However, at very least we should now have a clearer grasp of the dialectical situation involved in the metaepistemological debate between naturalists and rationalists, or at least insofar as the Siegel/Almeder dilemma is concerned.[28]

---

[27] See BonJour 1998 (142–46) where he repudiates the request for any sort of metajustification for rationalism. He proceeds to go back to the self-evidence criterion in order to support his repudiation. However, I think that he still falls prey to the objection here raised. We can still ask why the self-evidence of a proposition is conducive to its being the object of a justified belief. Other theories of a priori justification do not seem to have the available machinery to be self-justifying either. For example Bealer's account of the a priori probativity of intuition does not seem to be intuitively obvious. See, for example, Bealer 1992 and Bealer 1999.

[28] I would like to thank Risto Hilpinen, A.J. Kreider, Keith Lehrer, Peter Lewis, Jeremy Morris, and Mike Shaffer for very helpful and interesting conversations relating to the material in this paper. I would especially like to thank Harvey Siegel for discussion and in particular for motivating me to engage with his argument.

Appendix 1

Here is the reductio proof of premise 1 of the dilemma for arbitrary N.

1.	$(\forall e)\ (e \in E^* \leftrightarrow e \in S)$	Definition Schema (3).
2.	$(\exists e)\ (eJN\ \&\ e \in E^*\ \&\ e \notin S)$	Supposition for *Reductio*.
3.	$aJN\ \&\ e \in E^*\ \&\ a \notin S$	EI 2 a/e flag a.
4.	$a \in E^*$	&-E 3.
5.	$a \notin S$	&-E 3
6.	$a \in E^* \leftrightarrow a \in S$	$\forall$I 1 a/e.
7.	$a \in E^* \rightarrow a \in S$	$\leftrightarrow$-E 6.
8.	$a \in S$	$\rightarrow$-E 7,4.
9.	$a \in S\ \&\ a \notin S$	&-I 5,8.
10.	$\neg(\exists e)(eJN\ \&\ e \in E^*\ \&\ e \notin S)$	*Reductio* 2–9.

By simple classical manipulation we can see clearly that there can be no independent justification for any naturalistic thesis N if that thesis is in fact true; for as the proof demonstrates if for some N there is an independent justification then it is true that it is not the case that N is true. As noted above, however, we could substitute any epistemological theory in for N in the above proof and get the same result. Again, there seems to be an underlying criterion of adequacy for any epistemological theory that underwrites premise 1.

Appendix 2

Proof of the possibility of a self-justifying naturalized epistemology from (3'), (CA') and (PE) in terms of possible worlds semantics.

Let R be the accessibility relation between possible worlds and let @ be the actual world.

1.	$\Box\ (\forall Y)(\forall e)\ (e \in E^* \leftrightarrow e \in Y),\ @$	(3')
2.	$\Box\ (\forall X)(\forall e)(eJX \leftrightarrow e \in E^*),\ @$	(CA')
3.	$\Diamond(\exists X)(\exists e)(eJX\ \&\ e \in E^*),\ @$	(PE) $/\therefore \Diamond\exists(e)(eJN\ \&\ e \in S)$
4.	$(\exists X)(\exists e)(eJX\ \&\ e \in E^*),\ 1$	$\Diamond$-E R@1, 3.
5.	$(\forall Y)(\forall e)(e \in E^* \leftrightarrow e \in Y),\ 1$	$\Box$-E R@1, 1.
6.	$(\forall X)(\forall e)(eJX \leftrightarrow e \in E^*),\ 1$	$\Box$-E R@1, 2.
7.	$aJA\ \&\ a \in E^*,\ 1$	$\exists$I, 4 a/e, A/C.
8.	$a \in E^* \leftrightarrow a \in S,\ 1$	$\forall$I, 5 a/e, S/U.
9.	$aJA \leftrightarrow a \in E^*,\ 1$	$\forall$I, 6 a/e, A/C.
10.	$aJN \leftrightarrow a \in E^*,\ 1$	$\forall$I, 6 a/e, N/C.
11.	$a \in E^* \rightarrow a \in S,\ 1$	$\leftrightarrow$-E, 8.
12.	$aJA \rightarrow a \in E^*,\ 1$	$\leftrightarrow$-E, 9.

13. aJA	&-E, 7.
14. $a{\in}E^*, 1$	→-E, 12, 13.
15. $a{\in}S, 1$	→-E, 11,14.
16. $a{\in}E^* \to aJN, 1$	↔ E, 10.
17. $aJN, 1$	→-E, 13, 15.
18. $aJN \& a{\in}S, 1$	&-I, 15, 17.
19. $(\exists e)(eJN \& e{\in}S), 1$	EG, 18 e/a.
20. $\Diamond(\exists e)(eJN \& e{\in}S), @$	$\Diamond$-I R01, 19.

Again, in this proof I assume that accessible possible worlds are just those worlds with beings that are relevantly similar to actual humans in terms of cognitive abilities. It should be noted that the proof goes through in modal system K, and thus one cannot hope to invalidate the inference from (CA'), (PE), and (3') to $\Diamond(\exists e)(eJN \& e{\in}S)$ in a weaker modal system.

REFERENCES

Achinstein, P. 1962. The Circularity of a Self-Supporting Inductive Argument. *Analysis* 22: 138–41.
Almeder, R. 1998. *Harmless Naturalism*. Peru, IL: Open Court Publishing.
Bonjour, L. 1998. *In Defense of Pure Reason*. Cambridge: Cambridge University Press.
Bealer, G. 1999. The A Priori. In Greco and Sosa 1999, 243–70.
———. 1992. The Incoherence of Empiricism. *The Aristotelian Society Supplementary*, vol. 66: 99–138.
———. 1996. *A Priori* Knowledge and the Scope of Philosophy. *Philosophical Studies* 91: 121–42.
Black, M. 1958. Self-Supporting Inductive Arguments. *Journal of Philosophy* 55: 718–25.
Brown, H. 1993. A Theory-Laden Observation *Can* Test the Theory. *British Journal for the Philosophy of Science* 44: 555–59.
———. 1994. Circular Justifications. *Proceedings of the PSA*, vol. 1: 406–14.
Creath, R. 2004. Quine on the Intelligibility and Relevance of Analyticity. In Gibson 2004, 47–64.
Casullo, A. 2000. The Coherence of Empiricism. *Pacific Philosophical Quarterly* 81: 31–48.
French, P., T. Uehling Jr., and H. Wettstein, eds. 1994. *Midwest Studies in Philosophy* IX. South Bend, IN: University of Notre Dame Press.
Foley, R. 1994. Quine and Naturalized Epistemology. In French et al. 1994, 243–60.
Gibson, R., ed. 2004. *The Cambridge Companion to Quine*. Cambridge: Cambridge University Press.
Goldman, A. 1967. A Causal Theory of Knowing. *Journal of Philosophy* 64: 357–72.

———. 1979. What is Justified Belief? In Pappas 1979, 1–23.
Greco, John, and Ernest Sosa, eds. 1999. *The Blackwell Guide to Epistemology*. Oxford: Blackwell Publishing.
Haack, S. 1993. *Evidence and Inquiry: Towards Reconstruction in Epistemology*. Oxford: Blackwell Publishing.
Kitcher, P. 1992. The Naturalists Return. *Philosophical Review* 101: 53–114.
Kornblith, H., ed. 1997. *Naturalizing Epistemology*. 2nd ed. Cambridge, MA: MIT Press.
———. 1994. Introduction: What is Naturalized Epistemology? In Kornblith 1997, 1–14.
Laudan, L. (1996) *Beyond Positivism and Relativism: Theory, Method, and Evidence*. Boulder, CO: Westview Press.
Lehrer, K. 1999. Rationality. In Greco and Sosa 1999, 206–20.
———. 1990. *Theory of Knowledge*. Boulder, CO: Westview Publishing.
Pappas, G., ed. 1979. *Justification and Knowledge*. Dordrecht: Reidel Publishing.
Putnam, H. 1976. 'Two Dogmas' Revisited. Reprinted in Putnam 1983, 87–97.
———. 1983. *Realism and Reason: Philosophical Papers*, vol. 3. Cambridge: Cambridge University Press.
Quine, W.V.O. 1951. Two Dogmas of Empiricism. Reprinted in Quine 1953, 20–46.
———. 1953 *From a Logical Point of View*. 2nd ed. Cambridge, MA: Harvard University Press.
———. 1969a. *Ontological Relativity and Other Essays*. New York: Columbia University Press.
———. 1969b. Epistemology Naturalized. In Quine 1969a, 69–90.
Rosenberg, A. 1996. A Field Guide to Recent Species of Naturalism. *British Journal for the Philosophy of Science* 47: 1–29
Roth, P. 1983. Siegel on Naturalized Epistemology and Natural Science. *Philosophy of Science* 50: 482–93.
Shaffer, M., and J. Warnick. 2004. Bursting Bealer's Bubble: How the Starting Points Argument Begs the Question of Foundationalism Against Quine. *Canadian Journal of Philosophy* 34:87–105.
Shogenji, T. 2000. Self-Dependent Justification without Circularity. *British Journal for the Philosophy of Science* 51: 287–98.
Siegel, H. 1980. Justification, Discovery and the Naturalizing of Epistemology. *Philosophy of Science* 47: 297–321.
———. 1984. Empirical Psychology, Naturalized Epistemology, and First Philosophy. *Philosophy of Science* 51: 667–76.
van Fraassen, B. 2002. *The Empirical Stance*. New Haven, CT: Yale University Press.

[9]

A Reconsideration of the Status of Newton's Laws

DAVID J. STUMP

The longstanding controversy concerning the epistemological status of Newton's laws of motion can be stated by the question: Are all three laws empirical, a priori, or conventional, or are they collectively some mix of empirical, a priori and convention?[1] Even in the twentieth century, after Newton's laws were replaced with those found in the Special and General Theories of Relativity, a lively debate over the status of Newton's laws of motion took place in the philosophical literature, where their introduction was seen as an extremely important example of conceptual change (Toulmin 1961; Hanson 1965). The overthrow of Scholastic theories of motion by Newton was seen as instructive because shifts in what required explanation, such as continued motion, were implicated in the change in fundamental principles or laws. Understanding Newton's laws required a new way of thinking, not merely the acknowledgment of a new fact.

Newton's laws clearly play a foundational role in theories of motion, but the question of how they are grounded is open. I will argue that these laws should be treated as empirical in a very abstract sense, while still functioning as a priori knowledge.[2] Though actually coming closer to the Quinean position than to a defense of a priori knowledge, the picture of science developed here is very different from that developed in Quinean holism in that categories of knowledge are strongly differentiated. Newton's laws, for example, played a very special role that is not captured

---

[1] I will use the term 'law' in order to maintain the traditional terminology without taking any particular stand in this essay on the nature of laws or on whether or not they are a necessary part of science. I will not attempt to cite all of the papers or to rehearse all of the arguments on Newton's Laws, but rather focus on a particular treatment of a priori knowledge. See Pap 1946, Whitrow 1950, Shapere 1967, or Earman and Friedman 1973 for more complete surveys.

[2] Use of the term 'functional' in relation to the a priori is due to Arthur Pap (1946). I deal with some of the themes presented here in a different context in Stump 2003.

simply by saying that they are in the hard core of the web of belief. Rather, Newton's laws made a science of motion possible. For example, one cannot formulate Newtonian mechanics without the concept of instantaneous velocity and one cannot define instantaneous velocity without the calculus.[3] The change from Scholastic to Newtonian theories of motion required new mathematics. By contrast, for example, the current dispute between two theories of human origins (the pathway out of Africa) can be settled when enough data is collected, without requiring any new mathematics or changes in concepts. Furthermore, Newton's laws changed the standard for what kinds of motion required explanation and what kinds were considered to be natural.

The possible empirical grounding of Newton's First Law has been questioned on the basis that it describes the behavior of bodies not acted upon by any other body. Given Newton's theory of universal gravitation, however, it seems that no body has ever been in this unaffected state, let alone been observed in this state. On the other hand, Newton's laws cannot easily be taken to be a priori. The laws certainly seem to be testable and defeasable, if only because they clearly describe the states of physical bodies. Alternative theories do not seem to be ruled out a priori. Those who would claim that the laws have a priori grounding (in the classical sense—that they are synthetic a priori truths) will have a large burden of proof, I will argue. The idea that the laws could all be definitions or analytic and thereby a priori will also flounder.

Arthur Pap's idea of the functional a priori provides a way of breaking away from the general debates over the existence of a priori knowledge (the debate between empiricists and rationalists) and of considering a much more interesting question, namely how to describe the constitutive elements of a scientific theory. The elements in the hard core of a scientific theory are functionally a priori in the sense that they must be established prior to everything else and that they are very difficult to test or to eliminate, while the periphery of a physical theory can be tested and can be eliminated. The epistemological status of Newton's laws has attracted so much attention because they are an excellent example of principles (or laws) that function a priori and are therefore very difficult to classify. Yet, they are empirical, I claim, just not simply so.

1. Rationalism versus Empiricism

Since the distinctive trait of modern science is taken to be its combination of experiment and the application of reason, especially mathematics, to the

---

[3] Earman and Friedman deny that this is the case for Newton's original formulation of

study of nature, it may seem easy to give Newton's laws this role—a mixture of empirical and a priori. It seems impossible to justify classifying Newton as an empiricist, even if he did say, famously, that he will "frame no hypotheses." Indeed, many have argued that the most philosophically appealing aspect of Newton's methodology was his resistance to the extremes of empiricism and rationalism (Stein 1990), expressed in Newton's recognition of the need for both analysis and synthesis and for actually carrying out experiments (Hankins 1985). Still, the roles of reason and the senses in knowledge and in the formation of ideas is at stake in the philosophical debates over rationalism and empiricism precisely because of the inconsistent claims made about their roles in the new science. These debates can be seen as having been born out of the methodological reflections on the relative roles of experiment and reason in creating the success of the new science, thus it will be worthwhile to review briefly the debate of the role of reason and experiment here before considering specifically Newton's laws.[4]

The rationalist claims that some part of scientific knowledge about the physical world is a priori—known through reason or intellectual intuition—while the empiricist claims that knowledge about things in the world can only be obtained through experience. Both sides accept the ability of the mind to formulate and to understand representations of nature and acknowledge the role of perceptual knowledge in science and in everyday experience, however empiricists claim that reason is limited to what Hume calls the "relations of ideas," that is, the defining of one term by means of another or the discovery of the logical consequences of propositions (Hume 1966, IV). It is important to note that a rationalist need not be committed to a priori knowledge of the existence of anything, nor of the properties of any individual object, but rather only to general claims about the nature of things in the world. For example, a rationalist might claim that geometry expresses the real nature of space and the things in it, so any triangle (or even something that approximates a triangle) in nature must have certain characteristics that we can discover a priori. Once we know that a triangle is a three-sided figure, we can use pure reason to show that the sum of the three angles of any triangle must be equal to two right angles [Descartes 1984, 45; *AT* 64]. Rational intuition is supposed to tell us how the world must be, since the general principles and laws that the rationalist claims to discover are not contingent facts.

---

the First Law (331). I intend 'Newtonian' to refer to the standard development of Newtonian mechanics, not Newton's own formulations.

[4] I expand considerably on the material in this section in Stump 2005.

The burden of proof for the rationalist is to explain what rational intuition is and why we should think that it will reliably tell us something about the world. The burden of proof for the empiricist in this debate, especially after Kant, is to show how science can exist without any a priori knowledge. While Kant limited reason and acknowledged that experience is the main source of scientific knowledge, he also argued that there is a residual element of a priori synthetic knowledge, what we might now call the theoretical elements of a science that cannot be eliminated. For example, Kant argued that mathematics is both a priori and synthetic, that is, it tells us more than Hume's relations of ideas convey. Since mathematics is clearly central to science, it becomes a major stumbling block to the empiricist claim that there is no a priori element in science (Field 1980; Sober 1999). This suggests that a good way to investigate rationalism in science is to ask whether there are some elements of science that are intractably a priori. Mathematics, a few fundamental principles or laws of nature and other theoretical elements of science seem to be good candidates for a priori knowledge for which the empiricist will need to provide an account.

2. Newton's Laws

In a standard formulation, Newton's First Law says that a body free of impressed forces either remains at rest or else continues in uniform motion in a straight line. Pap claims that it is an empirical fact that Newton's First Law is unrealizable because of the constant presence of friction and of universal gravitation. Friction slows bodies down and gravity diverts them from a straight path. Pap is, of course, aware of the possibility of reducing friction to a minimum and coming close, experimentally, to Newton's idealized law. Galileo accomplished such a reduction of friction with his inclined plane experiments. We can also observe some bodies traveling in deep space, far from the gravitational attraction of other bodies. I would note, however, that it appears that the unrealizability argument can be strengthened by the a priori or conceptual point that the law cannot be empirically grounded if the body obeying the law and the observer are separate entities, given that they must affect each other. Thus, it seems impossible in principle to observe a body that is completely undisturbed by any other body. Many have argued that the existence of universal gravity and friction make Newton's First Law at best hypothetical or subjunctive: If there were a particle unimpeded by universal gravity or by friction, it would continue at rest or in uniform rectilinear motion forever.

What Newton's First Law tells us to expect is not what we usually observe. Newton can explain what we observe with the First Law in combination with universal gravity and/or with friction, but we never observe precisely what the law says that we should see. Therefore, Newton's First Law is not a simple inductive generalization, but rather it is an idealization, given that it cannot be a simple inductive generalization if it is not in accord with observation. There is no consensus about its status as a synthetic a priori principle, a definition and hence analytic, or an empirical statement in any straightforward manner.

Newton's First law is strange, perhaps, in that for bodies at rest, the law accords with everyday observation, but for bodies in motion it does not. Bodies at rest remain at rest until they are disturbed by some external force, but bodies in motion appear to slow down and eventually stop, from an everyday (and a Scholastic) perspective. So, one implication of Newton's First Law is that uniform motion is the same as rest, a claim that is consistent with what we now call Galilean relativity, that while traveling along with an object at constant velocity, one will notice no motion at all—the object can be considered to be at rest, relative to an inertial frame. How do with know what should be taken as natural motion and what needs to be explained? Perhaps it is easier to understand Newton's First Law as a standard for the kind of motion that needs to be explained rather than as a law (Ellis 1965; Toulmin 1962, 54–55). Newton claims that uniform rectilinear motion is the norm, with deviations from uniform rectilinear motion explained by external forces such as friction, gravity or impact with another body, while the Scholastics hold that continued motion after impact needs to be explained. Thus, for example, the Scholastics contend that the motion of a cannonball can be explained by the initial impact of the explosion of gunpowder, but also, according to the Scholastics, by the impetus that is imparted to the cannonball, which is necessary for its continued motion.

2.1. A Priori Arguments

The Scholastic Theory of impetus has often been ridiculed and called ad hoc, yet for someone making an a priori argument for Newton's First Law, I maintain that discounting the Scholastic Theory presents a real challenge. How does one know what kind of motion is natural? Why would motion in a straight line be considered natural rather than motion in the arc of a great circle, as per Galileo? The charge that the Scholastic theory of impetus is ad hoc can only be made when empirical considerations are used to test what happens to projectiles under conditions, for example, where friction varies. These arguments are not open to someone making a purely a priori case for Newton's first law. Furthermore, there are instances where the impetus theory seems to apply, such as in the case of the Atlata, an ancient type of spear thrower, eventually replaced by the bow and arrow, which consists of a short stick with a hook used to launch a flexible spear or 'dart'. The mechanical advantage gained by the launcher was long understood, but this alone does not explain the tremendous power of this weapon, which was said to be the only thing that Cortez and his men feared while conquering the New World—it could pierce Spanish armor from a great distance. It turns out that the flexibility of the dart is the key. At launch, the dart bends, then straightens out in flight, acting much like a spring, thus giving the dart much more momentum (Perkins 1998, Brown, et al. 1996). Unlike the cannon, the Atlata actually does impart a force to its projectile—a perfect example for the impetus theory, given that the launching of an Atlata dart changes the dart itself. It does not remain passive like a cannon ball, but rather plays a part in its own motion after it has been launched. While Newtonian theory can account, of course, for this case too, the Atlata provides an example in which Newton's theory of inertia is not incorrect, but rather it is not such an obviously superior theory to the Scholastic theory that came before it.

Russell Norwood Hanson makes use of Galileo's incline ramp experiments to construct an interesting a priori argument for Newton's First Law. Galileo found that a ball that was rolled down an inclined plane and then back up another inclined plane would roll up to (almost) the same height at which it began, a motion that is analogous to a pendulum. He then argued that on a completely frictionless surface, the height reached would be exactly the same height at which the ball started and that therefore the correct interpretation is that the ball will always reach its original height unless its motion is disturbed by an external force. Hanson notes that as the angle of the second ramp is lowered, the ball must travel farther to reach its original height, and that as the angle of the ramp approaches 0°, the distance traveled will approach infinity. Therefore, we must assume that on a flat surface, a ball encountering no resistance will continue at the same speed indefinitely (Hanson, 1965, 9–11). Although this is an interesting use of Galileo's incline plane experiments, we must remind ourselves that we do not know what happens on completely frictionless surfaces. More importantly, any affects of friction will be extended indefinitely as the distance that the ball must roll is extended. Any amount of friction will make it harder and harder for the ball to reach its original height if it has to travel a greater distance; therefore the friction to be overcome is infinite if the distance to be traveled is infinite. Hanson's argument does show what happens if friction is reduced, but not what happens when friction is zero.

Kant, of course, defends the view that Newton's laws were synthetic and a priori, but in the end this puts his position very close to the one that I defend in this paper. At least in the critical period, Kant understands the Newton's laws, or more precisely Kant's own formulations of them, as preconditions for any science of motion.[5] Michael Friedman expresses Kant's view as follows:

> Kant, since he rejects absolute space, conceives the laws of motion rather as conditions under which alone the concept of true motion has meaning: that is, the true motions are just those that satisfy the laws of motion. . . . Kant thus views the laws of motion as definitive or constitutive of the spatio-temporal framework of Newtonian theory, and this, in the end, is why they count as a priori for him. (1992, 143)

Where Kant errs is first by seeing his laws of motion as apodictically certain, despite the fact that there are conceptual alternatives, as we saw above in the discussion of other a priori arguments for the First Law. Second, Kant does not see that there is a scientific realist interpretation of physical spacetime that opens a way to make Newton's laws into empirical claims.

2.2. The First Law as a Definition

After Kant, Newton's First Law frequently has been thought to be best interpreted as a definition and hence as an analytic truth. To be true, Newton's First Law must be taken to refer to an inertial frame, given that bodies do not remain at rest or in uniform rectilinear motion in accelerated frames. However, we do not know whether inertial frames exist, or what they are. Newton solved this problem with Absolute Space, which he took to be the inertial frame against which all motion was measured. Barring acceptance of Absolute Space, many post-Kantian physicists and philosophers have suggested that the First Law be used to define the concept of inertial frame. Like Kant, they understood the First Law as specifying the meaning of the fundamental terms of Newtonian Mechanics, but unlike Kant, they understood the First Law as an analytic statement. An inertial frame is precisely one in which particles obey Newton's First Law. Earman and Friedman point out that this move is unnecessary, given that the concept of a straight line can be well defined in a four-dimensional version of Newtonian spacetime, since it is a four-dimensional Euclidean manifold. Thus, 'inertial frame' can be defined independently of the First Law, so the law can be given empirical status. Earman and Friedman summarize their account of the status of Newton's laws as follows:

> What is the status of Newton's First Law? Again the answer is clear: on all of the above formulations it is an empirical law—it says something about the affine

---

[5] See Watkins 1998 for a discussion of Kant's formulations of Newton's laws and for the arguments that Kant gives in the precritical period.

structure of space-time and how that structure constrains particle trajectories—but it is superfluous since it is a consequence of the Second Law. (1973, 337)

Essentially, Earman and Friedman interpret Newton's Laws within the context of the General Theory of Relativity, with the four-dimensional spacetime manifold as a mathematical description of physical spacetime. Since Earman and Friedman take a scientifically realist position about spacetime, Newton's Laws can be considered straightforwardly empirical. Even absolute space can be understood in a realist fashion that is as well defined and empirically grounded as physical spacetime in the General Theory of Relativity, the current best scientific theory that we have. In viewing Newton's Laws as essentially empirical, Earman and Friedman represent the current thinking of philosophers of science about spacetime. The remaining element of constitutive a priori in their account places their view closer to Pap's functional a priori than they might have thought.

2.3. The Role of Mathematics

The key issue here is the role of mathematics in Newtonian Mechanics, especially in the interpretation of Newton's Laws of Motion. The mathematical entities that the laws invoke seem not to be empirical, no more so than any other pure mathematical entity. They are, in fact, the constitutive elements, in Kant's sense, of Newton's theory. Pap notes that in comparison to the Scholastic theory of impetus, Galileo explained the motion of bodies geometrically, dividing the forces acting on a projectile into two components—friction acting in the direct opposite direction as the straight inertial path of the projectile, and gravity acting orthogonally to pull the projectile to the earth. These two forces can then be combined as the cross-product of two vectors:

> Galileo saw a simpler way of explaining the parabolic trajectory of projectiles. The law of inertia, originally established by extrapolation from experiment, thus functions as a rule for the geometric construction of actual motions. It is a statement about a hypothetical component of actual motions, just as the law of the parallelogram of vectors assumes the causal efficacy of vector components to which not isolated existence can be ascribed. . . . no given component can be said to *exist* physically, unless it can be identified with an approximately isolable physical force of gravity. . . . In Kantian language, it is synthetic a priori in the sense of being a "constitutive condition" of mechanics: motion is a possible object of mechanics only in so far as it is geometrically constructible . . . (Pap 1946, 43)

Earman and Friedman admit similar kinds of geometrical objects play a fundamental role in Newtonian Mechanics; they actually replace the physical, causal process with a mathematical one. Since the bodies in question become mathematical, they cannot be (noncontroversially) empirically justified.

> Thus, in using Kepler's Laws to find the force of attraction exerted by the sun, Newton replaces the continuously acting force by a sequence of impulses acting at intervals Δt, replaces the actual path of the planet by a sequence of inertial paths, and passes to the limits as Δt goes to zero. (Earman and Friedman 1973, 331)

Classical Newtonian mechanics also uses a single mathematical point as the center of mass of a body. All of these replacements could be seen as mere idealizations, but they are, nevertheless, examples of an important point: Newtonian Mechanics would be impossible even to formulate without these mathematical tools. It follows that the mathematics used in Newtonian Mechanics is ontologically and epistemological prior to the physical claims made in the theory and therefore functionally a priori in the sense that it is a precondition, or in Kantian language, it is constitutive.

3. The Functional A Priori or Empiricism with a Difference

Newton's laws were seen as good examples of a pragmatic or changeable a priori, a view that was most fully explored by Arthur Pap (1946). The key element of this view is to follow Reichenbach in retaining Kant's idea of the constitutive aspect of a priori knowledge while removing the idea of a priori knowledge as necessarily true (Reichenbach 1965, 48). Thus, fundamental conceptual change in science is seen as changes in fundamental principles that are necessary preconditions to scientific knowledge—principles that had been seen as synthetic and a priori by Kant—but eliminating their necessity, given that they have in fact changed during a scientific revolution. These elements of physical theory have a unique epistemological status as a functionally a priori part of our physical theory, despite the fact that they can change. Writing in the 1940s, Pap uses a heady mix of logical positivism, pragmatism, and idealism to interpret Poincaré's conventionalism and the idea of conventions to interpret the functioning of the fundamental principles of science as a priori truths. With his theory of a priori knowledge, Pap made great conceptual strides and he is also well known for his work on necessity. However, Pap takes Poincaré's conventionalism for granted as obviously correct, which it is not, assuming as well that the mathematics is conventional, apparently taking a formalist position in the philosophy of mathematics. In fact, showing that there are mathematical entities that replace physical ones just pushes the question of the status of Newton's Laws back to the question of the status of mathematics. By raising questions about Poincaré's conventionalism here, I will further the line of discussion that Pap began and clarify his notion of the functional a priori.

The first problem with Pap's interpretation of Poincaré's conventionalism is that it removes any empirical element from physical theory, a view from which Poincaré already distanced himself when his contemporary Édouard Le Roy interpreted his work in a similar way (Poincaré 1902). Indeed, a closer look at the central passages that Pap (and Hanson) uses to interpret Poincaré's conventionalism shows that he made clear that Newtonian mechanics always remains empirical, even if it is possible to interpret each of Newton's laws individually as a convention. Poincaré noted that Newton's laws and other basic laws of motion can each be taken as a definition and thus as a convention. For example, if we discover a body that accelerates at an unusual rate, we immediately assume that there must be some force other than gravity acting on it—the law has become a definition of free fall. Despite the fact that he has made very conventionalist claims about Newton's laws in chapter VI of *Science and Hypothesis*, he softens this stance in summing up this part of the book, saying that some empirical element always remains in mechanics, since it is an empirical science. Thus, he claims, the empirical part of a law of mechanics cannot be eliminated, it is simply shifted to another place in our total theory: "Then our law is separated into an absolute and rigorous principle which expresses the relation of A to C and an experimental law, approximate and subject to revision, which expresses the relation of C to B" (Poincaré 1913, 126). It follows that while any one of Newton's laws can be "hardened" into a definition, they cannot all be at once. The starting point is conventional, but the final theory will be the same. Much as we have a choice of which terms to take as primitive in a formal axiomatic system, we also have a choice as to which principles to take as definitions in science.

The second problem with Pap's interpretation of Poincaré's conventionalism is that it is now widely acknowledged that Poincaré's metric conventionalism requires a fully relational theory of space, yet none of the historically accepted space or spacetime theories—Newtonian, the Special or the General Theory of Relativity—have been fully relational in the required sense (Friedman 1983). Sklar would seem to agree with this point when he argues that the only possible way to defend metric conventionalism now is with (Quinean) holism (Sklar 1986). A striking constitutive element remains in spacetime theories however, for with the proper background theory, Poincaré's conventionalism would have been possible. It is a merely contingent empirical fact that uniform acceleration is detectable and unrelativizable, while uniform velocity is not. The most important point for this discussion is that the epistemological status of the metric of space or spacetime changed as we changed background theories. In this case, Newtonian theory and the General Theory of Relativity each set the epistemological status of space (or spacetime). In Newtonian theory, we know a priori that space is Euclidean, but in the General Theory of Relativity, the metric is determined empirically. If a relational account of spacetime had been developed, Poincaré's metric conventionalism would have been vindicated. Background theory and context determine what is a priori and what is empirical, that is, which parts of the theory function as a priori knowledge, however, the background theory is determined empirically, in a broad sense of the term, by which I mean that while there is no single test that shows that the General Theory of Relativity is superior to Newtonian theories of motion and gravity, the choice between the two theories is in part a result of the empirical consequences of each. Thus, the Newtonian theories of space and of motion are empirical theories, while the metric of space is Euclidean and functions as a priori knowledge within Newtonian theory, which is why I argue that Newton's Laws are still empirical, albeit only in a very indirect and abstract sense.

My view is, of course, close to Carnap's later views in that the background commitments of a scientific theory determine what is a priori and what is empirical. However, Carnap makes a mistake in considering the background commitments as a language. He sees a priori truths as analytic, leaving himself vulnerable to Schlick's critique of conventions as trivial, as well as to further critiques by Quine. I claim that the process of determining what is a priori and what is empirical is embedded within a physical, empirical theory. It is necessary to develop a considerable amount of theory before empirical tests are possible at all, and even then, it may seem that empirical tests have very little to do with, for example, the truth of Newton's Laws. Empirical tests will seem to have even less to do with the truth of the mathematics that makes the formulation of Newton's Laws possible. Nevertheless, Newtonian theory is ultimately empirical, that is, the change from Newtonian theory to the Special and General Theories of Relativity has an empirical basis, though a rather indirect one.

The constitutive elements of a physical theory are determined empirically, which means that a theory can be grounded empirically but still contain functionally a priori elements that cannot be directly tested and without which the theory could not be stated. On the one hand, we could start from the constitutive functionally a priori elements, pointing out that these are necessary, while on the other hand, we could start from the whole empirical theory, pointing out that different empirical theories have different constitutive a priori elements. The constitutive elements are therefore not determined a priori, nor are they determined conventionally, but rather empirically as embedded elements in a physical theory. For example, Newton's laws are necessary preconditions of Newton's theory of motion, seeming to be a priori, but at the same time, they are superseded by Einstein's theory of Relativity. Einstein's fundamental laws and the applications of mathematics that he uses are justified, in part, by the empirical success of the General Theory of Relativity.

What is wrong with Quine's holism? First, Quine and other empiricists might say that what was once called a priori is simply the hard core of our empirical theories. However, the constitutive principles are not merely more entrenched—they have *never* been directly tested. As Friedman notes, the difference between the core and the periphery is not at all a difference in the degree of justification, as Quine's model seems to imply (Friedman 2001, 46). Secondly, Quineans seem to assume that the possibility of alternative theories is more than a mere possibility. We know that all of empirical science is fallible, meaning that the most likely of our physical theories could be wrong and that the least likely of our physical theories could be true. Thus, for example, the General Theory of Relativity could be false and a fully relational theory of space could be true, but saying that this is possible is a long way from actually working out such a theory. Even though possibilities of change always remain open, science does change on the basis of empirical results. Observing how science works and analyzing the constitutive elements of science is a more interesting and informative project than pointing out that theories are, in a very unrealistic sense, salvageable no matter what the evidence says. Quinean holism can degenerate into mere skepticism.

In his more recent work, Friedman adopts a viewpoint of the relativized a priori (2001), which should be inconsistent with his early position staked out with Earman, away from which Friedman certainly sounds at times like he has moved. He goes too far, however, in attempting to defend a special position for philosophy with the notion of a relativized a priori, given that a priori knowledge is fully part of science. Indeed, if Newton's laws are a priori in the sense that I have been discussing here—they are constitutive preconditions of Newtonian mechanics—then certainly everyone will have to agree that some elements of science are a priori. It would be odd indeed to say that anything that science requires is nevertheless separate and not part of science.

Friedman may simply mean to underline the fact that both Carnap and Quine's versions of scientism failed, given that philosophy cannot be reduced to logic or to behaviorist psychology. However, the failure of both of these programs does not imply that the relativized a priori, i. e. the necessary preconditions, could not be viewed as either empirical or conventional, yet remain changeable in ways that will account for scientific revolutions. Scientists as well as philosophers need to be aware of the constitutive elements of scientific theories, since philosophers have no special ability to point out these elements. I take it that Friedman and I would agree that philosophy is a broad discipline that legitimately does far more than the Vienna Circle thought it could, but I see no reason to think that philosophy plays any special role. Indeed, it is important to avoid at all costs the notion of "first philosophy" or any role for philosophy as a separate activity that "grounds" scientific activity, a role which becomes superfluous if we relinquish the general concern about the grounding of science (is it wholly empirical or are there some a priori parts?) and focus instead on how science works, adopting an attitude that goes two steps beyond Kant and a step beyond the relativized a priori by conceding that even the constitutive elements of physical theory are empirical.

How could the constitutive elements of a physical theory *not* be empirical? Surely Newton's mechanics is a physical theory that has empirical consequences. If the theory cannot even be stated without the Laws and without the mathematics that are necessary for them, then these must be empirical as well. The only way to avoid this conclusion is to claim that the constitutive parts are merely analytic, in which case we are back to the same rationalism vs. empiricism dispute, or to argue that they are in some other way separable from the physical theory, for example, by arguing that the pure mathematics refers to one kind of object and the applied mathematics to another, which cannot be considered a solution, given that it merely pushes the issue back another step to the question of the epistemological status of applied mathematics. What is applied mathematics but a mixture of pure mathematics and physical theory? Some may want to argue that mathematics is merely the language of physics and therefore analytic, which then returns us to the problem of how to separate analytic from synthetic. The key point is that the a priori or constitutive elements of the theory do not fit comfortably as either analytic or synthetic, or as empirical or a priori. The fact that a theory has constitutive elements does not imply that it is not empirical, nor even that those elements are nonempirical. The constitutive parts of a theory are those that are only empirical when considered as parts of an empirical whole. Rather than consider the constitutive elements of a theory to require a special a priori justification, they can be considered to be justified by the role they play in the theory as a whole.

Michael Resnik's work on the philosophy of mathematics provides a way to think about the status of mathematics within a modified Quinean perspective. Resnik's main new additions to discussions in the philosophy of mathematics are a disquotational account of reference and truth—a reduced and subtle kind of realism in mathematics—and structuralism to account for the incompleteness of mathematical objects. Resnik's immanent account of reference and truth makes for a realism that some may consider incomplete, but clearly disquotational accounts are not antirealist, since the epistemic accounts of truth usually associated with antirealism are rejected. Of particular significance is the point that an immanent account of reference eliminates one of the strongest arguments against mathematical realism. A transcendental approach seems to require a causal theory of reference, and since mathematical objects are causally inert, it seems impossible to be a transcendent realist in mathematics.

By advocating structuralism, Resnik hopes to make the ontological and referential relativity of mathematics seem natural. Since mathematical objects are defined by the axioms and only up to isomorphism, there is an apparent problem for the mathematical realist: Typically multiple objects satisfy the axioms since there are infinitely many structurally identical models. Resnik argues that realism can account for the incompleteness of mathematical objects as well as other philosophies of mathematics do, so that he can argue that realism has other advantages as a philosophy of mathematics (**92**). His aim is to clarify the nature of mathematical objects, not to reduce them to one kind of object (**223**). Not only is structuralism intended to make the incompleteness of mathematical objects philosophically palatable, it is also taken to be compatible with Resnik's epistemology, or at least with his story of the genesis of mathematical knowledge.

Resnik defends the indispensability thesis and promotes Quinean holism, arguing that mathematics is not separable from the rest of science and that justification of mathematics, once we move away from local justifications within various branches of mathematics, ultimately involves the role that mathematics plays in science as a whole. Resnik defends epistemic holism by arguing that the objects of physics are not so different from those in mathematics and by accounting for the stability of mathematics pragmatically. Mathematics will be tinkered with less frequently than experimental hypotheses, becoming relatively a priori, that is, more likely to be taken for granted. However, Resnik admits that mathematics is never falsified (**133**), leading one to wonder whether this is not in itself prima facie evidence for a fundamental epistemic difference between mathematics and the rest of science. Merging the position that I have been advocating here with Resnik's philosophy of mathematics solves the enigma of the special status of mathematics in physical theory. When it is used in a physical theory, mathematics plays a constitutive role.

The overall ground of mathematics is a large and seemingly intractable question. Is mathematical knowledge synthetic a priori, analytic, or empirical? The three great schools in philosophy of mathematics—intuitionist, formalist, and empiricist—line up exactly with these three positions. I agree with Resnik that the justification of a particular element of mathematics in a given context is enough. Pure mathematics will be justified on the basis of consistency and intrinsic interest, whereas applied mathematics will be justified on the basis of its utility in a physical theory. No more is required in order to understand science. I suggest that a general answer to the question of what grounds mathematics is not required for an understanding of how science works. We can look instead to the justification of the mathematical elements of a theory that take place in a scientific context. In the case of pure mathematics, the justification will look more formal and a priori, while in the case of applied mathematics; it will look more utilitarian and empirical.

4. Conclusion

Functional accounts of a priori knowledge should be seen as analogous to minimal theories of truth. These are deflationary strategies that leave a core of beliefs about the term in question in place, but refuse to say too much. Regarding a priori knowledge, we can acknowledge that we must begin our inquiry from some principles, but we do not need to claim that the principles are certain, or that they are known by some special intuition. On the other hand, we cannot claim that these fundamental principles are just like any other part of empirical inquiry. Although the fundamental principles of science are synthetic, they are constitutive, making science possible, and they are also empirical because they are an uneliminable part of an empirical, physical theory, even if they are not directly testable.

REFERENCES

Brown, M. M., D. Pritchard, P. Chauvaux, and C. A. Hoyt. 2005. *Atlatl Literature Resources* [Webpage]. Ted Bailey 1996 [cited 2005]. Available from http://www.flight-toys.com/atlatl/atlatl_books.html.

Descartes, R. 1984. *Meditations on First Philosophy*. In *The Philosophical Writings of Descartes*, vol. 2, tr. J. Cottingham, R. Stoothoff and D. Murdoch, 1–62. Cambridge and New York: Cambridge University Press.

Earman, J., and M. Friedman. 1973. The Meaning and Status of Newton's Law of Inertia and the Nature of Gravitational Forces. *Philosophy of Science* 40: 329–59.

Ellis, B. D. 1965. The Origin and Nature of Newton's Laws of Motion. In *Beyond the Edge of Certainty: Essays in Contemporary Science and Philosophy*, ed. R. G. Colodny, 29–68. Englewood Cliffs, NJ: Prentice Hall.

Field, H. 1980. *Science without Numbers: A Defense of Nominalism*. Princeton: Princeton University Press.

Friedman, M. 1983. *Foundations of Spacetime Theories:Relativistic Physics and Philosophy of Science*. Princeton: Princeton University Press.

———. 1992. *Kant and the Exact Sciences*. Cambridge: Harvard University Press.

———. 2001. *Dynamics of Reason: The 1999 Kant Lectures at Stanford University*. Stanford: CSLI Publications.

Hankins, T. L. 1985. *Science and the Enlightenment*. Cambridge: Cambridge University Press.

Hanson, N. R. 1965. Newton's First Law: A Philosopher's Door into Natural Philosophy. In *Beyond the Edge of Certainty: Essays in Contemporary Science and Philosophy*, ed. R. G. Colodny, 6–28. Englewood Cliffs, NJ: Prentice Hall.

Hume, D. 1966. *Enquiries Concerning the Human Understanding and Concerning the Principles of Morals*. Oxford: Clarendon Press.

Pap, A. 1946. *The A Priori in Physical Theory*. New York: King's Crown Press.

Perkins, B. 2005. *Atlatl & Dart Mechanics* [Webpage]. Mac Maness, 2004, 1998 [cited 2005]. Available from http://www.abotech.com/Articles/Perkins02.htm.

Poincaré. H. 1902. Sur la Valeur Objective de la Science. *Revue de Métaphysique et de Moral* 10: 263–93. Rpt. in Poincaré 1913, *The Value of Science*, chs. 10 and 11, 321–55.

———. 1913. *The Foundations of Science: Science and Hypothesis, the Value of Science, Science and Method*. Lanham, MD: University Press of America, 1982.

Reichenbach, H. 1965. *The Theory of Relativity and A Priori Knowledge*. Berkeley: University of California Press.

Resnik, M. D. 1997. *Mathematics as a Science of Patterns*. Oxford: Oxford University Press.

Shapere, D. 1967. Newtonian Mechanics and Mechanical Explanation. In *Encyclopedia of Philosophy*, ed. P. Edwards, 115–19. New York: Macmillan.

Sklar, L. 1986. *Philosophy and Spacetime Physics*. Berkeley: University of California Press.

Sober, E. 1999. Mathematics and Indispensability. *Philosophical Review* 102: 35–57.

Stein, H. 1990. On Locke, the Great Huygenius, and the Incomparable Mr. Newton. In *Philosophical Perspectives on Newtonian Science*, ed. R. I. G. Hughes, 17–47. Cambridge, MA: MIT Press.

Stump, D. J. 2003. Defending Conventions as Functionally A Priori Knowledge. *Philosophy of Science* 20: 1149–60.

———. 2005. Rationalism in Science. In *Blackwell Companion to Rationalism*, ed. A. Nelson, 408–24. Oxford: Blackwell.

Toulmin, S. 1961. *Foresight and Understanding: An Enquiry into the Aims of Science*. Bloomington: Indiana University Press.

Watkins, E. 1998. Kant's Justification of the Laws of Mechanics. *Studies in History and Philosophy of Science* 29: 539–60.

Whitrow, G. J. 1950. On the Foundations of Dynamics. *British Journal for the Philosophy of Science* 1: 92–107.

[10]

The Constitutive A Priori and Epistemic Justification

MICHAEL J. SHAFFER

> Take up, therefore, the staff of experience, and leave behind the history of all the vain opinions of philosophers. To be blind and yet believe that you can do without this staff, is blindness at its darkest. . . . One can and should admire even the most useless efforts of those lofty geniuses: the Descarteses, Malebranches, Leibnizes, Wolffs, etc.; but what benefit, I ask you, has anyone gathered from all their profound meditations and works?
>
> —LA METTRIE, *Man A Machine*

1. Introduction

In one of its forms the recent revival of the interest in and the defense of a priori knowledge has borrowed significantly from both Kant and from traditional conventionalism. Michael Friedman (1999, 2000, 2001, 2002a, 2002b), Graciela DePierris (1992), Robert DiSalle (2002), and David Stump (2003) have all presented and endorsed the view that some propositions in the networks that represent our belief structures (especially in the context of physical theory) have a special status that amounts to their being accepted a priori. These propositions are alleged to be a priori in virtue of their special function and they are supposed not to be subject to empirical refutation in quite the same way that garden-variety empirical propositions are. This claim is made in direct opposition to the Quinean model of the web of belief, wherein, due to the alleged collapse of the analytic/synthetic distinction, all propositions face the tribunal of experience in the same way and differ only in terms of how deeply entrenched in the web they are. Moreover, as Friedman in particular is all too clear (2002b, 172), this claim is also intended to constitute a strong rejection of naturalized epistemology.

The view endorsed by Friedman and the other constitutivists holds that a priori principles are constitutive in their function, hence the expression 'constitutive a priori'. Such principles serve as framework principles in the manner suggested by Kant, Poincaré, Carnap, Reichenbach and, to some degree, Kuhn. They are principles without which theories could neither be formulated nor applied to real world phenomena. Most importantly such principles are alleged to function so as to make possible the formulation of certain law statements and, in virtue of their role in connecting theory to data, these principles thus make empirical testing possible. However, unlike Kant, and in accord with Carnap and Kuhn, the defenders of the constitutive a priori hold that these principles are rationally revisable. Like Kant, however, and unlike Carnap and Kuhn, the constitutivists appear to argue that such principles are epistemically justifiable in some substantial sense.[1] So while the conventionalist element of the constitutivist view allows for the possibility that radically different core assumptions can govern the constitution, operation, and extension of theories, the Kantian element of the constitutivist view is supposed to block the charge of irrationality typically leveled at purely conventionalist views.

Here it will granted to the defenders of the constitutive a priori that such principles do serve a function within the structure of our belief systems that is appreciably different from that of more pedestrian empirical propositions, but what will be critically scrutinized here are the following claims: (1) that such principles are, or can be, justified in any coherent sense of the term, (2) that such principles are rationally revisable in any substantive sense and (3) that given points (1) and (2) the constitutivist view poses no threat to a thorough-going naturalism. Specific attention will be paid to Friedman's particular treatment of the constitutive a priori, but the main critical points to be raised in the sequel can be applied to the views of the other defenders of the constitutive a priori given a bit of creative extrapolation.

2. The A Priorist Resurgence and the Constitutivist View

Prior to the presentation and critique of the constitutivist view, it will be both instructive and useful to step back and look at the broader epistemological context in which this philosophical theory has been proposed, especially as constitutivism is a rather new view that may be unfamiliar to many. The constitutivist view arose, as many views of the a priori recently have, as a critical reaction to the wave of naturalized epistemologies developed in the last few decades as extensions of Quine's views presented most notori-

---

[1] Stump (2003) is perhaps notable for his rejection of the latter point.

ously in his 1951 "Two Dogmas of Empiricism," his 1960 *Word and Object*, his 1969 "Epistemology Naturalized" and, with Joseph Ullian, in their 1970 *The Web of Belief*.² It is, however, a view that has been developed by paying careful positive attention to a number of scientific and philosophical sources, including the works of some traditional, positivistic, and post-positivistic thinkers. Specifically, Friedman's (1992, 1999, 2000, 2002b) and DePierres's (1988) treatments of Kant and Friedman's (1999, 2001) treatments of Kuhn, Carnap, and Reichenbach ground the view philosophically. In taking Kuhn seriously, in particular, the constitutivist's at the same time pay careful attention to the historical analysis of philosophy and to the details of actual physical theories and their historical genesis, most obviously to Newtonian and relativistic mechanics. That this is so, of course, should not be too surprising given the particular character and interests of the influences just noted. What the constitutivist view then amounts to is a very powerful scientific, historical and philosophical reaction to Quinean holism as the best theory of the structure and dynamics of scientific knowledge, both in the historical and the normative senses.³ In so far as Quine's naturalism is more or less welded to his holism, the constitutivist view then also poses a serious threat to Quinean naturalism.⁴

So, while awareness of the context in which the constitutive view was developed and the influences which it incorporates amply demonstrates that it is first and foremost a reaction to holistic naturalized epistemology, it also amply demonstrates that it is an importantly different, more scientifically inspired, sort of reaction than most other contemporary, and more narrowly philosophical, reactions to epistemology naturalized such those defended by, for example, Laurence BonJour (1998), George Bealer (1992, 2000), or Christopher Peacocke (2000, 2004).⁵ Those reactions to naturalized epistemology are more generally concerned with directly showing that there is substantial knowledge justified without appeal to experience. The constitutivists, however, drawing heavily on Reichenbach's view of the a priori, are more concerned with a priority in the more literal sense of contingent propositions that are necessary presuppositions of some theory.⁶ This does not, of course, imply that the

---

² See Kornblith 1994 and Boghossian and Peacocke 2000 for various perspectives on the matter.
³ See Friedman 2000 and 2001 for the most explicit statement of this aspect of the constitutivist view.
⁴ Friedman is especially clear about this in his 2001 and his 2002b.
⁵ The main manner in which Friedman's view differs from these other views is derived from the view of the a priori that is found in Reichenbach 1920. Reichenbach adopts the view that the a priori is to be identified with relatively necessary propositions that are constitutive of the objects of scientific knowing.
⁶ See Reichenbach 1920/1965, 48–60.

constitutivists must necessarily disagree with those who defend more philosophical views of the a priori when it comes to accepting the possibility of a priori knowledge. In any case, as the constitutivist view is more scientific in origin it appears, at least prima facie, to pose a rather more worrying threat to holistic naturalized epistemologies than that posed by the sorts of more philosophical defenses of the a priori just mentioned. That it does so can be attributed primarily to the claim that careful attention to the details of actual physical theories and the history of science supports the view that some propositions that constitute scientific theories have the status of a priori and not a posteriori propositions. If this is indeed correct, then it challenges the core thesis of many forms of naturalized epistemology, that there is only one kind of knowledge—a posteriori scientific knowledge, on the very basis of science itself.

3. The Function of Constitutive A Priori Principles and Empirical Propositions

Friedman's constitutivism is based on the fundamental recognition that different sorts of propositions serve different sorts of functions within the context of a given scientific theory; that theories have a stratified and therefore nonholistic functional structure. Most importantly, he presents and defends the antinaturalist view that certain types of propositions within such structured physical theories are a priori in nature. Such propositions are supposed to be a priori in the sense that they are not subject to immediate empirical revision and this is due to their special function within such theories. Moreover this immunity to empirical revision is not held to merely be the result of a greater degree of entrenchment. As such, Friedman borrows the notion of the functional a priori from Arthur Pap's rather sadly neglected 1946 monograph, *The A Priori in Physical Theory*, and he seeks to draw parallels between this work and the view of the nature and function of a priori propositions defended in Reichenbach's 1920 *The Theory of Relativity and A Priori Knowledge* and so the constitutivist views builds also on Reichenbach's concept of coordinating principles.

The crucial basic thesis Friedman defends in his novel theory of knowledge is, again, that different types of propositions serve different epistemic functions in physical theories and he specifically identifies three distinct functions that types of propositions have in the context of such theories, one of which importantly is alleged to entail that such principles are a priori in nature. In any case, despite Quine's attack on the analytic/synthetic distinction, Friedman still subscribes to something like the early Carnapian belief that we can identify a sort of logical division of labor among the propositions that make up a theory based on the purely functional differ-

The Constitutive A Priori and Epistemic Justification

ences between those propositions (2001, 33). The three functionally different types of propositions in our belief systems that Friedman identifies are as follows: properly empirical laws of nature, constitutive principles, and philosophical metaframework propositions. Propositions of each type then subserve different, but interrelated, roles within scientific research programs (i.e. theories) and these specific functions are to be understood as follows.

First, properly empirical laws are assertions about the way the world is and they are judged via conformity to observational evidence by rigorous empirical testing. Second, constitutive a priori principles are (a) the sorts of coordinating principles mentioned above (2001, 76–80) and (b) principles of pure mathematics. They are basic principles of mathematics, mechanics, and geometry that allow us to render precise the crude objects of sensory perception. Moreover, they are supposed to be necessary relative to a given empirical theory in the sense that without them there would be insufficient structure to the theoretical objects posited by a theory to formulate, apply or test properly empirical laws. Constitutive a priori principles are, most essentially, structure-generating tools required for the formulation of properly empirical concepts and hypothetical objects. Thus, within a given theory constitutive principles are presupposed, as without them there would *per se* be no such theory (2001, 74), at least qua empirical theory. In any case, the crucial function of such principles is to unify abstract, purely mathematical, structures and concrete empirical phenomena (2001, 76–83), thus endowing the mathematical structures with empirical content. The other primary function they have in this respect is to provide adequately precise mathematical structure to describe the qualitative theoretical objects posited by the theory so that they can be effectively tested. The coordinating principles and the purely mathematical structures are not, however, supposed to be subject to direct empirical refutation or confirmation in response to empirical testing of the properly empirical laws of nature that they make possible (2001, 80–81). Friedman's preferred examples of such constitutive a priori principles are Newton's laws in the context of Newtonian mechanics and the principle of equivalence in the context of relativistic mechanics. As the constitutivists see it, these principles, as well as, for example, mathematical principles like those that constitute the theory of Riemannian manifolds, are simply not implicated when the relevant mathematized empirical theories are confronted with the result of empirical observation, at least not directly.[7] They are, however, subject to refutation and revision in the sense that when a whole research program is ultimately rejected due

---

[7] Friedman 2001, 83–92.

to its empirical inadequacy both the retention and classification of such principles is up for grabs. Finally, philosophical metaframeworks are the overarching philosophical propositions that allow both for the generation of new theories and for the rational transition from one research program to another, and without which science would be crippled as a progressive endeavor. Essentially what such philosophical principles are supposed to do is to assure that prior theories are retained as special cases of later theories and that there is some source from which new theories can be naturally generated from old ones (2001, 23). In other words, this is essentially the assumption of Bohr's famous correspondence principle, or that of convergence in light of theoretical novelty coupled with the idea that new theories grow naturally out of older theories by a series of continuous transformations. Such philosophical principles are needed because the nature of scientific research is supposed to be cumulative and continuous, and so science progresses via a process of conservative revision whereby we retain as much of past empirical successes as we can while conjecturing new theories that correct the empirical inadequacies of prior theories. Such philosophical principles are supposed to guarantee a sense of understanding of prior theories by the members of later research programs despite the kind of Kuhnian incommensurability that inevitably arises from the breakdown of the shared network of presuppositions within a research program that occurs during radical theory change.[8]

However, Friedman is clear that despite his dual rejection of Quinean naturalism and holism in favor of his notions of this tripartite stratification of knowledge and the constitutive a priori, he concurs with Quine on one crucial point. Specifically, all of these three types of propositions just noted are revisable (2001, 46 ff.). It is also crucially important to for us to be clear that the identification of constitutive principles as being a priori in nature does not imply some greater degree of epistemic security (2001, 46). So rather, like Carnap, Kuhn, Reichenbach, and Kant, Friedman claims that certain core propositions necessary for the conduct of empirical science under the aegis of a research program requires our accepting certain principles as being regarded as a priori within that research program. However, they are not immune to revision in the sense that such research programs cannot be themselves rejected and replaced, but constitutive principles are not subject to direct empirical refutation because, as just described, they are not ordinary claims about empirical reality per se.

---

[8] This philosophically grounded sense of understanding that allows for rational theory change is a form of what Friedman calls communicative rationality, although in revision of whole research programs it is a very different sense of communicative rationality than that shared within a research program.

So while it is true that when revolutionary theory change occurs those propositions treated as being functionally a priori in an earlier research program can be either wholly rejected in a later research program or can change their status with respect to how they are categorized in terms of the tripartite functional distinction referred to above, this is supposed to be the kind of change that Carnap regarded as involving external questions and hence which are essentially conventional in nature. For example, a proposition categorized as constitutive and hence a priori relative to an earlier research program can come to be regarded as a properly empirical proposition in a later research program if that is what the new framework adopted by the scientific community requires. Friedman (2001, 2002a) and DiSalle (2002) point to a number of examples from the history of physics in support of this aspect of the constitutivist view and the alteration in the status of the principles of physical geometry in the context of the shift from Newtonian mechanics to relativistic mechanics serves as the primary example in both cases. In any case, with this rather brief and schematic introduction to the constitutivist view out of the way, attention can now be turned to its critique. Of course, the main reason for this critical examination of the constitutivism is to defuse this particular threat to a thoroughgoing epistemological naturalism of the sort endorsed by Quine and other naturalized epistemologists.

4. The Justification of Constitutive A Priori Propositions

The first critical point to be raised here against Friedman in particular and the other constitutivists in general concerns the application of the concept of epistemic justification to constitutive a priori principles. Recall that, due to their function, constitutive a priori principles are not justified in virtue of any empirical evidence but they not unrevisable either. Such principles are to be regarded as presuppositions of properly empirical laws of nature in the sense that they make the formulation and testing of theories possible. However, as described earlier they can be rejected when a research program as a whole becomes empirically indefensible. Whatever the plausibility of this view about the nature and function of constitutive principles, some troubling problems arise when we consider how such principles might be epistemically justified or rationally revised. This is especially troubling when one grants that Quine's attack on the analytic/synthetic distinction is successful. If it is, as Friedman perhaps grudgingly admits (2001, 33), then we cannot treat constitutive principles as being justified in the way that analytic propositions are supposed to be justified. This leaves then only two apparent options. First, the constitutivists might hold that such principles are empirically justified and, second, they might hold that they are conventional and so by their very nature are not epistemically justified.[9]

Friedman clearly rejects the first option outright even though he notes that such principles have some sort of empirical significance (2001, 84) and so it would appear that he must, on pain of incoherence, accept the second option. It then appears that Friedman's view implies that the adoption of constitutive principles is essentially a nonrational, or at least nonepistemic, endeavor. This contention is supported by much of what he has to say about the adoption of such principles. In speaking of these sorts of principles in the context of Einstein's revolutionary rejection of Newtonain mechanics, he says, "It is precisely here that an essentially nonempirical element of "decision" must intervene, for what is at issue, above all, is giving a radically new space-time structure a determinate empirical meaning—without which it is not even empirically false but simply undefined" (2001, 88). However, both Friedman and DiSalle (2002) attempt to avoid outright conventionalism by claiming that such principles are necessary in the sense that they are presupposed by properly empirical laws and hence are necessary components of the theory with special status; they are required before any empirical testing of any part of a theory can be done because they make the theory empirically meaningful (2001, 74 and 83). As a result, although they are not strictly speaking empirically contentful in the sense of being testable, they are alleged to have some sort of empirical significance if only in the meager sense that they are involved in applying theories to empirical phenomena.[10] As such, the implication is that while they are supposed to be conventions, they are not "mere" conventions in the pure sense as understood by, for example, Carnap and Poincaré. Rather, the advance of empirical research dictates their adoption even though they are not empirically testable. Echoing Friedman, DiSalle, specifically, argues for the following account of constitutive principles

> they are interpretive claims rather than empirical claims, for they propose certain characteristic physical phenomena be interpreted through certain geometrical structures. *Yet these definitions are in no sense mere conventions.* Instead, each arises from a conceptual analysis of procedures of spatiotemporal measurement; in each case the definition is not chosen from among empirically equivalent alternatives, but discovered to be implicit in current empirical principles at a critical moment in the history of physics. (2002, 194, my italics)

---

[9] See DiSalle 2002, 197.

[10] DiSalle (2002, 170) thus regards them as essentially interpretive and definitional in character, and so attempts to argue that such principles are conventional, a priori, but neither analytic nor synthetic in the ordinary senses of those terms.

As such, the constitutivists believe that these principles are supposed to be rationally held, although not rationally held in the manner that ordinary empirical propositions are held. Holding such principles is presumed to be rational in something like the following sense. It is supposed to be rational to adopt such principles because they are something like the presuppositions of a current theory that arose out of the ashes of earlier theories, or that they are principles that are implicit in some currently held theory.

Whatever its historical merits, this view of the constitutive a priori is perplexing to say the least, and, on closer scrutiny, it turns out to be painfully short on crucial epistemological details. What Friedman and the other constitutivists appear to hold is that empirical testing requires the assumption of various constitutive, quasi-empirical, principles and that absent such principles one would have a theory that is part of pure mathematics rather than a theory that is a part of empirical science. In a real sense, these principles serve to define what it is for a theoretical claim to be empirically contentful and so they are empirically significant in this rather rarified sense. As Friedman explains, "A constitutive framework thus defines a space of empirical possibilities (statements that can be true or false), and the procedure of empirical testing against the background of such a framework then functions to indicate which empirical phenomena are realized" (2001, 84). But, so described how are such principles then themselves the objects of rational acceptance? Why choose one set of constitutive principles rather than another?

Following Poincaré's work we should all be aware that for purely logical reasons, relative to one set of empirical phenomena there will often be a number of constitutive frameworks adequate to the task of rendering that theory empirical and testable by endowing the phenomenon with an adequately precise structure.[11] As such, the question of the epistemic justification of constitutive principles is an acute one and simply claiming that they are partly conventional and partly empirical in the manner suggested above will simply not do. Absent some coherent theory of the justification of constitutive a priori principles, the only answer open to Friedman and the other defenders of the constitutive a priori is that such propositions really *are* mere conventions despite their protestations to the contrary.[12] However, it is then hard to see how the constitutivist view is anything more than a nominally disguised and rather traditional conventionalist view like that of Poincaré or Duhem, or perhaps a form of more modern

---

[11] In his 2002a Friedman attempts to sidestep this issue by noting that in the particular case of relativistic mechanics, the choice of constitutive principles was limited to one set and forced and not a matter of arbitrary choice. Nevertheless, this neither shows how that principle is epistemically justified nor is it clear that the case generalizes.

[12] See Friedman 2002a and DeSalle 2002 in particular.

conventionalism like that of the Carnap of "Empiricism, Semantics and Ontology." More interestingly, since such propositions appear to be nothing more than disguised conventions, it is not at all clear that epistemological naturalists would need to disagree with anything Friedman and the other constitutivists claim concerning the a priori. Presumably, as conventions, such propositions are not epistemically justified in any way and so they are not a kind of non-a-posteriori knowledge, because they are not a kind of knowledge at all. If this is so, then so much for the radical rebellion against naturalism that Friedman, in particular, makes so much of. Nevertheless, on a more positive note, what Friedman and the other constitutivists may have constructively pointed out is that naturalists might well want to avail themselves of some of the tools of conventionalism if that view is indeed defensible.[13]

5. The Revision of Constitutive A Priori Propositions

The second critical point to be raised here against Friedman and the other constitutivists concerns the account of the rationality of the revision of constitutive a priori principles. Perhaps while there is no coherent sense in which constitutive principles are epistemically justified with respect to empirical data in the static sense, maybe there is some sense in which their revision is rational or rule governed so as to make their adoption something more than arbitrary. Friedman, specifically, appeals to the role of philosophical metaframeworks and to Jurgen Habermas's concept of communicative rationality in order to ground the claim that such revisions are not merely anarchical and essentially arbitrary in the way that the adoption of mere conventions is. This possibility seems promising as Friedman explicitly states that the main merit of the constitutivist view is that it makes better sense of the dynamic history of science than Quine's holistic naturalism does (2000, 373).

However, when we grant his claim that even philosophical metaframework propositions are revisable, it is difficult to see how there can really be any substantial and non-Whiggish sense in which such transitions could be epistemically rational. The point is not overly difficult to see and simply amounts to the recognition that if philosophical metaframework propositions are themselves required to make rational changes in properly empirical law propositions and constitutive principles, then how can the revision

---

[13] Stump (2003) is more candid about the identification of the constitutive a priori with the conventional, but he still stubbornly resists accepting that the view is only nominally different than Quine's. See Ben-Menahem 2001 and DiSalle 2002, as well as Friedman 2002a for discussions of conventionalism.

of philosophical propositions be rational without inviting viscous regress? If there are no unrevisable philosophical framework propositions and such propositions are not themselves empirical, then the very possibility of the justification of such principles is thrown into serious question. To wit, these philosophical principles seem as if they may simply be arbitrary and parochial in the manner that Peirce suggested in "The Fixation of Belief" and which Kuhn built his early philosophy of science on. Peirce famously tells us of the a priori method of fixing belief that, "It makes of inquiry something similar to the development of taste; but taste, unfortunately, is always more or less a matter of fashion" (1877, 119). More crucially that the constitutivists fail to offer even a rudimentary theory of justification with respect to philosophical framework propositions merely exacerbates the problems concerning the justification of constitutive a priori principles in the sciences discussed in the previous section, and the epistemic bona fides of such constitutive principles can be challenged from above as well as from below. If there are no conditions on the rationality of the principles by which constitutive propositions are revised and the acceptance of philosophical metaframework principles is nonrational then there is simply no compellingly rational reason to adopt one set of constitutive principles rather than another.

Nevertheless, from a retrospective perspective Friedman tells us that science is, by its nature, a continuous, cumulative, and convergent endeavor (2000, 379–81), even if there is more than one series by which this convergence could be achieved. This idea of how science progresses amounts to the claims that science obeys the following norms:

C1 [*continuity*] — any given series of temporally ordered theories in a given domain *should* exhibit continuous evolution (i.e. the historical progression of theories in any given domain should have no gaps).

C2 [*cumulativity*] — for any two theories related as precursor and successor, the successor theory *should* be the most conservative revision of the precursor theory that eliminates the precursor theory's empirical inadequacy (i.e. more sophisticated theories, should be minimally revised, corrected, versions of less sophisticated theories).

C3 [*convergence*] — the process of continuous and conservative revision should ultimately result in the production of a unique theory.[14]

---

[14] Friedman accepts this norm in a restricted sense. Specifically, he leaves the possibility open that there may be more than one such convergent sequence branching out as science progresses. So he accepts it only in the sense that for each continuous and conservative sequence that can be relatively isolated from other branches of the overall sequence, it will converge to some terminal theory (2001, 68).

The claim that properly conducted science obeys these norms is made in direct opposition to the purely relativistic interpretation of Kuhn, and Friedman argues that Kuhn himself was ultimately forced to concede that there were essential features of science (2001, 47–68). More importantly, the fact that science is supposed to be a series of theories exhibiting these features is precisely the reason why a sufficient degree of communicative rationality is preserved across revolutionary changes. Consider Friedman's claim:

> Let us first remind ourselves that, despite the fact that we radically change our constitutive principles in the revolutionary transition from one conceptual framework to another, there is still an important element of *convergence* in the very same revolutionary process of conceptual change . . . key elements of the preceding paradigm are preserved as approximate special cases in the succeeding paradigm.
>
> This type of convergence between successive paradigms allows us to define a *retrospective* notion of inter-framework rationality based on the constitutive principles of the later conceptual framework: since the constitutive principles of the earlier framework are contained in those of the later as an approximate special case, the constitutive principles of the later framework are thus fully contained in the earlier framework. (2000, 379)

Such changes are supposed to be rational because we can, from the perspective of a latter theory, capture the mathematical structure of the former theory as a special case, even if the theories are, from the perspective of content, incommensurable (2001, 379, 381). Moreover, once this is admitted Friedman then allows for a prospective account of the rationality of theory change. This essentially amounts to the claim that new constitutive frameworks grow naturally out of old theories by a series of continuous and conservative transformations governed by the specific philosophical metaprinciples in place at the time (2000, 379–83, 2001 60–68). Of this aspect of philosophy with respect to the sciences Friedman himself says that,

> Science, if it to continue to progress through revolutions, therefore, needs a source of new ideas, alternative programs, and expanded possibilities that is not itself scientific in this sense—that does not, as do the sciences themselves, operate within a generally agreed upon framework of taken for granted rules. For what is needed here is precisely the creation and stimulation of new frameworks of paradigms—new conceptions of what a coherent rational understanding of nature might amount to—capable of motivating and sustaining the revolutionary transition to a new first-level scientific paradigm. (2001, 23)

But, why should we accept these particular philosophical principles about theory change? More importantly why should we suppose either that they are justified or that they justify the resultant constitutive frameworks that they give rise to? This is especially troubling as metaframeworks are revisable and not necessarily true in the conventional sense of the expression. If, on the one hand, we interpret the commitment to C1–C3 in the sort of Quinean manner suggested in the passage above, i.e. that we simply accept that that is how science works (at least as it is currently understood),[15] then Friedman is again guilty of masquerading what appear to be pure philosophical conventions as rationally grounded principles at the level of philosophical frameworks. If, on the other hand, we take it not as a sort of definitional claim, but rather as a claim descriptive of actual practice, then, as Laudan (1981) in particular has so forcefully shown, the retrospective claim is simply false of the history of science and it is well known that theory revision does not necessarily yield unique results. Consequently, the prospective notion of rationality does little in the way of offering a concept of justification appropriate for constitutive principles that would yield the results desired by the constitutivists. With respect to this latter issue, consider Friedman claims that,

> the present conception of scientific rationality need not imply the elimination of contingency from scientific progress, in the sense that there is a single preordained route through the set of all possible constitutive principles, as it were, which the evolution of science necessarily follows at each stage. On the contrary, we can, if we like, imagine a branching tree structure at every point, so that *alternative future evolutions of our fundamental constitutive principles are always possible*. (2001, 68, my italics)

So Friedman and the other constitutivists cannot seemingly accept the descriptive tactic if they are to maintain that their methodological account of science is superior to its competitors on the basis that it offers a better explanation of the dynamic history of science. As a result, it appears as if the constitutivists must accept the former view.

The obvious consequence of this is then that the particular picture of science as prospectively continuous and retrospectively cumulative and convergent is at best a parochial convention that may happen to be in place at a given time, and thereby the various specific constitutive principles of scientific theories accepted at various periods in the history of science are accepted neither on the basis of direct empirical testing nor are they (necessarily) the result of the outcome of some fixed and rational rule-governed evolution. This must be the case because according to the constitutivists philosophical principles themselves are not fixed and unrevisable, and so at best what we have are something like relative, or instrumental, standards of

---

[15] See Shaffer and Warnick 2004 for discussion of Quine's view of science.

rationality adopted arbitrarily to appeal to as guiding science and it is surely a serious question whether that is any sort of rationality at all.[16] More importantly, it should be obvious that there is then a serious tension, if not outright, contradiction, in the constitutivist view. Science is supposed to be rational and our adoption of constitutive principles nonarbitrary because science is defined by the philosophical principles C1–C3 so that a minimal sense of communicative rationality is preserved across revolutions, but those philosophical principles are neither themselves the object of rational acceptance nor need science have this character, because the principles are themselves revisable. In other words science is supposed to be defined by C1–C3, but these principles are not, at the same time, essential features of science. Moreover, absent C1–C3 science would be anarchical and on a par with all sorts of allegedly less rational endeavors in the most extreme Feyerabendian sense. But, more importantly yet, without some justification for adopting these philosophical principles, there is simply no sense in which constitutive principles, and hence empirical laws, in the actual sciences are anything but conventions derived, but not even uniquely derived, from the arbitrary assumption of those philosophical principles.

Thus Friedman appears to be claiming that the adoption of constitutive principles is rational because science is governed by the philosophical principles C1–C3, but those principles are not (and cannot be) independently justified.[17] Moreover, what could we appeal to in order to justify the kind of epistemic conservatism suggested by these principles? Given the constitutivist view we cannot appeal to more philosophical reasons in order to justify philosophical metaframework principles without inviting a regress of arbitrary stipulations, and no empirical reasons can possibly do the job because Friedman tells us that,

> it is folly for philosophy to try to incorporate itself into the sciences (as a branch of psychology, say, or mathematical logic), for its particular role is precisely to articulate and stimulate new possibilities at the meta-scientific level, as it were, and it cannot, on pain of entirely relinquishing this role, itself assume the position of a normal science. (2001, 24)

---

[16] See Siegel 1996.

[17] To be sure, the simple undermining of the constitutivists view in the manner pursued here is not itself alone sufficient to warrant the endorsement of Quinean naturalized holism. If the arguments here show that the constitutivist view is really nothing more than a disguised version of Carnapian-style conventionalism, then that is still a far cry from Quine's view. To turn such an argument into a more thorough and supportive argument in favor of the Quinean view would require a serious rebuttal of Carnapian conventionalism. That is, however, not the purpose of this particular paper.

The only other options appear to be either that in such periods we simply accept certain philosophical principles without question or that they are a priori self-justified in some more substantial nonconstitutive sense. However, the latter option is not one that is obviously open to constitutivists as they appear to reject the view that such truths are necessary and that they are knowable a priori in the more traditional sense (i.e. independent of any empirical justification). What we are left with then is either an almost thoroughly skeptical conventionalism from top to bottom. As such, the illusion of objective rationality as it applies to constitutive principles is preserved *only* by the arbitrary imposition of C1–C3 as a panacea against radical incommensurability and dynamic anarchy, but in the same breath we are told (at least by implication) that those principles are ultimately up for grabs! So we are left with the view that it is "rational" to adopt certain constitutive principles of specific empirical theories at certain times because they contain prior rejected theories as special cases and out of which they smoothly evolved, and not because they are empirically verified. Why is this so? The adoption of such constitutive principles is supposed to be rational and not conventional because science is continuous, cumulative and convergent. Why is science like this? We are to suppose that it is (which is just false) and we are also asked to suppose that it need not really have this character as philosophical principles are revisable and cannot, without inviting regress, be rational in the scientific or philosophical sense.

6. An Awkward Balancing Act

So, it should be clear that while the constitutivists have attempted to offer a new, scientifically grounded, theory of a priori knowledge in opposition to the holistic naturalized epistemology of Quine and his intellectual followers, the account they offer is ultimately unsatisfactory from an epistemological perspective, whatever its historical merits. This seems to be the case, because they have failed to even address the issue of the justification of a priori propositions. In attempting to balance their view on the knife-edge between pure conventionalism and an outright Kantian acceptance of the synthetic a priori, they have inherited the worst aspects of both views. We are left with what amounts to a deeply skeptical view of a science saturated with conventions governed by arbitrary, and highly dubious, philosophical principles. As a result, the constitutivist view appears to be nothing more than a nominally disguised form of the most radical conventionalism, and, as such, in that it fails to show that a priori principles are at all epistemically justifiable, it poses no threat to a thorough-going naturalism.[18] What is not justifiable cannot be knowledge and what is not knowledge, cannot ipso facto be nonnaturalistic knowledge. [19]

REFERENCES

Bealer, G. 1992. The Incoherence of Empiricism. *The Aristotelian Society*, supp. vol. 66: 99–138.
———. 2000. A Theory of the A Priori. *Pacific Philosophical Quarterly* 81: 1–30.
Ben-Menahem, Y. 2001. Convention: Poincaré and Some of his Critics. *British Journal for the Philosophy of Science* 52: 471–513.
Boghossian, P., and C. Peacocke. 2000. *New Essays on the A Priori*. Oxford University Press: Oxford.
BonJour, L. 1998. *In Defense of Pure Reason*. Cambridge University Press: Cambridge.
DiSalle, R. 2002. Conventionalism and Modern Physics: A Re-Assessment. *Nous* 36: 169–200.
DiPierris, G. 1992. The Constitutive A Priori. *Canadian Journal of Philosophy* (suppl.) 18: 179–214.
Friedman, M. 1992. *Kant and the Exact Sciences*. Cambridge: Harvard University Press.
———. 1999. *Reconsidering Logical Positivism*. Cambridge: Cambridge University Press.
———. 2000. Transcendental Philosophy and A Priori Knowledge: A Neo-Kantian Perspective. In P. Boghossian and C. Peacocke 2000, 367–83.
———. 2001. *The Dynamics of Reason*. CSLI Publications: Stanford.
———. 2002a. Geometry as a Branch of Physics: Background and Context for Einstein's "Geometry and Experience." In *Reading Natural Philosophy*, ed. D. Malament, 193–230 Open Court: Chicago.
———. 2002b. Kant, Kuhn and the Rationality of Science. *Philosophy of Science* 69: 171–90.
Kornblith, H. 1994. *Naturalizing Epistemology*. 2nd ed. MIT Press: Cambridge.
Laudan, L. 1981. A Confutation of Convergent Realism. *Philosophy of Science* 48: 19–49.
Peacocke, C. 2000. Explaining the A Priori: The Program of Moderate Rationalism, in P. Boghossian and C. Peacocke 2000, 255–85.
———. 2004. *The Realm of Reason*. Cambridge: Clarendon Press.
Peirce, C. S. 1877. The Fixation of Belief. *Popular Science Monthly* 12: 1–15.

---

[18] The issue of how apparently philosophical normative principles of this sort can be justified in discussed in Shaffer 2007.

[19] The author would like to thank Hal Brown, Michael Veber and the participants of the A Priori Knowledge in Contemporary Epistemology conference arranged by the Canadian Society for Epistemology, Sherbrook, Québec, Canada 2004, where an earlier version of this paper was presented.

Reichenbach, H. 1920/1965. *The Theory of Relativity and A Priori Knowledge*. Berkeley: University of California Press.
Shaffer, M. 2007. Bealer on the Autonomy of Philosophical and Scientific Knowledge *Metaphilosophy* 38: 44–54.
Shaffer, M., and J. Warnick. 2004. Bursting Bealer's Bubble: How the Starting Points Argument Begs the Question of Foundationalism against Quine. *Canadian Journal of Philosophy* 34: 87–106.
Siegel, H. 1996. Instrumental Rationality and Naturalized Philosophy of Science. *Philosophy of Science* 63: 116–24.
Stump, D. 2003. Defending Conventions as Functionally A Priori Knowledge, *Philosophy of Science* 70: 1149–60.

[11]

A Priori Conjectural Knowledge in Physics: The Comprehensibility of the Universe

NICHOLAS MAXWELL

1

The a priori both must, and cannot possibly, play a role in physics. There are powerful arguments in support of both horns of this dilemma.

I begin with the well-known arguments against a priori knowledge. All our knowledge about the world is acquired via experience. A priori knowledge about the world—knowledge based on an appeal to reason, independently of experience—is thus impossible. Reason is not some kind of intellectual searchlight that can, independently of observation and experiment, illuminate the world and provide us with infallible knowledge about it. All propositions that can be known to be true with certainty, in an a priori way, independently of experience—propositions like "either it is raining or it is not raining" or "all bachelors are unmarried"—are empty of factual content. And all propositions which have some factual content, which say something about the world, can only be known with some degree of uncertainty as a result of our experience of or interactions with the world—as a result of observation or experiment. As Einstein once put it, "as far as propositions refer to reality, they are not certain; and as far as they are certain, they do not refer to reality."[1]

This unquestionably represents the orthodox view among scientists and philosophers of science. Not all philosophers would, however, be convinced by this bald statement of the case for the nonexistence of a priori knowledge in science. Some might claim that the case for a priori knowledge is supported by Kripke's (1981) argument that identity statements with rigid designators are necessary—a statement such as that water is identical to H_2O being, according to Kripke, despite its factual appearance,

---

[1] This generalizes Einstein's remark, which was restricted to *mathematical* propositions see Einstein 1973 (233).

nevertheless *necessary*. Kripke would not himself hold this; he makes it quite clear that necessity and the a priori must be sharply distinguished. And in any case, Kripke's case for the necessity of identity statements with rigid designators is, in my view, not valid, as I have argued in some detail elsewhere (see Maxwell 2001, appendix 2).

I should add, in passing, that the anti-a-priori view, just indicated, can readily accommodate the thesis that necessary connections may exist between successive events or states of affairs. For we may hold that necessary connections exist but cannot be known to exist in an a priori fashion, with certainty. Elsewhere I have argued, along these lines, that necessary connections in nature are indeed possible, and that theoretical physics should be interpreted as improving our knowledge of their character. (See Maxwell 1968; 1976a; 1985; 1988; 1998, 141–55 and ch. 7).[2]

2

So much for the case *against* the a priori in science. The argument *for* a priori knowledge in science is not nearly so well known. It is an argument I have been advocating for over twenty years, but so far this advocacy has not had much impact. Nevertheless the argument is, I believe, decisive. It goes like this. Whenever a fundamental physical theory is accepted as a part of theoretical scientific knowledge there are always endlessly many rival theories which fit the available evidence just as well as the accepted theory. Consider, for example, Newtonian theory (NT). One rival theory asserts: everything occurs as NT asserts up till midnight tonight when, abruptly, an inverse cube law of gravitation comes into operation. A second rival asserts: everything occurs as NT asserts, except for the case of any two solid gold spheres, each having a mass of a thousand tons, moving in otherwise empty space up to a mile apart, in which case the spheres attract each other by means of an inverse cube law of gravitation. There is no limit to the number of rivals to NT that can be concocted in this way, each of which has all the predictive success of NT as far as observed phenomena are concerned but which makes different predictions for some as yet unobserved phenomena.[3] Such "patchwork quilt" theories can even be concocted which

---

[2] Some years after my 1968 paper refuting Hume on causation, Armstrong and Tooley put forward anti-Humean accounts of laws and causation, taking no account of my earlier work: see Armstrong (1988) and Tooley (1977, 1987). Armstrong and Tooley have been, in my view, decisively criticized by van Fraassen (1989, Part I). Van Fraassen fails to take into account my earlier, 1968 refutation of Hume, and his criticisms of Armstrong and Tooley are not applicable to my account.

[3] All the possible phenomena, predicted by any dynamical physical theory, T, may be

are *more* empirically successful than NT, by arbitrarily modifying NT, in just this entirely ad hoc fashion, so that the theories yield correct predictions where NT does not, as in the case of the orbit of Mercury for example (which very slightly conflicts with NT).[4] And quite generally, given any accepted physical theory, T, there will always be endlessly many "patchwork quilt" rivals which meet with all the empirical success of T, make untested predictions that differ from T, are empirically successful where T is ostensibly refuted, and successfully predict phenomena about which T is silent (as a result of independently testable and corroborated hypotheses being added on).

As most physicists and philosophers of physics would accept, *two* criteria are employed in physics in deciding what theories to accept and reject: (1) empirical criteria, and (2) criteria that have to do with the simplicity, unity or explanatory character of the theories in question. What the argument just indicated demonstrates is that (2) is absolutely indispensable, to such an extent that there are endlessly many theories empirically more successful than accepted theories, all of which are ignored because of their "patchwork quilt" character, their lack of unity.

Now comes the crucial point. In persistently accepting unifying theories (even though ostensibly refuted), and excluding infinitely many empirically more successful, unrefuted, disunified, "patchwork quilt," rival theories, science in effect makes a big assumption about the nature of the universe, to the effect that it is such that no disunified theory is true, however empirically successful it may appear to be for a time. Furthermore, without some such big assumption as this, the empirical method of science collapses. Science would be drowned in an infinite ocean of empirically successful disunified theories.[5]

---

represented by an imaginary "space," S, each point in S corresponding to a particular phenomenon, a particular kind of physical system evolving in time in the way predicted by T. In order to specify severely disunified rivals to T that fit all available evidence just as well as T does, all we need do is specify a region in S that consists of phenomena that have not been observed, and then replace the phenomena predicted by T with anything we care to think of. Given any T, there will always be infinitely many such disunified rivals to T. This point is inherent in Nelson Goodman's "new paradox of induction" (see Goodman 1954), although the kind of empirically successful disunified rivals considered by Goodman in his discussion of "grue" and "bleen" are but one kind of a number of kinds of disunified theories, as we shall see in section 3. There is a vast philosophical literature on the underdetermination of theory by evidence: for an excellent recent discussion, and reference to further literature, see Howson 2000 (see especially ch. 1, 30–34, 75–77, and ch. 5). See also Lipton 2004.

[4] For a more detailed discussion of empirically successful ad hoc rivals to accepted theories, see Maxwell 1974, 1993 and 1998 (51–54).

[5] It may be objected that the universe might have been genuinely disunified, so that physics could consist only of a great number of physical laws. In this case, it may be argued, physics could not be construed as making a metaphysical assumption about underlying

If scientists only accepted theories that postulate atoms, and persistently rejected theories that postulate different basic physical entities, such as fields—even though many field theories can easily be, and have been, formulated which are even more empirically successful than the atomic theories—the implications would surely be quite clear. Scientists would in effect be assuming that the world is made up of atoms, all other possibilities being ruled out. The atomic assumption would be built into the way the scientific community accepts and rejects theories—built into the implicit *methods* of the community, methods which include: reject all theories that postulate entities other than atoms, whatever their empirical success might be. The scientific community would accept the assumption: the universe is such that no nonatomic theory is true.

Just the same holds for a scientific community which rejects all disunified or aberrant rivals to accepted theories, even though these rivals would be even more empirically successful if they were considered. Such a community in effect makes the assumption: the universe is such that no disunified theory is true. Or rather, more accurately, such a community makes the assumption: "the universe is such that no disunified theory is true *which is not entailed by a true unified theory (plus, possibly, true relevant initial and boundary conditions)*." (A true unified theory entails infinitely many approximate, true, disunified theories.) Let us call this assumption "physicalism."

On the face of it, physicalism constitutes a priori scientific knowledge. It is so firmly accepted that any theory which clashes with it is rejected *whatever its empirical success may be*. Far from being accepted on the basis of evidence, it is accepted, if anything, in the teeth of counterevidence, in that, given any accepted unified theory there will always be endlessly many *disunified* rival theories which will not be considered for a moment because they clash with physicalism. The evidence constantly shouts "nature is disunified," and science calmly ignores this evidence and persists in accepting the unity of nature (physicalism) against the clamor of disunity. And furthermore, science must do this. Without the persistent acceptance of physicalism (explicit or implicit) science would be drowned in an ocean of absurd, "patchwork quilt" theories. (For earlier, and in some cases more detailed, expositions of this argument see Maxwell

---

unity. But even in this counterfactual situation, endlessly many very much more disunified but empirically more successful rival laws could easily be formulated: these would have to be rejected on nonempirical grounds, or physics would drown in an ocean of rival laws. The persistent rejection of such much more disunified but empirically more successful rivals would involve the methods of physics making an implicit metaphysical assumption, to the effect that nature is unified to some extent at least (all grossly disunified laws being false). It is necessary to make some such assumption, however disunified the totality of accepted laws may be—even if the assumption made is rather weak in character, in that only gross disunity is denied.

1974; 1984, ch. 9; 1993; and especially 1998; 2004a, chs. 1 and 2, and appendix; and 1984, 2nd ed., 2007, ch. 14.)

That is the case *for* a priori scientific knowledge.

3

How is the dilemma with which we began to be resolved? This is not too difficult a question to answer. The argument against the a priori is against knowledge which can be established *with certainty* by reason independently of experience. The argument for the a priori is merely for knowledge which is accepted on grounds other than an appeal to experience, and which may well be *conjectural* in character. Thus in order to resolve the dilemma all we need do is agree that we have a priori knowledge in the sense of *conjectural* knowledge accepted on grounds other than evidence, but not in the sense of *indubitable* knowledge established by reason alone. All hope of having knowledge that has Kantian "apodictic certainty" must be abandoned.

It needs to be appreciated that this claim—that there is just one item of *conjectural* a priori knowledge, namely physicalism—though relatively modest, is nevertheless blatantly at odds with orthodoxy. It clashes with just about every philosophy of science one can think of put forward in the last century: logical positivism, inductivism, logical empiricism, hypothetico-deductivism, conventionalism, constructive empiricism, pragmatism, realism, induction-to-the-best-explanationism, Bayesianism, and the views of Duhem (1954), Popper (1959), Quine (1953), Kuhn (1962), Lakatos (1968), and most more recent authors on the subject. For all these views, diverse as they are in other respects, all accept that *no factual proposition about the world can be accepted permanently as a part of scientific knowledge independently of empirical considerations*. According to this view, the simplicity, unity, or explanatory power of a theory may influence its acceptance in addition to empirical considerations, but not in such a way as to commit science permanently to the thesis that nature herself is simple, unified, or comprehensible. This view (which elsewhere I have called *standard empiricism*) is starkly incompatible with the thesis that physicalism constitutes a priori knowledge.

If the above argument for a priori scientific knowledge is valid, then standard empiricism, and all the above views which incorporate standard empiricism (logical positivism, inductivism, etc.), must be rejected. But is the above argument valid? In what follows considerations will emerge which require that the argument is *revised*, but not *rejected*.

As it stands, the above argument for the a priori character of physicalism raises a number of questions. (1) What exactly does it *mean* to assert of a physical theory that it is unified? Once this question has been answered, we can go on to tackle the question (2) What ought physicalism to be interpreted to assert about the universe? The case for claiming that physicalism is an a priori conjectural presupposition of physics rests on the claim that physics only accepts unified theories: hence the need to answer (1) before we can answer (2). Closely related to (2) is the question: (3) What rationale is there for accepting physicalism as a part of scientific knowledge? And finally, and most germane to the subject of this essay, and this book, there is the question: (4) Is physicalism really wholly a priori in character? Can we not imagine circumstances in which science, or at least the pursuit of knowledge, would be possible even though physicalism is false and is rejected? Does not this suffice to establish that physicalism is not a priori? If it is not, is there any item of scientific knowledge that is wholly a priori in character, wholly untainted by the empirical?

The rest of this essay is devoted to answering these four questions in turn.

4

(1) *What exactly does it mean to assert of a physical theory that it is unified?* This is a notorious, long-unsolved problem in the philosophy of science. Einstein recognized the problem but confessed he did not know how to solve it (Einstein 1982, 23). J. J. C. Smart once declared it to be one of the most important unsolved problems in the philosophy of science (Salmon 1989, 4). Many attempts have been made at solving the problem, none satisfactory.[6] The main difficulty is that any given theory can be formulated in many different ways, some formulations being beautifully simple and "unified," others being horribly complex and "disunified." The crucial step that needs to be taken to solve the problem is to recognize that what matters is what a given theory asserts about the world. In assessing the simplicity or unity of the theory it is its *content* that is important; the form of the theory is irrelevant. What has made the problem so hard to solve is that those trying to solve it have been staring at the wrong thing, the theory itself, its linguistic or axiomatic structure, its pattern of deriva-

---

[6] For a criticism of the attempts of Popper (1959, ch. 7; 1963, 241), Friedman (1974), Kitcher (1981, 1989) and Watkins (1984, 203–13), see Maxwell 1998 (60–68). For criticisms of these and other attempts, see Salmon 1989. More recent, unsuccessful attempts at solving the problem are: McAllister 1996, Weber 1999, Schurz 1999, and Bartelborth 2002. For criticism of McAllister, see Maxwell 2004b and 2004c; for criticism of Weber, Schurz and Bartelborth see Maxwell 2004b.

tions, when they should have been looking at *what the theory asserts about the world.*[7]

The solution to the problem is in fact implicit in the above argument for the a priori character of physicalism. There, a distinction was drawn between unified and "patchwork quilt," disunified theories. This is the heart of the matter. A unified theory is one which makes the same assertion—which specifies the same dynamical laws—throughout the range of phenomena to which it applies. A disunified theory is one which makes different assertions—which specifies different dynamical laws—in different regions of phenomena to which the theory applies. If a theory, T, specifies N distinct dynamical laws governing the evolution of phenomena in N distinct regions of phenomena, than T is disunified to degree N. For unity we require $N = 1$.

But there is an important complication. It turns out that there are *different* ways in which the content, the dynamical laws, can be different as we move from one range of phenomena to another—some of these ways being much more extreme than others. Here are eight increasingly mild kinds of disunity.

A dynamical physical theory, T, is disunified to degree N if and only if:

(1) T divides space-time up into N distinct regions, $R_1...R_N$, and asserts that the laws governing the evolution of phenomena are the same for all spacetime regions within each R-region, but are different in different R-regions.
(2) T postulates that, for distinct ranges of physical variables (other than position and time), such as mass or relative velocity, in distinct regions, $R_1,...R_N$ of the space of all possible phenomena, distinct dynamical laws obtain.
(3) In addition to postulating nonunique physical entities (such as particles), or entities unique but not spatially restricted (such as fields), T postulates, in an arbitrary fashion, $N - 1$ distinct, unique, spatially localized objects, each with its own distinct, unique dynamic properties.
(4) T postulates physical entities interacting by means of N distinct forces, different forces affecting different entities, and being specified by different force laws. (In this case one would require one force to be universal so that the universe does not fall into distinct parts that do not interact with one another.)

---

[7] The solution to the problem of unity of theory—the problem of what it means to say of a theory that it is explanatory—outlined here, summarizes a more detailed account to be found in Maxwell 1998, chs. 3 and 4. See also Maxwell 2004a (Appendix, section [2]); 2004b; and 2004d.

(5) T postulates N different kinds of physical entity, differing with respect to some dynamic property, such as value of mass or charge, but otherwise interacting by means of the same force.

(6) Consider a theory, T, that postulates N distinct kinds of entity (e.g. particles or fields), but these N entities can be regarded as arising because T exhibits some symmetry (in the way that the electric and magnetic fields of classical electromagnetism can be regarded as arising because of the symmetry of Lorentz invariance, or the eight gluons of chromodynamics can be regarded as arising as a result of the local gauge symmetry of SU[3]).[8] If the symmetry group, G, is not a direct product of subgroups, we can declare that T is fully unified; if G is a direct product of subgroups, T lacks full unity; and if the N entities are such that they cannot be regarded as arising as a result of some symmetry of T, with some group structure G, then T is disunified.

(7) If (apparent) disunity of there being N distinct kinds of particle or distinct fields has emerged as a result of a series of cosmic spontaneous symmetry-breaking events, there being manifest unity before these occurred, then the relevant theory, T, is unified. If current (apparent) disunity has not emerged from unity in this way, as a result of spontaneous symmetry-breaking, then the relevant theory, T, is disunified.[9]

(8) According to GR, Newton's force of gravitation is merely an aspect of the curvature of spacetime. As a result of a change in our ideas about the nature of spacetime, so that its geometric properties become dynamic, a physical force disappears, or becomes unified with spacetime. This suggests the following requirement for unity: spacetime on the one hand, and physical particles-and-forces on the other, must be unified into a single self-interacting entity, U. If T postulates spacetime and physical "particles-and-forces" as two fundamentally distinct kinds of entity, then T is not unified in this respect.

For unity, in each case, we require $N = 1$. As we go from (1) to (5), the requirements for unity are intended to be accumulative: each presupposes

---

[8] An informal sketch of these matters is given in Maxwell 1998, ch. 4, sections 11 to 13, and the appendix. For rather more detailed accounts of the locally gauge invariant structure of quantum field theories see: Moriyasu 1983, Aitchison and Hey 1982 (part III), and Griffiths 1987 (ch. 11). For introductory accounts of group theory as it arises in physics see Isham 1989 or Jones 1990.

[9] For accounts of spontaneous symmetry breaking see Moriyasu 1983 or Mandl and Shaw 1984.

that N = 1 for previous requirements. As far as (6) and (7) are concerned, if there are N distinct kinds of entity which are not unified by a symmetry, whether broken or not, then the degree of disunity is the same as that for (4) and (5), depending on whether there are N distinct forces, or one force but N distinct kinds of entity between which the force acts.

(8) introduces, not a new kind of unity, but rather a new, more severe way of counting different kinds of entity. (1) to (7) taken together require, for unity, that there is one kind of self-interacting physical entity evolving in a distinct spacetime, the way this entity evolves being specified, of course, by a consistent physical theory. According to (1) to (7), even though there are, in a sense, two kinds of entity, matter (or particles-and-forces) on the one hand, and spacetime on the other, nevertheless N = 1. According to (8), this would yield N = 2. For N = 1, (8) requires matter and spacetime to be unified into one basic entity (unified by means of a spontaneously broken symmetry, perhaps).

As we go from (1) to (8), then, requirements for unity become increasingly demanding, with (6) and (7) being at least as demanding as (4) and (5), as explained above.[10] It is important to appreciate, however, that (1) to (8) are all versions of the same basic idea that T is unified if and only if the content of T is the same throughout the range of possible phenomena to which it applies. When T is disunified, (1) to (8) specify *different* kinds of difference in the content of T in diverse regions of the space, S, of all possible phenomena to which T applies. Or, equivalently, (1) to (8) divide S into sub-regions in *different* ways, T having a different content in each sub-region.[11]

5

(2) *What ought physicalism to be interpreted to assert about the universe?* (3) *What rationale is there for accepting physicalism as a part of scientific knowledge?* Before I answer these two closely interrelated questions, I must first

---

[10] The account of theoretical unity given here simplifies the account given in Maxwell 1998, chs. 3 and 4, where unity is explicated as "exemplifying physicalism," where physicalism is a metaphysical thesis asserting that the universe has some kind of unified dynamic structure. Explicating unity in that way invites the charge of circularity, a charge that is not actually valid see Maxwell 1998 (118–23 and 168–72). The account given in this paper forestalls this charge from the outset. See also Maxwell 2004a (appendix, section 2).

[11] It may be doubted that it is possible to distinguish unambiguously between theories that do, and theories that do not postulate *the same* dynamical laws throughout the range of phenomena to which the theory applies. Such doubts may stem from Goodman's arguments concerning "grue" and "bleen" (see Goodman 1954), and from other considerations. For a rebuttal of these doubts and arguments see Maxwell 1998 (ch. 4); 2004a (appendix, section 2).

consider how the account of unity of theory just given both clarifies and complicates the argument for the a priori of section 2. Two points in particular need to be made.

The first is this. Above it was more or less taken for granted that a single disunified theory cannot be turned into two or more unified theories merely by chopping it into a number of distinct theories, each of which is unified. If this assumption is incorrect, the methodological requirement that an acceptable theory must be unified is in danger of becoming one which can always be fulfilled quite trivially, by the simple device of chopping any disunified theory into many unified theories. For theories that are disunified in ways (1) to (3), the assumption is valid. Thus a theory disunified in space and/or time cannot be turned into a number of unified theories, each restricted to specific regions of space and/or time, since physical theories so restricted may be deemed to be disunified just because of that arbitrary restriction. In the case of a theory disunified in a type (4) or (5) way, however, it would be possible, so it would seem, to chop the theory into a number of distinct theories, each postulating just one kind of force, or one kind of entity, and thus each being unified in a type (4) or type (5) way.

In order to exclude this trivial maneuver, the methodological requirement that a theory must be unified to be acceptable must be reformulated so that it applies to the whole of fundamental theory in physics—to all those theories which, in sum, apply in principle to all physical phenomena. Today, this sum consists of the so-called standard model (the quantum field theory of fundamental particles and forces) and general relativity.[12] (If a range of phenomena has no fundamental theory associated with it, then laws governing the phenomena must be included among fundamental physical theory.) The methodological requirement of theoretical unity can now be stated like this: A new fundamental physical theory, in order to be acceptable on nonempirical grounds, must be such that, when added to the totality of fundamental physical theory (perhaps replacing one or more precursor theories), the disunity of this totality is decreased (or, as a bare minimal requirement, not increased).

The second point is this. The account of unity of theory of the last section makes clear that, even though this involves a single basic idea (a theory is unified if the dynamical laws it specifies are *the same* for all the phenomena it predicts), nevertheless there are at least eight *different* ways

---

[12] If dark matter and quintessence exist and cannot be accounted for by the standard model and general relativity, then a specification of these phenomena would need to be added to the current disunified "theory of everything." Dark matter is postulated to account for the anomalous rotation of galaxies, which rotate at a rate that would pull them apart unless invisible, unknown extra matter exists—so-called dark matter. Quintessence is a form of energy postulated to be inherent in space that has been postulated to account for the increase in expansion of the universe.

in which dynamical laws can differ, some of these differences being more serious, more substantial, than others. Unity of theory is, as it were, an eight-dimensional concept (at least). In assessing the disunity of a theory of everything, T, we must first assess the worst kind of disunity it suffers from, M = 8, 7, ... 1, and then assess its degree of disunity, N = 1, 2, ..., so that disunity is fixed by two numbers, (M,N). [I have adopted the convention that (8,2) – (7,1).] The smaller M is, the more serious the kind of disunity; the larger N is, the greater the degree of disunity. For perfect unity, we require (8,1).

The argument for the a priori of section 2 needs to be regarded, then, as establishing that physics presupposes physicalism interpreted to assert: the universe is such that the true theory of everything, T, has a less serious *kind* of disunity than the totality of current accepted fundamental physical theory (plus phenomena where there is no theory), and/or a lower *degree* of disunity (or, at the very least, a *kind* of disunity no more serious, and a *degree* of unity no greater, than current fundamental theory).

This clarifies the argument of section 2. But there is a complication. The argument establishes that physics makes metaphysical assumptions, but not that these assumptions are a priori.[13] As physics advances, and greater and greater unity of accepted fundamental physical theory is achieved, so physicalism is repeatedly reinterpreted so that it asserts underlying dynamic unity in stronger and stronger senses. But if physicalism is to be revised in this way, in the light of empirical research, how can it be regarded as a priori?[14]

I defer discussion of what, exactly, is a priori in physics, until later, and consider first the question of what physics *ought* to be taken as presupposing, in the light of what has been said so far, and what reasons there are for adopting such a supposition.

There are six considerations—six methodological principles—that must be taken into account in deciding what physics ought to be taken to be assuming about the nature of the universe—what metaphysical assumption(s) it ought to be taken to be making. I now specify these six

---

[13] Physicalism(M,N), for any relevant value of M and N, is a *metaphysical* thesis because it is too imprecise to be empirically falsifiable (and it is not verifiable either).

[14] It cannot even be argued that physics can be regarded as accepting "the true theory of everything is *at least* as unified as current fundamental physical theory" which, once accepted, may be added to, but will not be subsequently rejected, and may therefore be regarded as a priori. This thesis, for all we can know, may be rejected in the future, in that physicists find that progress in predictive power of theory requires an *increase* in the disunity of accepted fundamental physical theory. Perhaps the increase in theoretical unity in physics that we have witnessed since Galileo has been a lucky streak that will not continue into the future. Whether this is the case or not is an empirical matter, and therefore, on the face of it, not something that can be decided a priori.

considerations in turn, and in each case specify the metaphysical thesis that is picked out. It is vital to appreciate that the following considerations provide grounds for holding that the relevant theses should be *accepted* as a part of scientific knowledge granted that our aim is to discover truth, but do not provide grounds for holding that the theses themselves are *true*.

1. This first consideration is the one we have already encountered above. Physics should accept the least substantial thesis that is implicit in the persistent acceptance of unified theories when empirically more successful disunified theories are always available. This picks out Physicalism(M,N), where M corresponds to a kind of disunity less severe than (or equal to) the kind of disunity of the totality of accepted fundamental physical theory, and N is less than (or equal to) the degree of disunity of the totality of accepted theory.

2. Physics should accept that metaphysical thesis which must be true if the acquisition of knowledge is to be possible at all—knowledge of our local environment required in order to make life possible. This picks out the thesis: the universe is such that we can continue to acquire knowledge of our local environment sufficient to make life possible.

3. Assumptions that are substantial, problematic, influential, and implicit need to be made explicit so that they can be critically assessed and so that alternatives can be considered, in the hope that the assumptions can be *improved*. In the case of physics, that assumption needs to be made explicit which is implicit in the *persistent* choice of unifying theories when this persistence is *pushed to the limit*. The implicit assumption inherent in *persistently* accepting increasingly unifying theories, when pushed to the limit, is that there is underlying dynamic unity in all natural phenomena—that is, physicalism(8,1). The persistent search for greater and greater unity of theory can only be satisfied if physicalism(8,1) is true. (This is not an argument for the *truth* of physicalism(8,1). Rather it is an argument for accepting physicalism(8,1)—granted our aim is to discover truth—so that this thesis, the extreme implicit presupposition of our methodology, may be subjected to maximum critical scrutiny, giving maximum hope of improvement. If the search for unity must ultimately fail because physicalism(8,1) is false, the sooner we discover this fact, and find an improved rival thesis, the better.)

4. Given that some kind of metaphysical thesis must be accepted by physics, that thesis is to be preferred which (if true) holds out the greatest hope of scientific progress. On these grounds, physicalism (8,1) is to be preferred to physicalism(M,N), where (M,N) are the values of currently accepted fundamental physical theory (since the latter thesis holds out no hope of progress in theoretical physics at all).

5. Again, given that some kind of metaphysical thesis must be accepted by physics, that thesis is to be preferred which has supported the most

empirically fruitful scientific research program. This consideration, again, picks out physicalism(8,1). All the great contributions to theoretical physics have brought greater theoretical unity to the subject, and can thus be regarded as constituting stepping stones towards the discovery of underlying dynamic unity in nature. From the seventeenth century to today, theoretical physics constitutes an astonishingly empirically successful research programme progressively moving towards capturing a *unified* theory applicable in principle to *all* phenomena. Unification, in senses (1) to (8) above, is the persistent theme of all the great theoretical revolutions in physics. Thus Newtonian theory (NT) unifies Galileo's laws of terrestrial motion and Kepler's laws of planetary motion (and much else besides): this is unification in senses (1) to (3). Maxwellian classical electrodynamics, (CEM), unifies electricity, magnetism and light (plus radio, infrared, ultraviolet, X and gamma rays): this is unification in sense (4). Special relativity (SR) brings greater unity to CEM, in revealing that the way one divides up the electromagnetic field into the electric and magnetic fields depends on one's reference frame: this is unification in sense (6). SR is also a step towards unifying NT and CEM in that it transforms space and time so as to make CEM satisfy a basic principle fundamental to NT, namely the (restricted) principle of relativity. SR also brings about a unification of matter and energy, via the most famous equation of modern physics, $E = mc^2$, and partially unifies space and time into Minkowskian space-time. General relativity (GR) unifies space-time and gravitation, in that, according to GR, gravitation is no more than an effect of the curvature of space-time—a step towards unification in sense (8). Quantum theory (QM) and atomic theory unify a mass of phenomena having to do with the structure and properties of matter, and the way matter interacts with light: this is unification in senses (4) and (5). Quantum electrodynamics unifies QM, CEM, and SR. Quantum electroweak theory unifies (partially) electromagnetism and the weak force: this is (partial) unification in sense (7). Quantum chromodynamics brings unity to hadron physics (via quarks) and brings unity to the eight kinds of gluons of the strong force: this is unification in sense (6). The standard model (SM) unifies to a considerable extent all known phenomena associated with fundamental particles and the forces between them (apart from gravitation): partial unification in senses (4) to (7). The theory unifies to some extent its two component quantum field theories in that both are locally gauge invariant [the symmetry group being $U(1) \times SU(2) \times SU(3)$]. All the current programs to unify SM and GR known to me, including string theory or M-theory, seek to unify in senses (4) to (8).[15]

---

[15] For further discussion see Maxwell 1998 (80–89, 131–40, 257–65 and additional works referred to therein).

6. Finally, physics has made progress as a result of putting forward bold conjectures that are then subjected to fierce attempted refutation—precisely formulated theories that have immense empirical content and that are then subjected to severe empirical scrutiny. Just the same procedure should operate in the essential *metaphysical* domain of physics. Here too, precisely formulated, bold conjectures should be put forward which are then subjected to fierce critical scrutiny—the more precise and bolder the better, since these are all the more potentially vulnerable (if false) to criticism. This consideration favors physicalism(8,1) over physicalism(M,N), the latter being messy and indefinite (given uncertainties about dark matter and quintessence).

What is striking about these six considerations is that they point in different directions. Some (1 and 2) point in the direction of accepting the most modest, least substantial theses capable of fulfilling the specified role. Others (3 to 6) point in the direction of accepting one of the most immodest, substantial theses conceivable, namely physicalism(8,1). How can these conflicting desiderata all be satisfied?

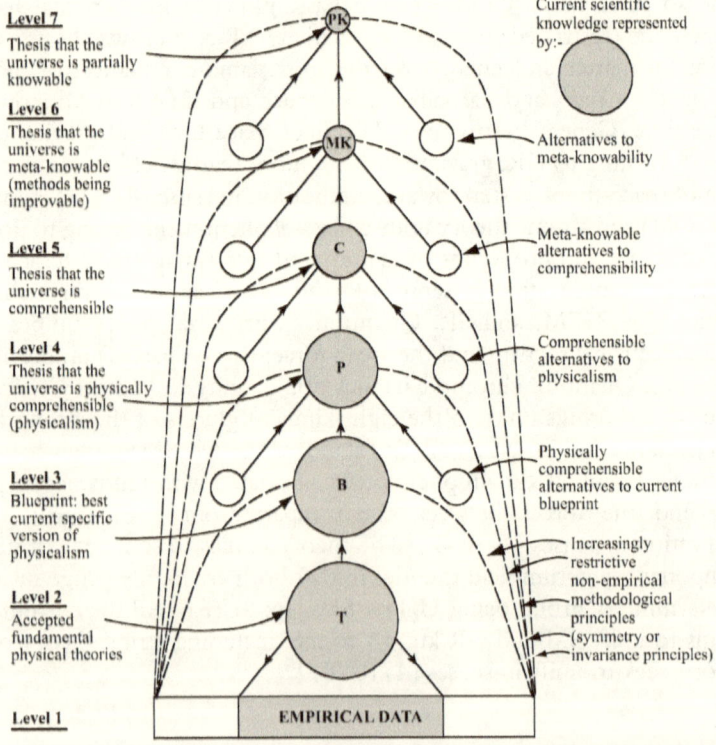

Figure 1. *Aim-Oriented Empiricism (AOE)*

The solution is to see physics as accepting, not just *one* thesis but a *hierarchy* of theses. At the top of the hierarchy there is an insubstantial thesis that must be true if physics, or the acquisition of knowledge more generally, is to be possible at all. As one goes down the hierarchy, the theses become increasingly substantial, potentially increasingly fruitful for the growth of knowledge, but also increasingly likely to be false, and thus increasingly in need of sustained critical scrutiny. One possibility is to take, as this hierarchy, the eight versions of physicalism corresponding to the eight types of unity specified in section 4 above. At the top there is the relatively insubstantial thesis physicalism(1,1), which asserts merely that the true theory of everything is unified in a type (1) way, to degree 1. Near the bottom of the hierarchy there is the very substantial thesis physicalism(8,1), which asserts that the true theory of everything is unified in a type (8) way, to degree 1. For a more detailed exposition and discussion of this version of the hierarchical view see Maxwell 2004d.

The problem with this version of the hierarchical view is that possibilities can be imagined which would render all eight versions of physicalism false, and yet life, the acquisition of knowledge, and even a kind of science, might still be possible. Perhaps God is ultimately in charge of the universe, and all versions of physicalism are false because God on occasions arranges for miracles to occur. Perhaps the universe is comprehensible but not *physically* comprehensible. Perhaps the universe is not comprehensible, all eight versions of physicalism being false, but knowledge can still be acquired. In order to take these possibilities into account, we need to adopt the following more general version of the hierarchical view: see diagram.

At the top of the hierarchy there is the relatively insubstantial assumption that the universe is such that we can acquire some knowledge of our local circumstances. If this assumption is false, we will not be able to acquire knowledge whatever we assume. We are justified in accepting this assumption permanently as a part of our knowledge, even though we have no grounds for holding it to be true. As we descend the hierarchy, the assumptions become increasingly substantial and thus increasingly likely to be false. At level 6 there is the more substantial thesis that there is some rationally discoverable thesis about the nature of the universe, which, if true and if accepted, makes it possible progressively to improve methods for the improvement of knowledge. "Rationally discoverable," here, means at least that the thesis is not an arbitrary choice from infinitely many analogous theses. At level 5 we have the even more substantial thesis that the universe is *comprehensible* in some way or other, whether physically or in some other way. This thesis asserts that the universe is such that there is *something* (God, tribe of gods, cosmic goal, physical entity, cosmic program, or whatever), which exists everywhere in an unchanging form and which, in some sense, determines or is responsible for everything that changes (all change and diversity in the world in principle being explicable and understandable in terms of the underlying unchanging *something*). A universe of this type deserves to be called "comprehensible" because it is such that everything that occurs, all change and diversity, can in principle be explained and understood as being the outcome of the operations of the one underlying *something*, present throughout all phenomena. At level 4 we have the still more substantial thesis that the universe is *physically* comprehensible in some way or other. This asserts that the universe is made up one unified self-interacting physical entity (or one kind of entity), all change and diversity being in principle explicable in terms of this entity. What this amounts to is that the universe is such that some yet-to-be-discovered unified physical theory of everything is true. In terms of the terminology indicated above, this thesis is physicalism(8,1). At level 3, we have an even more substantial thesis, the best, currently available specific idea as to how the universe is physically comprehensible. This asserts that everything is made of some specific kind of physical entity: corpuscle, point-particle, classical field, quantum field, convoluted space-time, string, or whatever. Given the historical record of dramatically changing ideas at this level, and given the relatively highly specific and substantial character of successive assumptions made at this level, we can be reasonably confident that the best assumption available at any stage in the development of physics at this level will be false, and will need future revision. Here, ideas evolve with evolving knowledge. At level 2 there are the accepted fundamental theories of physics, currently general relativity and the standard model. Here, if anything, we can be even more confident that current theories are false, despite their immense empirical success. This confidence comes partly from the vast empirical content of these theories, and partly from the historical record. The greater the content of a proposition the more likely it is to be false; the fundamental theories of physics, general relativity and the standard model have such vast empirical content that this in itself almost guarantees falsity. And the historical record backs this up; Kepler's laws of planetary motion, and Galileo's laws of terrestrial motion are corrected by Newtonian theory, which is in turn corrected by special and general relativity; classical physics is corrected by quantum theory, in turn corrected by relativistic quantum theory, quantum field theory and the standard model. Each new theory in physics reveals that predecessors are false. Indeed, if the level 4 assumption is correct, then all current physical theories are false, since this assumption asserts that the true physical theory of everything is unified, and the totality of current fundamental physical theory, general relativity plus the standard model, is notoriously disunified. Finally, at level 1 there are accepted empirical data, low level, corroborated, empirical laws.[16]

The idea is to separate out what is most likely to be true, and not in need of revision, at and near the top of the hierarchy, from what is most likely to be false, and most in need of criticism and revision, near the bottom of the hierarchy. Evidence, at level 1, and assumptions high up in the hierarchy, are rather firmly accepted, as being most likely to be true (although still open to revision): this is then used to criticize, and to try to improve, theses at levels 2 and 3 (and perhaps 4), where falsity is most likely to be located.

In order to be acceptable, an assumption at any level from 6 to 3 must (as far as possible) be compatible with, and a special case of, the assumption above in the hierarchy; at the same time it must be (or promise to be) empirically fruitful in the sense that successive accepted physical theories increasingly successfully accord with (or exemplify) the assumption. At level 2, those physical theories are accepted which are sufficiently (a) empirically successful and (b) in accord with the best available assumption at level 3 (or level 4). Corresponding to each assumption, at any level from 7 to 3, there is a methodological principle, represented by sloping dotted lines in the diagram, requiring that theses lower down in the hierarchy are compatible with the given assumption.

When theoretical physics has completed its central task, and the true theory of everything, T, has been discovered, then T will (in principle) successfully predict all empirical phenomena at level 1, and will entail the assumption at level 3, which will in turn entail the assumption at level 4, and so on up the hierarchy. As it is, physics has not completed its task, T has not (yet) been discovered, and we are ignorant of the nature of the universe. This ignorance is reflected in clashes between theses at different levels of AOE. There are clashes between levels 1 and 2, 2 and 3, and 3 and 4. The attempt to resolve these clashes drives physics forward.

In seeking to resolve these clashes between levels, influences can go in both directions. Thus, given a clash between levels 1 and 2, this may lead to the modification, or replacement of the relevant theory at level 2; but, on the other hand, it may lead to the discovery that the relevant experimental result is not correct for any of a number of possible reasons, and needs to be modified. In general, however, such a clash leads to the rejec-

---

[16] I first expounded and defended a version of this hierarchical view in Maxwell 1974. It was further elaborated in Maxwell 1976b, 1984 and 1993. A more elaborate version still is expounded and defended in great detail in Maxwell 1998. For a more detailed defense of the version indicated here, see Maxwell 2004a (chs. 1 and 2 and appendix); and 1984 (2nd ed., 2007, ch. 14). In Maxwell 2005 I argue that this view is a sort of synthesis of the views of Popper, Kuhn and Lakatos, but an improvement over the views of all three.

tion of the level 2 theory rather than the level 1 experimental result; the latter are held onto more firmly than the former, in part because experimental results have vastly less empirical content than theories, in part because of our confidence in the results of observation and direct experimental manipulation (especially after expert critical examination). Again, given a clash between levels 2 and 3, this may lead to the rejection of the relevant level 2 theory (because it is disunified, *ad hoc*, at odds with the current metaphysics of physics); but, on the other hand, it may lead to the rejection of the level 3 assumption and the adoption, instead, of a new assumption (as has happened a number of times in the history of physics, as we have seen). The rejection of the current level 3 assumption is likely to take place if the level 2 theory, which clashes with it, is highly successful empirically, and furthermore has the effect of increasing unity in the totality of fundamental physical theory overall, so that clashes between levels 2 and 4 are decreased. In general, however, clashes between levels 2 and 3 are resolved by the rejection or modification of theories at level 2 rather than the assumption at level 3, in part because of the vastly greater empirical content of level 2 theories, in part because of the empirical fruitfulness of the level 3 assumption (in the sense indicated above).

It is conceivable that the clash between level 2 theories and the level 4 assumption might lead to the revision of the latter rather than the former. This happened when Galileo rejected the then current level 4 assumption of Aristotelianism, and replaced it with the idea that "the book of nature is written in the language of mathematics" (an early precursor of our current level 4 assumption). The whole idea, however, is that as we go up the hierarchy of assumptions we are increasingly unlikely to encounter error, and the need for revision. The higher up we go, the more firmly assumptions are upheld, the more resistance there is to modification.

This hierarchical view, called by me *aim-oriented empiricism* (AOE), does justice to all six of the conflicting considerations spelled out above. But there is more to it than that. Its real merit is that it makes explicit metaphysical assumptions implicit in the manner in which physical theories are accepted and rejected, and which, at the same time, facilitates the critical assessment and improvement of these assumptions with the improvement of knowledge, criticism being concentrated where it is most needed, low down in the hierarchy. Within a framework of relatively insubstantial, unproblematic, and permanent assumptions and methods (high up in the hierarchy), much more substantial, problematic assumptions and associated methods (low down in the hierarchy) can be revised and improved with improving theoretical knowledge. There is something like positive feedback between improving knowledge and improving (low-level) assumptions and method—that is, knowledge-about-how-to-improve-knowledge. Science adapts its nature, its assumptions and methods, to what it discovers about the nature of the universe. This, I suggest, is the nub of scientific rationality, and the methodological key to the great success of modern science.

In summary, then, the argument in support of AOE is this. Some kind of more or less substantial metaphysical assumption is implicitly accepted by physics given that unifying theories are persistently favored *against the evidence*. This metaphysical assumption is very likely to be false. We need to array metaphysical assumptions in such a way that we subject them to maximum critical scrutiny, criticism being concentrated where it is most likely to be needed—those theses being favored either which must be true for the acquisition of knowledge to be possible at all, or which are most fruitful from the standpoint of promoting the growth of knowledge. The hierarchical structure of AOE succeeds uniquely well in doing what is required. No other view facilitates *improvement* of metaphysical assumptions and associated methods in response to the improvement of scientific knowledge as well as AOE does. (I put the matter like this to challenge the reader to think up something better.)

6

Granted AOE, as depicted in the diagram, what has become of a priori knowledge in physics? If "a priori knowledge" is to mean anything, it must mean at least, surely, "knowledge accepted independently of evidence." The whole point of AOE, however, is that the metaphysical theses in the hierarchy are *revised* in the light, in part, of evidence. This would seem to preclude any of these theses constituting a priori knowledge.

But this is not the case. The top two theses in the hierarchy, at levels 7 and 6, are accepted on grounds entirely independent of empirical considerations, revisable, if at all, in the light of improved non-empirical arguments only. These constitute a priori items of (conjectural) scientific knowledge. Three arguments establish this point.

(1) The level 7 thesis of partial knowability is a thesis that science, or the pursuit of knowledge more generally, is justified in accepting permanently, whatever may occur. Accepting this thesis as a part of knowledge can only aid, and can never impede, the acquisition of knowledge, in any circumstances whatsoever. If the thesis is false, then we cannot acquire knowledge, and hence cannot live, whatever we assume. This thesis is an authentic item of a priori (conjectural) knowledge: its acceptability is entirely unaffected by any empirical consideration. (This is, of course, not an argument for the *truth* of the thesis of partial knowability, but only for its *acceptance* as a permanent item of knowledge granted our aim is to acquire knowledge of factual truth, insofar as we can.)

(2) AOE demands that there is an item of a priori knowledge high up in the hierarchy. Without this, AOE collapses. For, if all the theses in the hierarchy were accepted on the basis of empirical considerations (of the kind indicated by 2 to 5 of section 5 above) then, whatever hierarchy is accepted on this basis, there will always be many (in principle infinitely many) *rival* hierarchies, composed of rival *disunified* theses, just as acceptable on purely empirical grounds. For example, if NT is accepted at level 2, and NT* is some equally empirically successful disunified variant of NT, then a rival hierarchy of disunified metaphysical theses can easily be concocted which favors NT* and excludes NT as unacceptable. The argument of section 2 above simply reappears, in a slightly modified form, with full force. Given any empirically successful, accepted theory, T, there will be infinitely many equally empirically successful (or more empirically successful) disunified rivals, $T_1^*, T_2^* \ldots T_\infty^*$, each with its associated hierarchy of appropriately disunified metaphysical theses, $\{M_1^*\}, \{M_2^*\} \ldots \{M_\infty^*\}$. Whatever purely *empirical* arguments there are for accepting T and its associated hierarchy of theses {M}, these will be echoes by equally valid, purely empirical arguments for favoring T_1^* and $\{M_1^*\}$, T_2^* and $\{M_2^*\} \ldots$ and T_∞^* and $\{M_\infty^*\}$. AOE, in short, collapses. This collapse can only be avoided if a thesis is accepted, high up in the hierarchy of AOE, on entirely a priori, nonempirical grounds—this thesis being such that it rules out all *disunified* rival hierarchies, and renders only one unified hierarchy acceptable (once empirical considerations are taken into account as well). The thesis that performs this function is the level 6 thesis of metaknowability. This thesis asserts that there is some "rationally discoverable" metaphysical thesis, which, if accepted, leads to improved methods for the improvement of knowledge. Here "rationally discoverable" means that the thesis in question is not an arbitrary choice from infinitely many analogous theses. The level 5 thesis of perfect comprehensibility satisfies this requirement. Disunified rivals—theses that assert "broken" comprehensibility (some phenomena being incomprehensible, or phenomena occurring in accordance with two or more distinct pattern of comprehensibility incapable of being unified into *one* unified pattern of comprehensibility) fail to satisfy the requirement. These theses, given the level 6 thesis of metaknowability, are unacceptable because they are *not* rationally discoverable. Each is an arbitrary choice from infinitely many analogous theses (the disunified elements being adjustable in infinitely many different ways, in the sort of way we saw in section 2 above).

Given the fundamental role that this level 6 thesis of metaknowability has within AOE, it is clearly of crucial importance to know what the nonempirical, a priori grounds are for accepting this thesis as a part of scientific knowledge. This issue will be discussed in a moment.

(3) If AOE is acceptable, it must be possible to solve the problem of induction within its framework—in so far as it is possible to solve the prob-

lem at all. There is an elementary argument which seems to show that the problem of induction cannot possibly be solved granted AOE—at least if AOE appeals only to empirical considerations in justifying acceptance of theses at various levels in the hierarchy. Any attempt to solve the problem of induction in this way must be circular. For it involves appealing to metaphysical theses in order to justify acceptance of scientific theories, and then appealing to scientific theories in order to justify acceptance of metaphysical theses. A purely empirical version AOE can only provide some slightly more intricate variant of such a hopelessly viciously circular argument, as a candidate for the solution to the problem of induction. The hopeless invalidity of this kind of circular argument is highlighted by the argument spelled out in (2) above. Given that acceptance of NT us justified (in part) by an appeal to the unified thesis of physicalism at level 4, acceptance of any equally empirically successful NT* can be justified equally well by an appeal to an appropriately disunified variant of the level 4 thesis of physicalism. In order to solve the problem of induction, in short, it is essential to acknowledge the existence of a priori knowledge. We require there to be a metaphysical thesis that is accepted for purely nonempirical, a priori reasons. This is the level 6 thesis of metaknowability.[17]

What exactly ought this crucial level 6 thesis to be taken to assert, and what are the nonempirical grounds for accepting it as a part of scientific knowledge? In order to answer this question we need first to answer another: What is the least substantial thesis that must be true if AOE is to be implementable?[18] Actually, we need to answer a somewhat broader question: What is the least substantial thesis that must be true if *generalized* AOE (GAOE) is to be implementable? I have used "AOE" to refer to the hierarchy of theses indicated in diagram 2. But in order to discuss the a priori character of the level 6 thesis of metaknowability, we need to consider much broader possibilities. Physicalism might be false, but the level 5 comprehensibility thesis might be true, a hierarchy of theses might be acceptable, and it might be possible to improve aims and methods in the light of improving knowledge in the way so characteristic of AOE. This might be the case even if the level 5 thesis of comprehensibility is false. We need in short to generalize AOE to take into account such possibilities. "Implementable" in the above question does not mean that GAOE meets with success, just that any specific version of GAOE, with some appropriate thesis M at level 5, is not sabotaged by some grossly disunified, ad hoc

---

[17] Elsewhere I have argued in some detail that AOE succeeds in solving the problem of induction, insofar as it can be solved see Maxwell 1998, ch. 5; 2004a, appendix, section 6; and especially 1984, 2nd ed., 2007, ch. 14.

[18] The more insubstantial the thesis is, other things being equal, the easier it becomes to provide an a priori justification for its acceptance.

variant of M being true. AOE, or GAOE more generally, is only implementable if the falsity of grossly disunified, ad hoc rivals to any acceptable level 5 thesis can be taken for granted.

It is at once clear, in broad outline at least, what the level 6 thesis of metaknowability must assert: *No grossly disunified, ad hoc variant of a potentially acceptable level 5 thesis is true*. We do not require that metaknowability asserts that some acceptable level 5 thesis is true, merely that all grossly ad hoc variants are false.

At once at least three questions arise about this thesis. I indicate, briefly, how, in my view, these questions are to be answered.

1. How do we decide whether a thesis, M, is a candidate level 5 thesis? Answer: M must either be the thesis that the universe is comprehensible, or some rival thesis about the overall nature of the universe of comparable generality that has the potential for supporting GAOE research. If some thesis M* is a special case of a more general thesis M that satisfies this condition, then M is the candidate level 5 thesis, and not M*.

2. Are there rivals to the level 5 thesis of comprehensibility that amount to candidate level 5 theses? Answer: Two examples are as follows. M_1: the universe is such that theoretical physics, in order to make progress, must go through an endless series of theoretical revolutions, each revolution being such that, after it, the number of distinct fundamental physical theories goes up by one. M_2: there are three fundamental forces governing all phenomena, each being such that its nature can be specified increasingly accurately as a result of theoretical revolutions, infinitely many such revolutions being required, however, before any force can be specified precisely. In view of the answer to 1, however, M_1 and M_2 should perhaps be regarded as different versions the level 5 thesis: the universe is such that infinitely many theoretical revolutions in physics are required before the true theory of everything can be formulated, the series of revolutions having associated with it some simple series of numbers, each being the number of distinct theories required for that revolution.[19]

3. How do we distinguish unambiguously between candidate level 5 theses that are, and are not, grossly disunified and ad hoc? Answer: Relevant here are some of the points made in section 4 above concerning the unity of physical theory. Thus, in order to distinguish between unified and grossly disunified or ad hoc candidate level 5 theses we must attend to the *content* of these theses, to what they assert about the world, and not to their linguistic form. Let us now, to begin with, restrict our attention to candidate level 5 theses that assert that the universe is physically comprehensible,

---

[19] See Maxwell 1998 (169–71) for a list of twenty metaphysical theses which either fail to imply, or are incompatible with, the thesis of comprehensibility.

either in a grossly disunified way or not in a grossly disunified way. How is the line between these possibilities to be drawn? In order to answer this question, we need to appeal to the different kinds of disunity of physical theory, distinguished in section 4 above. The true physical theory of everything, T, might be disunified in ways (4) to (7), and still AOE science (or GAOE science) might be possible—as long as the degree of disunity, N, is not too large. What undermines AOE science is T being disunified in ways (1) and (2). We might call this severe kind of disunity "aberrance." If nature is aberrant, then the laws of nature can, at any instant, be transformed utterly into something quite different, there being no possibility of predicting beforehand that this transformation will take place.[20] It is this severe kind of disunity, or aberrance, that we must be able to exclude from consideration if AOE science is to be possible. What about disunity of type (3)? In some cases, given a physical universe disunified in a type (3) way, it might still be possible to do AOE science: this possibility cannot, it seems to me, be excluded on a priori grounds. We are led, then, to interpret "grossly disunified" to mean "aberrant," i.e. "disunified in ways (1) or (2)." I assume that this notion of "aberrance," as it arises in the context of physical theory and physical comprehensibility, can be generalized so that it applies equally to theses that assert that the universe is more or less comprehensible in nonphysical ways, or that the universe is such that GAOE is implementable because of some level 5 thesis other than that of comprehensibility.

The conclusion, then, is this. The level 6 thesis of metaknowability is to be interpreted as asserting: The universe is such that no candidate level 5 thesis that is *aberrant* (i.e. disunified in ways [1] or [2]) is true.

GAOE, and thus AOE, become possible if—but only if—metaknowability, so defined, is acceptable on a priori grounds. But what are these a priori grounds? Here are three arguments intended to establish that metaknowability is acceptable as an item of a priori scientific knowledge.

1. Granted that there is *some* kind of general feature of the universe which makes it possible for us to acquire knowledge of our local environment (as guaranteed by the thesis at level 7), it is reasonable to suppose that we do not know all that there is to be known about what the *nature* of this general feature is. It is reasonable to suppose, in other words, that we can improve our knowledge about the nature of this general feature, thus improving methods for the improvement of knowledge. Not to suppose this is to assume, arrogantly, that we already know all that there is to be known about how to acquire new knowledge. Granted that learning is

---

[20] Prediction might be possible in the case of type (2) aberrance, as long as the conditions for an aberrant phenomenon to occur are not so complex and precise that it is impossible to reproduce them.

possible (as guaranteed by the level 7 thesis), it is reasonable to suppose that, as we learn more about the world, we will learn more about how to learn. Granted the level 7 thesis of partial knowability, in other words, metaknowability is a reasonable conjecture—even if we have so far failed to improve our methods for improving knowledge.

2. If the universe is *aberrant*, in the sense explicated above then, at any given moment, there can be no rationale for favoring one factual hypothesis or law as a basis for action over another. For, if the universe is aberrant, anything may happen at any moment. There will always be aberrant theories—empirically more successful than nonaberrant rivals—that predict that an aberrant event will occur at the next instant, whatever we may do. Empirical considerations favor the acceptance of such an aberrant theory at any instant, and if it is accepted that the universe is, in general, aberrant, no grounds exist for rejecting such a theory. In order for knowledge, and life, to be possible, the thesis that the universe is aberrant must be rejected.

3. Accepting metaknowability can only help, and can never, in any circumstances, harm the pursuit of knowledge. For even if phenomena occur which appear to be aberrant, it can never help the pursuit of knowledge to accept, or to entertain as a possibility, that the universe is aberrant. Once this is accepted, or allowed as a possibility, the rationale for rejecting empirically successful aberrant theories disappears, and the pursuit of knowledge is sabotaged by a flood of empirically successful aberrant theories, in the kind of way discussed in section 2 above. Even if phenomena occur which appear to be aberrant, the pursuit of knowledge requires that it is assumed that there is some underlying, as yet undiscovered, nonaberrant cause for the ostensibly aberrant phenomena.

Considerations 2 and 3 are strengthened, at least as far as the exclusion of type (1) aberrant theses is concerned, once it is recognized that anti-Humean necessary connections between successive events are possible. Suppose, to begin with, that Hume is right and no meaning can be given to the idea that necessary connections can obtain between successive states of affairs. In this case there does not seem to be such a big difference between a universe in which the same laws govern all phenomena at all times and a universe in which there is a slight, inexplicable change in the laws at some definite time. For, if Hume is right, there can be no explanation as to why laws are obeyed by natural phenomena. Deriving laws from more general laws just increases the mystery. Anything might happen at any moment, and it would seem just as big a mystery that phenomena occur in accordance with the same laws *at all times*, as that phenomena occur in accordance with same laws at all times *except for a slight change in the laws at some given time*. Grant, now, that Hume is wrong, and it *is* meaningful and possible that that which exists at one instant determines necessarily (deterministically or probabilistically) what exists at the next instant (see Maxwell 1968; 1976a; 1985; 1988; 1998 [141–55 and ch. 7 for the demonstration that this is indeed the case]).[21] Granted this, there *is* now an explanation as to why phenomena occur in accordance with laws: it is that the physical entities of which the universe is composed possess necessitating properties which determine that the laws are obeyed. If these entities exist with these properties, then the laws *must* be obeyed. Granted that we live in a universe that seems to exhibit lawfulness, as our universe does, it would be absurd, profoundly irrational indeed, to believe that nature will continue to be lawful and at the same time deny that necessitating properties exist which would explain why lawfulness does exist. But if there is an inexplicable, type (1) change in the laws at some specific time, this establishes that necessitating properties do not exist. Accepting that such a change has occurred would involve abandoning the idea that there exists something, in the constitution of things, that is responsible for the continuing lawfulness of nature. Anything might happen at any moment, and the persistent lawfulness of nature would be a mystery. There would be no rationale for choosing one set of factual hypotheses as a basis for action in preference to any other. The price that must be paid for acknowledging that the laws of nature have inexplicably changed, in a type (1) way, at some instant is, in other words, that one has to abandon the idea that what exists at one instant determines what exists next, and thus abandon the idea that there can be a rational basis for action. This provides additional grounds for rejecting a priori any thesis disunified in a type (1) way—a thesis that postulates an inexplicable change in the laws of nature at some specific time.

What if empirical science seems to establish aberrance, of type (2) let us say, on very firm empirical grounds? If some specific physical state of affairs is brought into existence, basic physical laws seem to change, and this effect occurs repeatedly, and resists all attempts at theoretical (i.e. non-aberrant, unifying) explanation. Should not metaknowability be rejected in these circumstances? The answer is no. Metaknowability should continue to be accepted, and the incompatibility between accepted theory, at level 2, and metaknowability, at level 6, should be noted, and attempts to eliminate it by the development of new theory should continue. Incompatibility between levels is, as I have already noted, a standard feature of AOE. It exists in the current version of AOE, in that level 2 is incompatible with levels 4 and 5.

---

[21] This requires that the true theory of everything remains true when interpreted essentialistically, as specifying necessitating properties possessed by the fundamental physical entity (or entities) postulated by the theory. The laws of the theory are true analytically, and the empirical import of the theory is bound up with the assertion of the theory: the world is made up of such and such physical entities possessing the necessitating properties specified by the theory.

These three arguments for accepting metaknowability as a part of scientific knowledge on a priori grounds are rather weak, and may well be challenged. It is important to appreciate, however, that unless metaknowability (defined more or less as above) *is* accepted as a part of theoretical scientific knowledge on a priori grounds, AOE science becomes impossible. The three arguments I have given seem to me to be just about the best that can be given in support of the a priori status of metaknowability.[22]

There are, then, two theses that deserve to be accepted as a part of scientific knowledge on a priori grounds: the level 7 thesis of partial knowability, and the level 6 thesis of metaknowability.

I conclude this section by remarking that "a priori" may be interpreted in a more liberal, relational manner, the outcome being that more theses emerge as having "a priori" status. The arguments above have assumed that if a thesis has to be accepted as a part of knowledge if the pursuit of knowledge is to be possible at all, then that thesis deserves to be accepted on a priori grounds (even if there are no arguments for the truth of the thesis). We may, however, interpret "a priori" somewhat differently, so that a thesis is a priori if its truth is required for the success of *physics*, or the possibility of *science*. Thus, if theoretical physics is to continue to be as successful as it has been since Galileo in developing increasingly empirically successful and unifying theories, it is necessary that physicalism is true. Relative to the continuing existence of physics, construed in these terms, physicalism may be said to be a priori. On the other hand, we might require only that physics continues to make some progress, but does not make progress towards capturing a true unified theory of everything. Relative to this less demanding notion of physics, physicalism is not a priori, but a more or less disunified version of physicalism (disunified in ways [4] to [8]) is a priori.

7

The history of western philosophy is split to its core by a longstanding, fundamental dispute. On the one hand there are the so-called empiricists, like Locke, Berkeley, Hume, Mill, Russell, the logical positivists, A. J. Ayer and Karl Popper, who hold empirical considerations alone can be appealed to in justifying, or providing a rationale for, claims to factual knowledge, there being no such thing as a priori knowledge—items of factual knowledge that are accepted on grounds other than the empirical. And on the other hand there are the so-called rationalists, like Descartes, Spinoza,

---

[22] For an earlier attempt at justifying acceptance of metaknowability see Maxwell 1998 (186–93). See also Maxwell 1984 (2nd ed., 2007, ch. 14, section 6).

Leibniz, Bradley, McTaggart, who hold that a priori knowledge does exist, and even plays a crucial role in science. Kant, famously, sought to resolve this debate by means of his claim that we do possess a priori knowledge of the world of appearance (since this must conform to the conditions required for it to be consciously experienced), but possess no knowledge whatsoever of the world of reality, the noumenal world of things in themselves. But Kant's attempted resolution of the debate fails. Perhaps our experiences must exhibit a certain degree of order, and cannot be completely chaotic, if these experiences are to be *consciousness*, and are to be interpretable as experiences of a world distinct from the experiencing subject. If so, propositions ascribing such a degree of order to the world can never be refuted by experience because such refuting experiences would not be conscious. These propositions deserve to be regarded as being known a priori, their truth being a necessary requirement for there to be any conscious experiences at all. But any such propositions, a priori on Kantian grounds, fall far short, in content and specificity, of Kant's own candidates for a priori propositions (such as that space is Euclidian), and fall far short of what is required to be accepted on a priori grounds in order to make science possible. A highly aberrant world, in which objects abruptly and inexplicably disappear and appear, could easily be sufficiently orderly for conscious experience to be possible, but science as we know it would not be possible. Thus Kant fails to resolve the empiricist/rationalist dispute.

This longstanding dispute has been resolved, however, by the line of thought developed in this essay. The empiricists were right to deny the existence of a priori knowledge where this means factual knowledge of apodictic certainty justified independently of any appeal to experience. They were wrong, however, to deny the existence of a priori knowledge where this means *conjectural* items of factual knowledge whose acceptance is justified independently of any appeal to experience. Science requires there to be a priori knowledge in this latter sense, and two items of such knowledge have been exhibited: the level 7 thesis of partial knowability, and the level 6 thesis of metaknowability.

In addition to resolving the empiricist/rationalist dispute, this essay has also developed a new conception of science—aim-oriented empiricism—and solved the longstanding problem of what it means to say of a theory that it is *unified* or *explanatory*. Furthermore, aim-oriented empiricism does not just change our *conception* of science; it requires that *science itself* needs to change. Science needs to become much more like the seventeenth-century conception of natural philosophy, intermingling consideration of testable theories with consideration of untestable metaphysical, epistemological, and methodological ideas. The whole relationship between *science* and *the philosophy of science* is transformed. The philosophy of science, construed as the exploration and critical assessment of rival ideas about what the aims and methods of science ought to be, ceases to be a metadiscipline, and becomes an integral part of science—or natural philosophy—itself. Rigor requires that, because of the inherently problematic character of the basic aim of science of improving knowledge about the universe *presupposed to be comprehensible,* even *physically comprehensible,* science and philosophy of science need to influence each other within the general framework of aim-oriented empiricism. There is, in addition, a major increase in the *scope* of scientific knowledge. The thesis that the universe is physically comprehensible (physicalism) ceases to be a mere metaphysical speculation, and becomes a central, firmly established tenet of (conjectural) theoretical scientific knowledge, more firmly established, indeed, than any physical theory, however empirically successful, such as quantum theory, general relativity, or the so-called standard model (the current quantum field theory of fundamental particles and forces).

Elsewhere I have shown that the line of thought developed in this essay is the first step in an argument, of much greater importance and scope, which demonstrates that there is an urgent need to change, not just science, but the whole of academic inquiry. In order to create a kind of inquiry rationally designed to help humanity learn how to make progress towards a better world, the aims and methods of academic inquiry need to be changed so that the basic aim becomes to promote wisdom by intellectual and educational means, wisdom being the capacity to realize what is of value in life for oneself and others, wisdom thus including knowledge, technological know-how and understanding, but much else besides. This broader argument for an intellectual revolution was first set out in Maxwell 1976b, and was given its definitive formulation in Maxwell 1984. The argument has been brought up to date in Maxwell 2004a. For summaries of the argument see Maxwell 2001, ch. 9 (a slightly improved version of Maxwell 2000), Maxwell 2003 and 2010.

REFERENCES

Aitchison, I. J. R., and A. J. G. Hey. 1982. *Gauge Theories in Particle Physics.* Bristol: Adam Hilger.
Armstrong D. 1988. *What is a Law of Nature?* Cambridge: Cambridge University Press.
Bartelborth, T. 2002. Explanatory Unification. *Synthese* 130: 91–107.
Duhem, P. 1954. *The Aim and Structure of Physical Theory.* Princeton: Princeton University Press.
Einstein, A. 1973. *Ideas and Opinions.* London: Souvenir Press.
———. 1982. Autobiographical Notes. In *Albert Einstein: Philosopher-Scientist,* ed. P. A. Schilpp, 1–94. La Salle, IL: Open Court:

Friedman, M. 1974. Explanation and Scientific Understanding. *Journal of Philosophy* 71: 5–19.
Goodman, N. 1954. *Fact, Fiction and Forecast*. London: Athlone Press:
Griffiths, D. 1987. *Introduction to Elementary Particles*. New York: John Wiley.
Howson, C. 2000. *Hume's Problem*. Oxford: Oxford University Press.
Isham, C. J. 1989. *Lectures on Groups and Vector Spaces for Physicists*. London: World Scientific.
Jones, H. F. 1990. *Groups, Representations and Physics*. Bristol: Adam Hilger.
Kitcher, P. 1981. Explanatory Unification. *Philosophy of Science* 48: 507–31.
———. 1989. Explanatory Unification and Causal Structure. In *Scientific Explanation, Minnesota Studies in the Philosophy of Science*, vol. 13, ed. P. Kitcher and W. Salmon. Minneapolis: University of Minnesota Press, 428–48.
Kripke, S. 1981. *Naming and Necessity*. Blackwell: Oxford.
Kuhn, T. S. 1962. *The Structure of Scientific Revolutions*. Chicago: Chicago University Press.
Lakatos, I. 1970. Falsification and the Methodology of Scientific Research Programmes. In *Criticism and the Growth of Knowledge*, ed. I. Lakatos and A. Musgrave, 91–195 Cambridge: Cambridge University Press.
Lipton, P. 2004. *Inference to the Best Explanation*. London: Routledge.
Mandl, F., and G. Shaw. 1984. *Quantum Field Theory*. John Wiley: New York.
Maxwell, N. 1968. Can there be Necessary Connections between Successive Events? *British Journal for the Philosophy of Science* 19: 1–25. Reprinted in Swinburne 1974, 149–74.
———. 1974. The Rationality of Scientific Discovery. *Philosophy of Science* 41: 123–53 and 247–95.
———. 1976a. Towards a Micro Realistic Version of Quantum Mechanics, Parts I and II. *Foundations of Physics* 6: 275–92 and 661–76.
———. 1976b. *What's Wrong With Science? Towards a People's Rational Science of Delight and Compassion*. Frome, England: Bran's Head Books.
———. 1984. *From Knowledge to Wisdom: A Revolution in the Aims and Methods of Science*. Oxford: Blackwell (2nd ed., 2007, London: Pentire Press).
———. 1985. Are Probabilism and Special Relativity Incompatible? *Philosophy of Science* 52: 23–44.
———. 1988. Quantum Propensiton Theory: A testable Resolution of the Wave/Particle Dilemma. *British Journal for the Philosophy of Science* 39: 1–50.
———. 1993. Induction and Scientific Realism: Einstein versus van Fraassen. *British Journal for the Philosophy of Science* 44: 61–79, 81–101, and 275–305.
———. 1998. *The Comprehensibility of the Universe*. Oxford: Oxford University Press.
———. 2000. Can Humanity Learn to become Civilized? The Crisis of Science without Civilization. *Journal of Applied Philosophy* 17: 29–44.
———. 2001. *The Human World in the Physical Universe*. Lanham, MD: Rowman and Littlefield.
———. 2003. Do Philosophers Love Wisdom? *The Philosophers' Magazine*, Issue 22, 2nd quarter, 22–24.
———. 2004a. *Is Science Neurotic?* London: Imperial College Press.

———. 2004b. Non-Empirical Requirements Scientific Theories Must Satisfy: Simplicity, Unification, Explanation, Beauty.
http://philsci-archive.pitt.edu/archive/00001759/.
———. 2004c. Comprehensibility rather than Beauty. http://philsci-archive.pitt.edu/archive/00001770/.
———. 2004d. Scientific Metaphysics.
http://philsciarchive.pitt.edu/archive/00001674/ .
———. 2005. Popper, Kuhn, Lakatos and Aim-Oriented Empiricism. *Philosophia* 32: 181–239.
———. 2010. *Cutting God in Half—And Putting the Pieces Together Again: A New Approach to Philosophy.* London: Pentire Press.
McAllister, J. 1996. *Beauty and Revolution in Science.* Ithaca: Cornell University Press.
Moriyasu, K. 1983. *An Elementary Primer for Gauge Theory.* Singapore: World Scientific.
Popper, K. R. 1959. *The Logic of Scientific Discovery.* London: Hutchinson.
———. 1963. *Conjectures and Refutations.* London: Routledge and Kegan Paul.
Quine, W. V. O. 1961. *From a Logical Point of View.* Cambridge, MA: Harvard University Press.
Salmon, W. 1989. *Four Decades of Explanation.* Minneapolis: University of Minnesota Press.
Schurz, G. 1999. Explanation as Unification. *Synthese* 120: 95–114.
Swinburne, R., ed. 1974. *The Justification of Induction.* Oxford: OxfordUniversity Press.
Tooley, M. 1977. The Nature of Law. *Canadian Journal of Philosophy* 7: 667–98.
———. 1987. *Causation: A Realist Approach.* Oxford: Oxford University Press.
van Fraassen, B. 1989. *Laws and Symmetry.* Oxford: Oxford University Press.
Watkins, J. 1984. *Science and Scepticism.* Princeton: Princeton University Press.
Weber, E. 1999. Unification. *Synthese* 118: 479–99.

[12]

Terror of Knowing:
Can an Empiricist Avoid Unwanted
A Priori Knowledge?

ÜMIT D. YALÇIN

0. Preamble

One needs to know whom one is trying to scare.[1] For example, one cannot scare Quine by telling him: "You know what, your semantic theory cannot account for a priori knowledge!"[2] You cannot even scare him by saying "Your account allows the possibility of *a priori knowledge of the empirical*": he will just tell you that you are utilizing a category he does not countenance, and which cannot be formulated in his system. So if one is trying to scare people by saying something like "your account of X allows for the possibility of a priori knowledge of the empirical," it had better be someone who minimally (a) accepts the empirical/a priori distinction; (b) uses these terms in the sense you use them (for we all know that there are many senses of these terms in the literature), and (c) denies that there can be a priori knowledge of the empirical in the relevant sense.

Perhaps this is obvious, but let me say something more about what I mean by a priori "in the relevant sense." Can one just ignore the relevancy condition I am trying to uphold by saying "So much the worse for the traditional use of a priori, why should I care?" I think not. Obviously, if her target is someone in a tradition that accepts the a priori/empirical dichotomy, she needs to generate that difficulty in accordance with how that tradition understands those terms. I will say more about this below, but let me quickly illustrate. It is of course possible to use 'a priori' in such a way that even in Quine's system, 'a priori' becomes an adjective that can

---

[1] The original name of this article was "Fear of Knowing." I was subsequently informed by the editors of a recent work by Paul Boghossian by the same name: hence, the present, more picturesque title.

[2] I do consider Quine as having a semantic theory, albeit not a theory of the traditional sort. For more on this see Yalçın 2001.

be applied to something or another. Assume that I commence to use 'a priori' to mean "is furthest away from the fringes of one's system of beliefs." Then I can say that Quine allows for the existence of a priori knowledge and the "charge" would stick. But I submit that Quine would not be terrorized in the least.[3]

So we are looking for those who use 'a priori' in the relevant sense, and who deny that there can be a priori knowledge of the empirical in *that* sense. Radical empiricists like Quine and Mill will not do. Neither will members of the Rationalist tradition. It seems like the intended audience of our scare-scenario are members of moderate empiricism, arguably the dominant tradition in philosophy at least for the last couple of hundred years: Someone in this tradition who uses the word 'a priori' in a sense close to what would be considered the relevant sense, and who would deny that there could be a priori knowledge of the empirical in that sense. Who might these people be? Who is there in the moderate empiricist tradition that can be scared upon hearing the words "You are committed to the existence of a priori knowledge of the empirical!"

I will answer this question in detail in the body of my discussion. But the answer will be mostly in the negative: I will show why many people would not be touched or scared of such a charge. To some extent, I will leave it to the reader to decide who else is left.

1

Externalism with respect to propositional attitude contents (*externalism*, or *anti-individualism*, for short), like many philosophical positions that try to improve on the commonsense view of the world, does funny things with the mind—or should I say *to* the mind.[4] An interesting comparison helps to highlight what I mean: Consider phenomenalism, a position that maintained the reality and epistemic accessibility of the external world to the mind by bringing the latter *into* the mind. Putting aside the cost issue for the moment, the phenomenalist gamble was supposed to have a simple payoff: constitute the supposedly nonmental out of the mental, and you have a ready-made account of how you can know the things you know about the "external" world. You know it just the way you know your mind (assuming you already have an account of how you know your own mind).

---

[3] I would also have to argue that 'knowledge' is a term that can be used in Quine's system, which is a formidable undertaking in the first place. See Quine 1984, 295.

[4] Of course, this type of *content* externalism has to be distinguished from *epistemological* externalism. When the occasion demands, I will use the proper adjectives, but otherwise, 'externalism' will be used in this essay to refer to content externalism.

There is a similar reshuffling of the boundaries of the mental with the nonmental in externalism. In externalism, portions of the world hitherto considered distinctively nonmental *invade* the mind, so to speak.[5] Yet, in doing so, the nonmental does not lose its distinctively nonmental character—it is an invasion in which the invader is supposed to retain its identity, avoiding assimilation.

One should also expect *this* reshuffling of the boundaries of the mental with the nonmental to have "out of the ordinary" consequences. Depending on one's epistemic attitude towards the mental and/or the nonmental, there are a number of interesting possibilities. For example, if you are an externalist who believes that our knowledge of the nonmental is problematic, it is only natural that you should expect knowledge of (at least the invaded portions of) the mental to become problematic. Or, if you continue to believe that one has easy epistemic access to all things mental, then you should expect certain portions of the nonmental to be easily epistemically accessible. Without getting tangled up in loaded philosophical terminology, you would have mental-style knowledge of the nonmental invaders of the mental.

The thought that externalism undermines some of our basic intuitions about the nature and possibility of what is generically referred to as "self-knowledge" is not new (I will call those who defend this claim *incompatibilists*). The tension between externalism and self-knowledge was first hinted by Putnam (1975), and later explicitly countenanced by other externalists (e.g., Davidson 1984, 1987; Burge 1982, 1988; Heil 1988, 1992). In this essay, I shall focus on one type of argument, of relatively recent vintage, that aims to highlight one aspect of this tension.

There will be occasion to investigate the details of anti-individualism in due course, but for now, I take the following to be an adequate working formulation of its main thesis:

(CE) Some cognitive states that are ascribed by *de dicto* attitude sentences (for example, those that involve natural kind terms, etc.) necessarily depend on or presuppose the existence of objects external to the person to whom the state is ascribed, where the objects in question are specifically related to the particular contents of the cognitive states in question.[6]

---

[5] With certain accounts of higher-order belief, the latter, more often than not, end up having the content they have by virtue of their relation to other mental states, such as first-order beliefs. This complication is not directly relevant to the point I am making here.

[6] McKinsey 1991 uses the following formulation of externalism: "(B) Some neutral cognitive states that are ascribed by *de dicto* attitude sentences (e.g., 'Oscar is thinking that water is wet') necessarily depend on or presuppose the existence of objects external to the person

A succinct version of the incompatibilist argument I will focus on challenges the anti-individualist to maintain the consistency of the following triad of propositions (McKinsey 1991, 12):[7]

(1) Oscar knows a priori that he is thinking that water is wet.
(2) Oscar can know that the proposition that Oscar is thinking that water is wet necessarily depends upon E.[8]
(3) The proposition E cannot be known a priori.

Here, E is supposed to be "the 'external proposition' whose presupposition makes Oscar's thought that water is wet a wide state" (12). E is supposed to be a proposition like 'There is water in my environment', a proposition that asserts the existence of an object external to the individual, and is thereby decidedly only empirically knowable. (1) is supposed to be supported by the traditional thesis that one has privileged access to one's own mental states, and (2) is supposed to be a conceptual consequence of the externalist thesis formulated by (CE), or a suitably amended version of it. The incompatibilist believes that the triad is inconsistent because (1) and (2) putatively entail that

(4) Oscar can know a priori that E,

that supposedly contradicts (3).

I will argue that this specific incompatibilist argument fails. The reasons for this failure are complex. The incompatibilist argument is essentially an *ad hominem* against those who, among other things, accept the traditional distinction between empirical and a priori knowledge. (1)–(3), and their logical implications, are supposed to create a problem for precisely those who would like to understand (1)–(3) with the traditional interpretation of

---

to whom the state is ascribed" (10). For reasons I cannot go into in the present context, I find this formulation to be too broad, and suggest the formulation in the text. Very briefly, the specificity requirement in my formulation prevents externalism to be true in a possible world in which there is one mind (thinking of butterflies) and one atom. I do assume that historically, externalists did not intend externalism to be true in such a world.

[7] Discussion of similar incompatibilist arguments are also to be found in McKinsey 1994, Brown 1995 and Boghossian 1997.

[8] (2) is weaker than the second proposition in McKinsey's original triad, which just says that *the proposition that Oscar is thinking that water is wet necessarily depends upon E*. But if we leave it at that, it turns out that (4) is entailed by (1) and McKinsey's (2) only if we presuppose closure of a priori knowledge under entailment. Since this is as controversial as closure of knowledge (in general) under entailment, I weaken (2) to its present form. This way, only closure of a priori knowledge under *known* entailment is presupposed. I do need to point out that although closure under known entailment is less controversial than closure under entailment, it is still not fully exonerated. See Hales 1995.

their key terms. Yet, putting it simply, if we are careful not to equivocate on 'a priori', we discover that there is no reading of (1)–(4) which:

(a) sustains the prima facie plausibility of (1)–(3);[9]
(b) ensures that (3) and (4) are inconsistent; and
(c) secures the putative entailment from (1) and (2) to (4).

Before I commence to argue for these claims, I will briefly describe two ongoing disputes about the correct formulation of the externalist thesis, and defensive strategies against the incompatibilist argument associated with them. I believe that this will help put the strategy I am pursuing in this essay in proper perspective.

2

The first controversy centers on the nature of the dependency relationship between mental contents and the external entities invoked by the externalist thesis. Is the dependency conceptual, or a weaker sort of "metaphysical" dependency? Burge (1988), and more recently Brueckner (1992) argue for the latter interpretation. Their strategy, then, is to appeal to Kripkean arguments that purport to show that metaphysical necessities need not be knowable a priori. But if the externalist thesis (or, specific instances of it) cannot be known a priori, the support for the claim that (2) can be derived from the externalist thesis is undermined. A crucial premise of the incompatibilist argument, namely (2), is implicated.

I will sidestep this defensive strategy, and the associated interpretation of (2), for three reasons. First, there is good cause to believe that the externalist thesis can and should be cast as expressing a conceptual necessity (Brown 1995). Second, even if one grants that Kripkean arguments are strong enough to convince us that metaphysical necessities are *often* only knowable a posteriori, this is not the same as actually showing that the externalist thesis, even if interpreted as a metaphysical necessity, cannot be known a priori. A separate argument is needed, but is not provided, in the specific case of that thesis. Third, I intend to show that the incompatibilist argument is unsound even if (2) can be interpreted as invoking a stronger conceptual dependence relation. If correct, this is a point very much worth emphasizing.

The second controversy is about the scope of the externalist thesis. Is the thesis applicable to natural kind concepts (Putnam 1974), to some

---

[9] This is required for the dramatic effect of the argument. If (1)–(3) are not prima facie plausible, why should the fact that you have to deny one of them cause any consternation?

nonnatural kind concepts (Burge 1979, 1982) to atomic concepts (Boghossian 1997), to concepts that incorporate indexical components (Putnam 1988) or to all concepts (Brown 1995)?

To appreciate the significance of the scope question to the incompatibilist argument, consider the following: Let us assume that the externalist thesis applies only to natural kind concepts. So the thesis asserts, roughly, that if C is a natural kind concept, then the existence of cognitive states involving C necessarily depends on the existence of Cs in the environment. And let us also assume that a person can know that they are thinking about water. But before this person can utilize the externalist principle to reason, in this particular case, that there is water in her environment, she also has to know that *water* is a natural kind concept. The incompatibilist has to provide additional reasons to sustain the claim that this further fact (if *water* is in fact a natural kind concept) can be known a priori. More needs to be done to uphold the credibility of the incompatibilist argument.

I will also sidestep this complicating maneuver. The incompatibilist argument might be shown to be defective by some suitable refinement or qualification of the scope of the externalist thesis; but I intend to show that it is ineffective for an independent and more fundamental reason. The incompatibilist argument fails even if the aforementioned externalist defenses prove deficient.

3

In order to show that the incompatibilist argument still fails under conditions optimal for its success, and in line with the strategy I just outlined, I will make two assumptions that favor the incompatibilist. First, I will assume that according to externalism, the relation between a person's thought contents and propositions about her environment is the conceptual entailment relation. Second, I will assume that the externalist thesis applies to all concepts. Of course, the latter assumption has some counterintuitive consequences, for example, that one cannot think of golden mountains without such things existing. Yet, as I indicated earlier, I am willing to set such problems aside in order to show that the incompatibilist argument fails even under conditions optimal for its success. Hence, from now on, let the following be the externalist thesis:

(CE_2) If X has a thought part of the content of which is comprised by a concept C, then this entails that X is in an environment that contains instances of C.

One consequence of (CE$_2$), among others, is that Oscar's thinking a thought involving the concept of water entails that there is water in his environment. This by itself does not yet establish anything like the epistemic claim in premise (2) of the incompatibilist argument. We have to establish also that Oscar can know this entailment. In fact, we can do more.

Entailment relations are traditionally taken to be paradigm examples of (relational) facts one can grasp or apprehend by means of pure thought or reason. Hence, even if Oscar does not at present know that his thinking that water is wet entails the existence of water in his environment, this is something he can come to know if he is prepared to exert the necessary mental effort and has the requisite mental capacities. Of course, to become aware of this particular entailment between his thoughts involving the concept of water, and the existence of water in his environment, Oscar has to be able to discover the truth of externalism—but this is not an insurmountable task. After all, externalists have discovered the truth of externalism by apparently a priori thought experiments. So imagine that Oscar is one of those people who is capable of exerting the requisite mental energy, who can come to know that externalism is true, and who can also appreciate that the truth of externalism has specific implications about, say, his thoughts involving water. Thus, we are justified in believing that Oscar can know the specific entailment between his water-thoughts and the existence of water in his environment, and know it just by thinking. We can now reformulate the incompatibilist's inconsistent triad as follows:

(1) Oscar knows a priori that he is thinking that water is wet.
(2*) Oscar *can* know a priori that his thinking that water is wet entails that there is water in his environment.
(3) The proposition *E* cannot be known a priori.

So far so good, but we cannot afford to ignore that whether (1) and (2*) jointly entail:

(4) Oscar can know a priori that that there is water in his environment, and thus generates a conflict with (3) still depends on the following closure principle pertaining to knowledge:

(PC) If X knows *a priori* that P, and X can know *a priori* that P entails Q, then X can know *a priori* that Q.

(PC) is akin to the principle that knowledge is closed under known logical entailment. The existence of the modality makes it weaker, while the fact that the kind of knowledge in question is a priori knowledge renders it more complicated.

As it stands, (PC) is more like a schema—for 'a priori' is a term with a long history during which it has acquired many senses. Various closure principles, some perhaps acceptable and some not, can be generated from it depending on which sense or senses of 'a priori' one uses in the three occurrences of that term in (PC). Accordingly, I now turn to the incompatibilist literature for clues.

4

One of the main proponents of the anti-individualist argument, McKinsey, calls knowledge "obtained independently of empirical investigation," a priori knowledge. He further characterizes this kind of knowledge as obtainable "just by thinking," "without launching an empirical investigation," or "without making any assumptions about the external physical world" (1991, 9). (I should emphasize that McKinsey uses 'just by thinking' in place of the more traditional 'by pure reason', and I follow him in taking these two expressions to be interchangeable). Yet some other participants of the debate on incompatibilism take their cue from the fact that traditionally, one's knowledge of one's own mental states is also considered to have two additional important properties: such states are thought to be "purely introspective" and "noninferential" (or "immediate"). So they use 'a priori' in one of these senses (e.g., Boghossian 1989). Accordingly, I begin with the following provisional characterizations of 'a priori':

(A1) X's knowledge that p is a priori if only if X can know that p *just by thinking*.

(A2) X's knowledge that p is a priori if only if X can know that p *without launching (independently of) an empirical investigation*.

(A3) X's knowledge that p is a priori if only if X can know that p *without making any assumptions about the external* world.[10]

(A4) X's knowledge that p is a priori if only if X can know that p *purely introspectively*.

---

[10] I change McKinsey's 'external physical' to 'external' to avoid a gratuitous commitment to physicalism. In doing this, I assume both that anti-individualism in the philosophy of mind and the compatibilist challenge to anti-individualism are supposed to be independent of the truth of physicalism. At least, this better be true about anti-individualism if Putnam-style anti-skeptical arguments, deriving from anti-individualist principles, are supposed to avoid begging the question against external-world skepticism.

(A5) X's knowledge that *p* is a priori if only if *X* can know *noninferentially* that *p*.

However, a closer examination reveals that some of these can be readily eliminated.

(A2) is not very useful unless we already know what 'empirical' means. Obviously, it will not do to define 'empirical' as that which cannot be known a priori, since this will only yield a circular definition of 'a priori'. Since it is also obvious that any attempt to explicate 'empirical' without invoking the notion of *a priori* will also provide an independent explication of a prioricity to some extent, let us turn to (A1) and (A3) to see if they succeed on this count.

(A1) does not seem to be confronted by any immediate difficulties, and in fact, seems to present the appropriate sense of 'a priori' for the second occurrence of that term in (PC). For the second occurrence of 'a priori' in (PC) is related to the second premise of the incompatibilist argument, namely (2*). And in (2*), what can be known is an entailment between two propositions. Traditionally, knowledge of conceptual, logical and mathematical facts and relations between such facts have been thought of as knowledge one can attain purely (just) by thinking. Of course, there is much more that can be said about how much is packed into the expression "purely by thinking" (and some of it will be said below), but this will do for the time being.

I believe we can utilize (A1) also to explicate the third occurrence of 'a priori' in (PC), which is related to the use of that term in (3). The clue is to be found in the putative relationship between (3) and (4). If these propositions are supposed to be contradictory, then the sense of 'priori' in (3) must be a sense of this term that contrasts with the sense of 'empirical' in (4). But whatever else 'empirical' might mean in this context, it should be clear that 'empirical' does not contrast either with noninferential or introspective, the senses that would be supplied by the other remaining alternatives, (A4) and (A5). Moreover, knowledge obtainable by pure thinking is often contrasted in the tradition that utilizes these concepts, with empirical knowledge. Hence, it seems that the third occurrence of 'a priori' in (PC) can also be provisionally replaced with 'purely by thinking', thus yielding:

(PC) If *X* knows *a priori* that *P*, and *X* can know *purely by thinking* that *P* entails *Q*, then *X* can know *purely by thinking* that *Q*.

Yet, (A1) falls short of being satisfactory for the first occurrence of 'a priori' in (PC), the occurrence related to the use of the term in premise (1) of the incompatibilist argument. That premise is about Oscar's knowledge of the contents of his own mind, i.e., his knowledge of what he happens to be thinking about. The tradition that embraces the empirical/a priori distinction does not conceptualize what it would consider introspective and direct (immediate, noninferential) knowledge of the contents of our own minds as being on a par with knowledge of conceptual and logical facts. The latter may be acquired just by thinking, but the former are not.[11] Insofar as the empirical/a priori distinction in this tradition is based on a distinction in human faculties (roughly) between sensing and thinking, introspective knowledge belongs with sensing rather than thinking (or, more circumspectly, it does not belong with thinking; whether it should also be distinguished from sensing and thus placed in a category of its own is a matter for further investigation.)[12] The salient point is that knowledge that depends for its justification on such introspective knowledge is not thereby rendered a priori in the traditional sense). This is clearly codified in Kant by his use of 'inner sense' when talking about knowledge of the mind, and the tradition is continued by the neo-Kantian card-carrying empiricists of the twentieth century.

Of course, if the incompatibilist insists on using 'a priori' in (1) in the sense indicated by (A1), he can do so. Yet this is a costly move that turns (1) into a proposition that will not be accepted by an overwhelming majority of philosophers who embrace the empirical/a priori distinction. But as the foregoing discussion indicates, both (A4) and (A5) provide suitable senses of 'a priori' for (1), and hence the first occurrence of that term in (PC). Consequently we have two versions of (PC) to consider:

(PC_1) If X knows *introspectively* that P, and X can know *purely by thinking* that P entails Q, then X can know *purely by thinking* that Q.

(PC_2) If X knows *noninferentially* that P, and X can know *purely by thinking* that P entails Q, then X can know *purely by thinking* that Q.

Unfortunately, both (PC_1) and (PC_2) are false under the standard intended interpretations of their key terms in the tradition that utilizes these terms. The former is false because empiricism has often sought to ground empirical knowledge in justification-conferring inferential relations (entailment, induction, abduction) from self-knowledge to empirical

---

[11] Of course, this is somewhat simplistic, and there are major difficulties in characterizing precisely what the distinction comes to. But still, the distinction between sensing and pure thinking I depend on is not too crude to cast a shadow on the important distinctions I make in this essay.

[12] Shoemaker 1994 argues that introspection cannot be understood in terms of a sensory or perceptual model.

beliefs about the external world. But this does not commit traditional empiricism to the paradoxical-sounding conclusion that empirical beliefs are after all acquired just by thinking. Or if there is some unusual sense in which it does, this means that the existence of empirical beliefs acquired just by thinking in this unusual sense is not something that needs to worry the externalist more than anyone else in this tradition. And the same goes for (PC_2): given the standard understanding of 'noninferential', it is false that what is deductively inferred from noninferential beliefs is thereby acquired just by thinking.

Consider the following examples in connection with (PC_1). When Chisholm argues for an empiricist foundationalism where the foundation consists of justified beliefs about one's own present states of consciousness, and these foundational beliefs transmit their justification to beliefs of other kinds by virtue of *synthetic* a priori epistemic principles, he is not committed to the claim that empirical beliefs are known a priori in the sense of *known just by thinking*. Minimally, he is not committed to such a conclusion in terms of the tradition that drew the empirical/a priori distinction in the first place. In similar fashion, despite their attempt to justify all empirical beliefs in terms of self-knowledge (knowledge of sense data, of the given, etc.), phenomenalists of the early twentieth century were not committed to the claim that empirical knowledge is a priori in the sense of *known just by thinking*.

Quinton's epistemology serves to highlight the problem with (PC_2). Quinton considers what he calls "logically intuitive beliefs" to be noninferential perceptual beliefs that form the basis of empirical knowledge. But Quinton's logically intuitive noninferential perceptual beliefs are not introspective beliefs: such beliefs are paradigmatically beliefs about publicly observable objects, and not about the contents of our consciousness. Moreover, logically intuitive beliefs can be utilized to (inferentially) justify other beliefs about the external world. But this does not mean that the latter, inferential beliefs are thereby beliefs obtained just by thinking. They are, after all, inferred from perceptual beliefs.

Can the incompatibilist wave aside my appeal to "the tradition" and say "So much the worse for the tradition?" I grant that there are some possibilities. For example, he can emphasize that the tradition I am invoking does not have a monolithic sense of 'a priori', which is a point I already concede by seriously considering more than one interpretation of that term. Thus, if the incompatibilist believes that there is a marginal sense of 'a priori' different from the main senses in which the term is used in the tradition, but which nevertheless applies to self-knowledge, he can clearly define that marginal sense and proceed to apply it to self-knowledge (this seems to be what Boghossian is implicitly doing when he uses 'priori' to mean *introspective*). Or, he can perhaps argue that the tradition is wrong in placing self-knowledge and thinking in different categories. But these strategies need to be backed up by argument. In the former case, we need to be told why it is significant that, in this marginal sense of 'a priori' there can be a priori knowledge of the external world (after all, the incompatibilist argument supposedly aims to create a problem for anyone who wishes to accept both externalism and self-knowledge, not only for those who additionally have an unusual sense of 'a priori'). In the latter case, we need to have good reason to give credence to the novel categorization. Without any such argumentation, there is no basis to take him seriously.

I also grant that there could be philosophers who deny that we can have knowledge of the external world by inferring such knowledge from introspective or noninferential knowledge. They might also be externalists. They might also accept that some knowledge is acquired purely by thinking (remember the occurrence of 'a priori' in [2*]). These philosophers may be bothered by the fact that (1) and (2*) jointly entail, via (PC_1) and/or (PC_2), that one can have introspective and/or noninferential knowledge of the external world. Suffice it to say that I do not know of any that satisfy all of the above desiderata.[13]

A different problem confronts (A3). To put it succinctly, (A3) entails that knowledge of the external world can be empirical only if knowledge of the external world cannot exist (i.e., some form of skepticism with respect to the external world is true). To see this, assume that knowledge of the external world is possible. This means that there is some justification of beliefs about the external world that does not depend on a question-begging inference.[14] In turn, the existence of such a noncircular justificatory argument means that there is some justification of beliefs about the external world that does not depend on any assumptions about the external world. But according to (A3), any justified belief that satisfies the additional desiderata for knowledge (whatever these may be) will also qualify as a priori, and hence will not be empirical knowledge! This surely indicates that (3) is too restrictive as a definition of 'a priori'.

5

The incompatibilist may accept what I have had to say so far, but suggest a further sense of our key term that might be sustained by traditional usage:

---

[13] Just as a mental exercise, consider Burge, who seems to believe in "privileged access" to one's own mind in some sense of this term. Does Burge believe that he has noninferential knowledge of his own mind? Does he believe that he has introspective knowledge of his own mind? Does Burge believe that he knows certain things just by thinking?

[14] I am aware of, but not convinced by recent attempts to generate a notion of virtuous epistemic circularity.

(A6) X's knowledge that *p* is a priori if only if *X* can know that p *without depending on the senses*.

The incompatibilist can argue that (A6) can be used to interpret all three occurrences of 'a priori' in (PC). First, introspective and immediate knowledge of one's own mind does not depend on the senses. Second, knowledge of entailment relations does not depend on the senses. And third, if one can know a proposition like "There is water in my environment" without depending on the senses, it would be easy to accept that the latter is thereby not obtained by empirical investigation. Hence, this sense of 'a priori' would also generate the desired inconsistency between (3) and (4). So the incompatibilist argument would now look like:

(1) Oscar knows *without depending on the senses* that he is thinking that water is wet.

(2*) Oscar *can* know *without depending on the senses* that his thinking that water is wet entails that there is water in his environment.

Hence,

(4) Oscar *can* know *without depending on the senses* that there is water in his environment.

Which would apparently conflict with:

(2) The proposition "There is water in my environment" cannot be known *without depending on the senses*.

And the corresponding closure principle would be:

(PC3) If *X* knows *without depending on the senses* that *P*, and *X* can know *without depending on the senses* that *P* entails *Q*, then *X* can know *without depending on the senses* that Q.

(PC3) cannot be readily dismissed. If introspective knowledge is not based on the senses, then what is inferred from such knowledge through the (nonsensory) grasping of entailment relationships would also be independent of the senses. So (PC3) seems to be an acceptable closure principle. Hence, (1) and (2*) appear to entail (4).

At this point, I will neither challenge the correctness of (PC3), nor the entailment from (1) and (2*) to (4) (but such a challenge will be issued below). Instead, I will argue that many philosophers who would accept (4) on the basis of (1) and (2*) would also simultaneously reject (3) (or more precisely, they would reject (3) when it is interpreted in a way that would make it inconsistent with [4]). To put it succinctly, my argument depends on exploiting an ambiguity in the expression 'depending on the senses'.

I will, once again, remind the reader of the prevalent tendency in traditional empiricism that tries to generate knowledge of the external world on the basis of what is known about one's own states of consciousness, including one's occurrent thoughts (and yes, such attempts to generate knowledge of the external world tend to fail, but that is beside the point). Consider an empiricist of this sort who is able to come to know of the existence of entities, say water, outside of his mind. He might say to himself, "Lo and behold, I have come to know something about the world without using my senses, isn't that great!" He might even concede that in one sense, this knowledge was gained "without launching an empirical investigation" if the latter means that the existence of sense organs were not assumed in the process. But this would not vex our imaginary philosopher: this is, after all, the fulfillment of his wildest dreams. He has managed to prove the existence of a world outside his mind without launching an empirical investigation. Thus, anyone who believes in (3) must be wrong!

The response of our imaginary philosopher is best understood by highlighting the ambiguity I mentioned above. To do this, let me once again focus on a concrete example.

According to one reading, Hume is a philosopher of the sort I have described above, i.e., one who would like to generate knowledge of the external world on the basis of what he knows about his own states of consciousness. Now, when Hume advances his thesis that all ideas depend on (sense) impressions, he is not in a position to define what he means by the 'senses' in terms of the sense organs of an external body. If he were to invoke such sense organs, his epistemological quest would be threatened by circularity. So he has to give an internal account of the senses, and the various sensory modalities (it is not clear that he bothers to do the latter, but that is not relevant to our concerns). To put things somewhat anachronistically, even if the knowledge we start with is introspective knowledge of the contents of our sense impressions, the latter cannot be assumed to have arisen from the operation of extramental sense organs.

Nevertheless, it is possible that the sense impressions are actually causally generated by sense organs. Although Hume is not entitled to assume this at the beginning of his epistemological quest, there might be an external world and sense organs in it, and the latter might be causally responsible for the sense impressions we end up with as part of our mental economy. Consequently, the introspective perusal of one's sense impressions could be possible only because the sense impressions are in fact causally generated by the operation of the as-yet-unknown sense organs.

So in one sense, the introspective knowledge one gains through such perusal is dependent on the sense organs. Moreover, Hume is also a concept empiricist, and would insist on the causal dependency of thoughts (ideas) on the "sensory" manifold (impressions) he is presented with. Hence, his thoughts would also be potentially causally dependent on his sense organs.

This indicates that the expression 'without depending on the senses' is ambiguous between 'without causally depending on the sense organs' and 'without epistemically depending on the sense organs'. An empiricist such as Hume cannot accept (1) interpreted as:

(1a) Oscar knows *without causally depending on sense organs* that he is thinking that water is wet,

because for all he knows and hopes, they actually might be. But he can accept (1) if it is interpreted to mean that his knowledge of his thoughts and the external world are epistemically independent of the sense organs (i.e., the existence of the sense organs is not assumed in the production of either type of knowledge):

(1b) Oscar knows *without epistemically depending on sense organs* that he is thinking that water is wet.

Of course, (1b) and (2*) jointly entail:

(4b) Oscar can know *without epistemically depending on sense organs* that there is water in his environment.

At the same time, such an empiricist may accept:

(3a) The proposition "There is water in my environment" cannot be known *without causally depending on sense organs*.

But he will not accept:

(3b) The proposition "There is water in my environment" cannot be known *without epistemically depending on sense organs*,

since accepting (3b) is tantamount to giving up his epistemological quest to generate knowledge of the external world purely on the basis of evidence pertaining to the contents of his present states of consciousness. So our empiricist, at best, might be forced to accept (4b) and (3a), which are not inconsistent.

So why should we be bothered by the problems Hume faces in his epistemological quest? Why is all this relevant to the epistemology, metaphysics, and the philosophy of mind in the twenty-first century? Because the twenty-first century also has to face up to the ambiguity Hume has to untangle. And once he does, he has to make a choice.

Can a content externalist reasonably accept (1a)? It seems to be quite difficult. Once an externalist accepts (CE), i.e., that one's mental states "depend on or presuppose the existence of objects external to the person," he also has to have an explanation of this dependency. Presumably, the contents of the mind depend on these external objects because the latter have a causal role to play in the genesis of the former. And presumably, the causal chain from external object to mental content traverses the sense organs. If this is the way things happen, both the mental contents and the knowledge thereof seem to causally depend on the sense organs.

Please do not think that I claim that the content externalist is committed to such an account of the dependency of the mind on external physical objects. As it stands, (CE) is even consistent with hard-core Platonism. One can be an externalist while maintaining the existence of Platonic forms, and invoking them as the extramental constituents of one's mental contents. While doing this, one can also deny that there can be any kind of causal connection between such Platonic forms and humans minds—there is good reason to believe that "causation" is not a relation that can hold between necessary entities and contingent entities.

But who is the content externalist the incompatibilist aims to target? Is it the Platonist I just sketched, or the well-behaved empiricist who gives the standard causal and perceptual account of object-dependent thought that goes all the way back at least to Locke and Hume? If it is the latter, then it is clear that such and externalist will reject (1a). The incompatibilist, in turn, is not entitled to force (1a) on such an externalist.

So the incompatibilist can saddle the well-behaved externalist mentioned above at best with (1b), and hence (4b). Can he also cast the externalist as being committed to (3b), and thus claim victory due to the ensuing inconsistency? This depends on the epistemology of the externalist in question, and particularly, on his attitude towards the problem of Humean external-world skepticism. If he is interested in finding an answer to Humean skepticism on its own terms, then he has to reject (3b) to avoid begging the question.

What is the alternative? I don't know. I am an epistemologist at heart, and I believe that the onus of proving the skeptic wrong falls on me and my kin. I also believe that one cannot do anything in philosophy in isolation—one cannot do philosophy of mind without at least issuing promissory notes in epistemology and metaphysics. But I also know that there are a significant number of souls in philosophy who seem to assume the opposite. These, perhaps, might accept (3b), and hence become legitimate targets of the incompatibilist.

In short, interpreting 'priori' in terms of (A6) also fails to uphold the incompatibilist argument against externalism if one is a well-behaved externalist who, from the perspective of the present author, takes his epistemology seriously.

With this, I believe that I have exhausted all reasonable construals of 'a priori' in this context. Barring future surprises, I conclude that there is good reason to believe that there is no sound version of the argument that hits a significant target. The incompatibilist has to look for some other way of exploiting the putative tension between content externalism and self-knowledge.

REFERENCES

Boghossian, P. 1989. Content and Self-Knowledge. *Philosophical Topics* 17: 5–26.

———. 1997. What The Externalist Can Know *A Priori*. *Proceedings of the Aristotelian Society*, supp. 86: 161–75.

Brown, J. 1995. The Incompatibility of Anti-Individualism and Privileged Access. *Analysis* 55: 149–56.

Brueckner, A. 1992. What an Anti-Individualist Knows *A Priori*. *Analysis* 52: 111–18.

Burge, T. 1979. Individualism and the Mental. In *Midwest Studies in Philosophy 4*, ed. P.A. French, T.E. Uehling Jr., and H.K. Wettstein, 73–121. Minneapolis: University of Minnesota Press.

———. 1982. Other Bodies. In *Thought and Object: Essays on Intentionality*, ed. A. Woodfield, 97–120. Oxford: Oxford University Press.

———. 1986. Intellectual Norms and Foundations of Mind. *Journal of Philosophy* 83: 697–720.

———. 1988. Individualism and Self-Knowledge. *Journal of Philosophy* 85: 649–63.

Chisholm, R. M. 1982. *The Foundations of Knowing*. Minneapolis: University of Minnesota Press.

———. 1990. The Status of Epistemic Principles. *Nous* 24: 209–16.

Davidson, D. 1984. First Person Authority. *Dialectica* 38: 101–11.

———. 1987. Knowing One's Own Mind. *Proceedings and Addresses of the American Philosophical Association* 60: 441–58.

Hales, S. D. 1995. Epistemic Closure Principles. *The Southern Journal of Philosophy* 33: 185–201.

Lewis, C. I. 1955. Realism or Phenomenalism. Reprinted in *Collected Papers of Clarence Irwing Lewis* (1970), ed. J. D. Goheen and J. L. Mothershead, J. L., 335–47. Stanford: Stanford University Press.

Kripke, S. 1972. Naming and Necessity. In *Semantics of Natural Language*, ed. D. Davidson and G. Harman, 253–355. Dordrecht: D. Reidel Publishing Co.

McKinsey, M. 1991. Anti-Individualism and Privileged Access. *Analysis* 51: 9–16.

———. 1994. Accepting the Consequences of Anti-Individualism. *Analysis* 54: 124–28.
Putnam, H. 1975. The Meaning of 'Meaning'. In *Mind, Language and Reality: Philosophical Papers*, vol. 2, 131–93. Cambridge: Cambridge University Press.
Quinton, A. 1973. *The Nature of Things*. Boston: Routledge and Kegan Paul.
Shoemaker, S. 1994. Self-Knowledge and 'Inner Sense.' *Philosophy and Phenomenological Research* 54: 249–90.

Name Index

Achinstein, P., 120n24
Aitchison, I.J.R., 218n8
Almeder, R., 158–59, 163, 165n17, 166–68, 170–72
Antony, L., 11n3
Armstrong, D., 212n2
Ayer, A.J., 2, 3, 6

Banton, M., 141
Bartelborth, T., 216n6
Bealer, G., 6, 3, 13, 15, 17, 20, 22, 22n15, 22n16, 26–28, 45, 50, 88, 163n15, 172n27, 195
Benacerraf, P., 90, 90n3, 120
Ben-Menahem, Y., 202n13
Black, M., 170n24
Boghossian, P., 19, 20, 20n14, 28n20, 45, 195n2, 241n1, 244n7, 246, 248, 251
BonJour, L., 3, 16, 17, 20, 22n15, 28–29, 46, 50–51, 85–88, 92, 95, 112, 113, 135, 171n26, 172n26, 172n27, 195
Brandom, R., 72
Brandt, R., 33–36
Brown, H., 137–54, 170n24
Brown, J., 244n7, 245, 246
Brueckner, A., 4, 5, 85–92, 111–22, 135n5, 245

Burge, T., 22, 26, 243, 245, 246, 252n13
Bruzzaniti, G., 150

Carey, S., 108
Casullo, A., 4–6, 8, 85–92, 93–109, 111–35, 171
Chalmers, D., 64n1
Chisholm, R., 146n8, 251
Creath, R., 163n14

Davidson, D., 243
Dehaene, S., 108n10
Descartes, R., 148–49, 179, 193, 236
Devitt, M., 3, 4, 9–30, 42–43, 61–63
DiSalle, R., 193, 199, 200, 200n9, 200n10, 202n13
Dryden, W., 36
Duhem, P., 12, 21, 52, 54, 139, 162–63, 165n17, 201, 215
Dummett, M., 19

Earman, J., 177, 178n3, 183–85, 188
Einstein, A., 142, 188, 200, 211, 211n1, 216
Ellis, B.D., 181
Erwin, E., 4, 33–59

259

Fajans, K., 150
Field, H., 16, 18n11, 19n12, 69, 180
Friedman, M., 61, 62, 142, 147, 177n1, 178n3, 183–90, 193–208, 216n6

Galison, P., 151
Gallistel, C.R., 108, 108n10
Garber, D., 149
Gelman, R., 108, 108n10
Gendler, T.S., 15n9
Gettier, E., 64, 66
Gladwell, M., 14n8
Glymour, C., 69
Goldman, A., 12n3, 160n9
Goodman, N., 149, 213n3, 219n11
Gould, S., 143
Greenwood, J., 139
Griffiths, D., 218n8
Guiot, J., 150

Haack, S., 159n7
Hacking, I., 150
Hales, S., 244n8
Hankins, T.L., 179
Hanson, N.R., 177, 182, 186
Harman, G., 16n10, 46, 47, 50–51
Heathwood, C., 41
Herschel, W., 150
Hersh, R., 147
Hey, A.J.G., 218n8
Holmes, J., 35
Howson, C., 213n3
Hoyningen-Huene, P., 153
Hume, D., 147, 179, 180, 212n2, 234, 236, 254, 255, 256

Isham, C. J., 218n8

Jackson, F., 64, 64n1, 76–78
Jeshion, R., 5, 6, 93–110, 111, 122–35
Jones, H.F., 218n8

Kant, I., 6, 7, 91, 111, 113, 120, 140, 142–48, 151, 180, 182, 183–85, 189, 193–95, 198, 207, 237, 250
Kitcher, P., 113–14, 146n8, 160n9, 216n6
Kornblith, H., 14n7, 22n15, 151n1, 159n5, 160n9, 216n6
Kovel, J., 35
Kripke, S., 45, 64, 66, 91–92, 120–22, 211, 245
Kuhn, T., 6, 12, 152–55, 194–95, 198, 203, 204, 215, 227n16

Lakatos, I., 152n13, 215, 227n16,
Laudan, L., 151, 152n13, 160n9, 205
Lehrer, K., 170n25, 172n28
Lewis, C.I., 96
Lewis, D., 76
Lewis, P., 28
Lindley, R., 35
Lipton, P., 213n3
Locke, J., 61–62, 236, 256

Mackie, J., 41, 44
Mandl, F., 218n9
Maxwell, N., 7, 211–40
McAllister, J., 216n6
McKinsey, M., 243n6, 244, 244n7, 244n8, 248, 248n10
Moriyasu, K., 218n8

Oakley, S., 153–55

Pap, A., 177n1, 178, 180, 184, 185–86, 196
Papineau, D., 4, 19, 61–83
Peacocke, C., 3, 25–26, 45, 137n2, 195, 195n2
Peirce, C.S., 203
Perkins, B., 182
Plantinga, A., 27, 88, 113

Name Index

Poincaré, H., 185–87, 194, 200–201
Popper, K., 139, 215, 216n6, 227n16, 236
Psillos, P., 19
Putnam, H., 6, 28, 42, 43, 87, 98, 101, 105, 105n9, 106, 123–25, 127, 152, 153, 163n14, 243, 245, 246, 248n10

Quine, W.V.O., 2, 3, 9, 11, 12, 18, 21, 42–44, 51–56, 69, 70–71, 75, 80, 139, 152-153, 157, 158, 159n8, 162–65, 177, 187–90, 194–96, 198–99, 202, 205, 206n17, 207, 215, 241, 241n2, 242
Quinton, A., 251

Reichenbach, H., 142, 185, 194–96
Resnik, M.D., 189–90
Rey, G., 11n3, 12, 22n15, 28n20, 29n22
Rituo, H., 141
Robotti, N., 150
Rosenberg, A., 160n9
Roth, P., 164n17, 165n17

Salmon, W., 216, 216n6
Schurz, G., 216n6
Scriven, M., 41
Sellers, W., 6, 152, 152n14, 153
Shaffer, M., 1–8, 163n15, 172n28, 193–208
Shapere, D., 177n1
Shaw, G., 218n9
Shoemaker, S., 250n12
Shogenji., T., 170n24
Siegel, H., 158–59, 163–72
Silverman, L., 55

Sklar, L., 186
Soames, S., 104n7
Sober, E., 180
Soddy, F., 150
Sosa, E., 89
Stein, H., 179
Stump, D., 177–92, 193, 194n1, 202n13
Summer, L., 42

Thompson, A., 35
Tooley, M., 212n2
Toulmin, S., 152n13, 177, 181
Tsivkin, S., 109n10
Tymoczko, T., 147n9

Ullian, J.S., 52–53, 195

Van Fraassen, B.C., 9n1, 17, 140, 159n6, 212n2
Veber, M., 1–6, 57, 208n19

Warnick, J., 163n15, 205n15
Watkins, E., 183n5
Watkins, J., 216n6
Weatherson, B., 67
Weber, E., 216n6
Weinberger, J., 55
Wetzels, W., 150
Whithrow, G.J., 177n1
Williamson, T., 65
Wisniewski, E., 14
Wolpe, J., 37
Woods, J., 42
Wright, C., 20, 20n14

Yalçin, U., 7–8, 241–58

www.ingramcontent.com/pod-product-compliance
Lightning Source LLC
Chambersburg PA
CBHW022011300426
44117CB00005B/125